NORTHEAST
GARDENING

NORTHEAST GARDENING

THE DIVERSE ART AND SPECIAL CONSIDERATIONS OF GARDENING IN THE NORTHEAST

— ELVIN McDONALD —

Macmillan Publishing Company
New York

Collier Macmillan Canada
Toronto

Maxwell Macmillan International
New York Oxford Singapore Sydney

To some of my earliest editors
Grandma King, Grandmother McDonald, Mama, Beth, Aunt Ella,
Aunt Eulice, Miss Colbert, Mrs. Whipple, Miss Nicholson,
Billie Godley, Peggy Schulz, Gretchen Harshbarger, Olga Rolf
Tiemann, Fay S. Payne, Ernesta Ballard, Rachel Snyder, Carol
Woodward, Eleanor Hepburn Noall, Kate Steichen, Helen Van Pelt Wilson, Clara
Claasen, Bernice Brilmayer, Kathleen Bourke, Elaine Cherry,
and Sarah Tomerlin Lee

And especially

Harriet Glass

who helped

gardens grow in Brooklyn

and beyond

Macmillan Publishing Company
866 Third Avenue
New York, NY 10022

Collier Macmillan Canada, Inc.
1200 Eglinton Avenue East, Suite 200
Don Mills, Ontario M3C 3N1

Library of Congress Cataloging-in-Publication Data

McDonald, Elvin.
    Northeast gardens: the diverse art and special
considerations of gardening in the Northeast/Elvin
McDonald.
        p. cm.
    Includes bibliographical references and index.
    ISBN 0-02-583125-9
    1. Gardening—Northeastern States. 2. Gardens—
Northeastern States. I. Title.
SB453.2.N82M33   1990
635'.0974—dc20   90-6159
                                        CIP

Macmillan books are available at special discounts for bulk purchases for sales promotions, premiums, fund-raising, or educational use. For details, contact:

    Special Sales Director
    Macmillan Publishing Company
    866 Third Avenue
    New York, NY 10022

NORTHEAST GARDENING
was produced by
Running Heads Incorporated
55 West 21 Street
New York, NY 10010

Editor: Charles de Kay
Designer: Kingsley Parker
Managing Editor: Lindsey Crittenden
Production Manager: Linda Winters

All photographs by Elvin McDonald except photograph on page 38 by Bill Mulligan.

10 9 8 7 6 5 4 3 2 1

Typeset by Dix Type Inc.
Color separations by Hong Kong Scanner Craft Company
Printed and bound in Singapore through Palace Press

ACKNOWLEDGMENTS

In my dedication I named some of the individuals who guided my earliest efforts in gardening, journalism, and getting on with my life in general. Here I want to thank the individuals and institutions who helped make *Northeast Gardening* possible:

Pam Hoenig, the editor at Macmillan who conceived the idea and sought me out to produce the manuscript and photographs; and Running Heads Incorporated, in particular Sarah Kirshner, the editor who saw me through the selection of photography, Kingsley Parker, the designer who laid out the pages, and Charlie de Kay, who copy-edited the manuscript and saw the book through production.

On a continuing basis I have always to thank my agent, Carla Glasser, who works out the details; David Glasser, lawyer, who gives me peace of mind; Helen Henry, banker; Anne Fitzroy Stewart, accountant, who looks favorably on artists; Hila Paldi, bodycoach for Pilates-type exercise, who happens also to be an apartment gardener and participant in the Brooklyn Botanic Garden's Signature Seeds program; Arthur Wooten, whose hands-on gestures of healing through shiatsu massage help me let go; Joseph A. Vargas, Houston-based doctor who specializes in wholistic health care; and Bill Mulligan, actor, writer, musician—my toughest editor and best friend.

Special thanks to the owners of the gardens whose names appear in the captions, who welcomed my cameras with a minimum of laments that the best had passed or was yet to be, and as well fed, sheltered, entertained, and enlightened me. I am especially grateful to Lea Davies, C. Z. Guest, Hope Hendler, and Lawrence Power for permitting me to work in their gardens as if they were mine. Finally, I thank the staff and volunteers who have helped make the Brooklyn Botanic Garden my professional base, most of all Donald E. Moore, whose vision that I would work a season as though I were one of the Garden's professional gardeners will not be fully realized until publication of another book in which I will detail my experiences while gardening with the best at BBG.

Elvin McDonald
New York City
March 1990

CONTENTS   NORTHEAST

GARDENING

CONTENTS

INTRODUCTION

Throughout most of the twentieth century a large percentage of the gardening and plant books published in America have originated from publishers based in the Northeast, in particular Boston, New York, and Philadelphia. At least until the 1970s, a large proportion of the books' authors were those who gardened as well in the Northeast, yet the books themselves have been mostly marketed as being applicable all across our diverse land. *Northeast Gardening* turns this tradition inside out and attempts no more than to share the ways we are gardening today in the Northeast, the problems we are trying to solve, and where we hope to go—or grow—into the third millennium.

During the past year, much of my energy has been spent gathering the materials that have become *Northeast Gardening*. Besides interviewing all kinds of gardeners in the Northeast and photographing the fruits of their labors, I have amassed a small mountain of newspaper and magazine clippings and photocopies from books of all ages, which, together with my own hands-on gardening experience, constitute the raw materials that have now been organized into this book.

Perhaps a decade after the end of the Second World War, there appeared in the *New Yorker* magazine a cartoon that showed two suburbanites visiting over a backyard fence. One said, "The state the world's in, I'm planting only annuals this year," which, despite its irony, sums up the hopefulness inherent in the act of gardening. There have always been cries that doomsday was near, yet some individuals always pushed on, planting seeds, literal or figurative encapsulations of faith, hope, and charity, that feed, house, clothe, heal, purify the air, and uplift our spirits. Even among the lost (or suppressed) teachings of Jesus we find words to the effect that the life force in a plant is the same as that in us. I have also read that the DNA in a begonia is not all that different from the DNA in each of us humans. Is it any wonder then that gardeners find peace and sustenance when we are in the company of plants? Or that those of us who live in the crowded, polluted Northeast corridor are gardening with a passion that may yet exceed that of any previous generation of Americans?

On a map of North America, *Northeast Gardening* is about the Northeastern quadrant generally, but more specifically an area pinpointed around Philadelphia, fanning out up the Atlantic coastline into Canada, then across to Buffalo, and back down to Pennsylvania. For plant cold hardiness, I have chosen the newly issued map from the United States Department of Agriculture and the National Arboretum, which is located in Washington, D.C. As compared to the 1965 edition, in the 1990 map, which is reproduced here on page 154, five states are registering slightly cooler temperatures on average; these states are Connecticut, New Jersey, New York, Pennsylvania, and Rhode Island. The new map shows a slightly warmer Maine and New Hampshire, with Delaware and Vermont remaining about the same. How much has actually changed in the twenty-five years between the maps is a moot point, since the 1990 version is based on more data and is presumably more accurate than its predecessor.

Cold hardiness and the ability of plants to survive temperatures below freezing if not below zero, are the major factors we associate with winter in the Northeast, which can vary, depending on where one lives, from the relative mildness of Zone 7, to the serious snows and deep freezing of Zone 3. In Brooklyn and on Long Island where I have done a great deal of outdoor gardening, we regularly enjoy a frost-free gardening season of six to seven months, while in the coldest regions of the Northeast everything has to happen in as little as ninety days. Whether the growing time is short, long, or in-between, the gardening year as a whole will still have seasons that we characterize as spring, summer, fall, and winter. Spring, in a most simplistic way, is for planting, summer is for growing, harvesting, and sheer pleasure, fall is also for planting but focuses more on final harvesting and putting the garden to rest, and winter is for getting through, which gardeners manage by reading colorful seed and nursery catalogs, sketching ideas for spring, and devoting themselves to indoor gardening.

There is a rhythm and flow to each gardening season in every community. If on any given day you should feel puzzled as to what might be an appropriate activity for your garden, observe what is going on in your neighbors' plantings and see what's happening at the local nursery or garden center.

Gardening is an activity that has something for everyone at every age and stage of life. Sometimes we think it is not possible to garden unless we have land and a large amount of money, but in fact, the miracle can be experienced with next to nothing. For example, a dried bean seed taken from the kitchen can be planted in a tin can or paper cup of soil, watered lightly, kept at room temperature, and soon it will be breaking through the surface, unbending, flexing, and putting forth leaves. Being part of this process makes us feel good, no matter our age or who we are.

Through the chapters of *Northeast Gardening*, I have set out the fundamental basics in Chapter One, and then focused on nine specific types of gardens, each with its own set of challenges and opportunities. In order to get the most information within the allotted space, various subjects such as soil preparation, planting, pruning, pest management, and specialty plants are treated as appropriate throughout the book. While one or more chapters may be uniquely suited to your particular gardening situation, I hope you will read all of them in order to have a more complete overview.

Presuming that you have the inclination to garden, there are only two necessities: You must have a place to garden and you must be healthy and strong enough to sustain the physical activity required.

As to place, the best advice I've heard came from Miss Elizabeth Cornelia Hall, during an interview conducted at the New York Botanical Garden in January 1988, about two months before her ninetieth birthday: "You must be adaptable and set about gardening where you are versus where you aren't. Otherwise, you'll be frustrated instead of fulfilled. We all have handicaps and challenges."

Recent studies have shown that the physical activity of gardening constitutes beneficial all-around exercise, and can be counted as part of a fitness regimen the same as swimming, running, walking, or bicycling. Moreover, we never lose our joy at contact with the soil, so when age or any physical impairment necessitates, the garden can be modified to suit. Those who have difficulty bending over, or getting down on hands and knees, can tend raised planting beds. For shut-ins, there is the enticing world of miniature horticulture, which can run the gamut of the gardening experience, including flower arranging.

The emotional benefits of gardening have been formally studied for more than a hundred years. A nineteenth-century prison warden in England observed that prisoners assigned to work in the kitchen garden were happier, better adjusted, and generally more productive than inmates assigned other tasks. After Miss Hall graduated in 1924 from the Pennsylvania School of Horticulture for Women (now the Ambler campus of Temple University), she went to work in a hospital for patients with mental and nervous diseases and became an oc-

engaged in any activity that could produce an unexpected flying object, such as while brush-cutting and compost shredding. If you have trouble seeing up close, say to transplant tiny seedlings or to determine where to make a crucial pruning cut, have your eyes checked. Being able to see clearly will reduce the amount of tension you feel from the act of gardening itself. Of course, it has been conjectured that Gertrude Jekyll's failing eyesight helped her achieve painterly results with the colors and textures of the plants she arranged in her fabled gardens and landscapes.

When your gardening involves spraying or dusting, wear a mask. Say no to the use of toxic pesticides and you won't have to dress for Armageddon, but don't take any chances with those judged safe either. Wear a cotton handkerchief tied across your nose and mouth when spraying plants with anything stronger than water and when engaged in any dust-producing

cupational horticultural therapist. The director told her, "When I've had a big day here I go up to my garden and pull weeds. There is nothing that relaxes you like pulling weeds."

Apart from general fitness, gardeners benefit from paying particular attention to these body parts and functions:

It has been said that for all the requisite stooping over, the gardener needs to come outfitted with a stainless steel back hinge. Statistics suggest that the majority of back problems are rooted in stored tension. The ideal physique for a gardener is a strong back counterbalanced by a strong midsection or abdominal muscles.

Before you charge out into your garden on any fine, sunny day, take a minute to rub sunscreen on all exposed parts, especially your face, neck, arms, and backs of hands. Renew as necessary. It also helps to wear a big straw hat in the height of summer.

Wear shatter-proof goggles when you are

activity, such as handling dry potting mix ingredients or cultivating dry soil.

Gardeners have a way of getting wet, especially about the feet, knees, and hands. Being cold and wet at the same time may exacerbate the pains of arthritis. Hands and feet that are damp or wet for long periods of time will inevitably develop painful cracks and may invite the invasion of harmful organisms.

Rubber-soled shoes or boots of the Wellington type will help keep your feet dry from the outside. Wearing athletic socks designed to draw moisture away from the feet will help dissipate your own sweat. When bathing, scrub all foot parts, especially between the toes, with a brush or terry cloth, then dry well, again with special emphasis between the toes. Apply anti-fungal powder as necessary against athlete's foot. If possible, let each pair of shoes dry out for a day or two between wearings. Keep your toenails clipped short, wear only shoes that feel comfortable and supportive.

Spring and fall are perhaps the primary times when gardeners' hands take a beating. Potting,

repotting, pot-cleaning, digging in the earth, pruning—all offer potential pitfalls that mostly we ignore. Here are some friendly gestures to make toward your hands:

1) Wear heavy-duty gloves when you work with roses or other thorny plants. Thorn punctures are painful; worse are thorns that break off and remain buried in your flesh.

2) Gardeners are often outdoors working when the weather is cold and damp. Wearing

Front yards in the Northeast are being changed from large areas of lawn, foundation plantings of shrubbery, and shade trees to inviting gardens and outdoor living rooms, OPPOSITE ABOVE. The elements here are spring-flowering dogwood and magnolia trees, beds of bulbs and perennial flowers, and a wicker chair. Toolsheds can be both functional and picturesque, OPPOSITE BELOW, as in this Quebec garden of Mr. and Mrs. Francis H. Cabot. The trees are poplar; the vine is Dutchman's-pipe, Aristolochia durior. Quick-from-seed, sow-and-grow annuals such as these red zinnias and blue larkspur, ABOVE, provide color in the garden and an abundance of blooms for bouquets.

gloves without fingertips allows the tactile sensations we need, yet keeps the hands warm.

3) Resist the impulse to use your thumb as a scrubber when cleaning pots and seed trays. Use a stiff brush, or a pot scrubber from the kitchen. (Soaking mineral-encrusted pots overnight in vinegar water works wonders, 1 cup vinegar to 1 gallon water.)

4) Potting mediums for orchids and other epiphytic or air plants can be highly abrasive. Wear adhesive bandages around the tips of the fingers that you use most.

5) Keep your nails trimmed short and buffed smooth. Long nails gather rather than resist dirt and are more likely to be torn.

6) Begin gardening by pulling your fingernails across a bar of soap. Afterwards, a little nail brushing with soap and warm water, followed by gentle rubbing and massaging with a moisturizer and your hands will feel refreshed.

7) It's been said that gardeners buy more gloves than we wear, and that a cracked thumb, more than a green one, is the sign of a practicing gardener. To help heal a cracked thumb, wrap adhesive tape around it before gardening. Afterwards, remove the tape, clean hands in warm water, dry, then rub well with a moisturizer containing Vitamin E. (A friend says her solution is better: Take a long trip visiting other gardens and don't even think about dirtying your own hands for the duration.)

Come in, Mission Control

A certain amount of paperwork goes with any serious gardening effort. There are inevitably catalogs to be dug through, orders to be written out, and bills to be paid. Keeping records is a way of repeating successes instead of failures. A guru has said the myth of the green thumb lies in the instinctive ability of some gardeners to do the right thing at the right time, without consulting past records or the

Almanac. My system is to keep one datebook that serves all my needs, business and personal. I make appointments to plant seeds and clip the topiaries on the same page with deadlines for newspaper columns and travel plans.

Catalogs are a constant source of information and inspiration, and not in the New Year alone. No season is without catalogs, hardly any week or day for that matter. I mark what interests me and may immediately place an order or not. In any event the catalogs to be kept are filed alphabetically and the rest are discarded.

Every gardener also needs at least a good-sized bookshelf if not a library. Size of budget and storage space do not necessarily mesh. More to the point is a need for quick access to the information you need, when you need it. I maintain a small library of gardening and botanical reference books. The rest I read or look at the pictures and then pass along to friends.

Laying in the plant materials and supplies needed for any gardening project requires planning ahead. The best days for gardening outdoors are probably the worst for shopping. On a sunny Saturday morning, finding a parking spot at my garden center can take longer than it takes to plant a tree. A rainy weekday morning will find the place nearly vacant. This is the time to shop so that when the sun shines the most can be made of every gardening minute.

Storage for gardening tools, equipment, and supplies can also be planned so as not to cause unnecessary frustrations. The system I have devised as an apartment gardener is described in Chapter Ten. A pleasure in rainy or cold weather, this organization prepares you for the times when plants become your top priority.

Besides dry storage for supplies and equipment, the ideal being a place for everything and everything in its place, a garden work center needs above all a large, sturdy potting bench, set at the height most comfortable for the person who will be using it. A bench that is too low can wreak havoc with the lower back; one that is too high unnecessarily stresses the upper back and arms. Add adequate lighting, to facilitate seeing exactly what you are doing at night or in overcast weather. Over my bench there is a sign: *Don't put it down, put it away.* Since the needs of living plants come first, this dictum must on occasion be ignored, but it is fundamentally sound policy.

Besides storage and a potting bench, it helps to have an area with one or more raised nursery beds and shelves or tables on which to set young container plants. Often a garden work center can be right next to the garden itself, the outdoor living area, or the dwelling, screened off by trelliswork or plantings. This becomes the place for processing cut flowers, herbs, and vegetables before taking them inside, and also for grooming or training potted specimens. It helps if this area has sharp drainage and a hose for cleaning pots, or, ideally, a stainless steel sink with running water.

Gardening Knowledge Is Primary

Ultimately, a perfect body and place, with all the right plants and tools, will not make you a successful gardener. Taking courses, reading books, and studying videos can impart knowledge and even inspiration, but motivation is the magic ingredient that leads to the actual practice of gardening. Near the end of a lifetime of practicing, Thomas Jefferson observed, "I may be an old man, but I am a young gardener."

The geographical area represented by *Northeast Gardening* varies not only in maximum low and high temperatures, but also presents all kinds of terrain, from flat, to rolling hills, to mountainous, with soils ranging from clayey to sandy, and from acid to alkaline. We can choose to grow plants adapted to the site, or we can attempt to change the site in order to suit the plants we want to grow. In practice, most of us do some of both, the idea being not so much one of compromise but of achieving harmony between what we like and the resources at our command.

Of all the tremendous resources we have for gardening today in the Northeast, none is more precious than water. There have always been periodic droughts in this territory, but some recent periods, during which water rationing has been in effect for millions of us, have brought home the necessity for conservation. Since neither plants nor people can live without water, one way to conserve is to plan our gardens so they are not unduly dependent on irrigation during the normally dry seasons. When we do apply water, we can do it as efficiently as possible, through drip irrigation. The single word that describes this ecologically sensitive approach to gardening is Xeriscape (zee-ris-scape, the first "e" sounded as in "here"), which means, "water conservation through creative landscaping." The concept, which originated in 1981 at the Denver Water Department, is widely applicable since lists of plants suited to Xeriscaping must be highly localized. Plants uniquely adapted to the site are appropriate, native or otherwise. Also to be considered are good design principles, soil improvement, the aforementioned efficient irrigation systems, reduction of turf areas, the use of mulches, and sensitive plant management, all of which are discussed in the pages that follow.

One of the perceived benefits of gardening in the Northeast is that we have four definite seasons, each in turn bringing weather conditions that encourage, slow, halt, or kill the plants in our gardens. Each season in the garden has a distinct personality, knowledge of which helps us know when to plant and when to harvest and when to give the garden and ourselves a rest. When Miss Hall spoke at a summer resort for blind people, she recalled, "It was amazing how relaxed they were, and how able to show me around. We felt and smelled the fragrances together, and exchanged feelings about herbs. If you know how gardening feels, you'll know better what's going on than if you merely look." Enjoy!

CHAPTER ONE

THE ABSOLUTE BASICS

First, Develop a Plan

Whether or not it is committed to paper, every garden has a plan. Form follows function, but success also involves motivation, inspiration, knowledge, vision, and experience. The primary purpose is to establish goals and priorities, so that everything you set in motion has the potential of a satisfying achievement. Adaptability and flexibility also come into play, for rigidly fixed plans can become frustrating if not entirely unworkable.

Motivation. What is the purpose of the garden you are planning? Pleasure we take for granted, but this can be skewed by unrealistic expectations or questionable motives.

Inspiration. A little inspiration goes a long way in garden planning. Russell Page, the late English landscape gardener, more often than not sketched his first inspirations for a site on the back of any envelope that happened to be in his jacket pocket. Working plans, incorporating refinements and details, came later.

Knowledge. Jean Woodhull, a director of the American Horticultural Society, has said, "Many people do not realize it, but we all live in a garden, the earth." This being the case, it does not seem too farfetched to suggest that each of us is born with a consciousness of gardening that can be raised by visiting gardens, studying books and magazines, taking courses, and then practicing what we have absorbed.

Planning and designing your own garden mandates getting to know the site. Consult a compass if you are not sure which direction is due North; study intensity and duration of sun (and shade) and how they may be affected by seasonal changes such as leaves coming and going from deciduous trees and shrubs. Pinpoint where you live on the USDA Plant Hardiness Zone Map; the most recent version, issued in 1990, is reproduced on page 154. The

A place to garden: A dry stone retaining wall in the Hartwood garden in New Jersey holds a bark-mulched ground cover planting of heather (Calluna vulgaris cultivars), with variegated lacecap hydrangea (Hydrangea macrophylla 'Mariesi Variegata') in the foreground. The young tree is Japanese tree lilac (Syringa reticulata), with oakleaf hydrangea (Hydrangea quercifolia 'Snow Queen') blooming at left. An open-lattice fence frames the cottage garden with Edwardian greenhouse that opens to both garden and house.

map cannot foretell the future, but it does tell you whether a plant is likely to survive winters in your region. Study climate and weather, not today or this season alone, but over the long haul. Pay particular attention to the microclimates that exist in your own garden: There are likely to be many. The more you are aware of them, the more you will be able to select plants that will thrive without undue pampering. Examples of conditions that foster microclimates include: A site against a south-facing wall warms earlier in spring and may escape earliest frost in the fall, in effect becoming a hardiness zone warmer than the surrounding landscape; a storm breaks a large branch from a tree, and its removal results in a spot of ground that—at least for some time—will be sunnier than before; an area where the soil is boggy or even inundated, but rarely dry, surrounded by well-drained soil, or vice versa; soil next to building foundations may be considerably more alkaline than elsewhere in the garden.

Vision. It is invaluable to know exactly what you want before executing a garden plan, otherwise those who mean to help may alter your course and diminish the end results. Well into the eighth decade of my grandfather King's life he announced plans for a new orchard. Family, friends, and neighbors lost no time advising him of his folly: He could not expect to live to see the trees bear fruit. Grandfather King persisted and before he died at age ninety-six the orchard had validated his vision through a decade of productive harvests.

Experience. Planning a garden in the mind or on paper is a pleasant activity that gardeners and would-be gardeners find especially therapeutic in the dead of Northeast winters when little can be accomplished outdoors. Nevertheless, the wisdom of experience can be gained only through the process of turning a plan or dream into reality, yours or someone else's. If your own garden is presently in the dream stages, seek experience by helping others achieve their goals.

Soil, Fertilizer, and Waste Management

Healthy soil must be the basis for every healthy garden. No matter how vigorous your plants may be when you buy them, their ultimate success depends on the soil in which they are planted. If (by nature or through abuse) the soil is of poor quality, this condition stresses the plants and makes them more susceptible to decimation by insects, disease, or air pollution.

A common mistake is to assume that applications of fertilizer will make up for any inadequacies in the soil. There is much more to it. Good garden soil should be of a texture that will hold plants securely; release plant foods to the roots slowly over a long period; and retain moisture, while at the same time allowing any surplus to drain away. The three basic types of soil are loam, clay, and sand. "Loam" suggests a balanced combination of soil, which includes both clay and sand, as well as humus from decaying organic matter. It is likely to have a moderately acid to neutral pH, which is to say between around 6.0 to 7.0 on the pH scale. "Clay" is dense, sticky when wet, rocklike when dry, and inclined to the acid side, which is to say a pH of 6.0 or lower; it can be improved for plant life by the addition of sand and humus. "Sandy" soil is porous, fast-draining, and often alkaline, with a pH of 7.0 or higher. In most cases in the Northeast soil can be rendered suitable for planting by digging deeply, from 8 to 20 inches, and incorporating generous quantities of well-rotted compost or sphagnum peat moss and clean, sharp sand to break up dense clay.

Moisture content of the soil at the time of cultivation is critical, particularly on soils with relatively large amounts of clay. Tilling a clay loam or finer textured soil when too wet or too dry often results in large rocklike clods. At an intermediate water content the soil can usually be broken without destroying the natural structure. The proper moisture content can be determined very easily. Dig up a handful of soil. Squeeze it. If it crumbles, the moisture is right for cultivation. If it remains in a tight ball, it is too wet to disturb.

Most of us have little choice in selecting the soil for our gardens. More often than not, the original surface soil has been disturbed or is of poor quality. So, you must build a soil to suit the plants you want. Composts and mulches are very important in soil building. Compost is the partially decomposed remains of plants. Worked into soil, compost loosens the structure for easier penetration of plant roots, water, and air, and increases the capacity of the soil to hold water. Mulches are surface coverings applied to soil to prevent moisture loss, increase water intake, moderate soil temperatures, and discourage weeds. Well-rotted compost may be used as mulch, as well as bark chips, licorice root, and a variety of other organically based commercial products.

Any garden can benefit from its own compost pile, where all vegetable waste, including that from the kitchen, can be returned to the soil—and the needs of growing plants. The site for the compost pile should be an out-of-the-way corner of the garden, readily accessible to wheelbarrow or garden cart, yet screened from view, yours and the neighbors'. You can make a satisfactory compost pile without any retaining structure, but some type of box or frame is helpful. One simple solution is to take heavy wire fencing and create a cylinder, 4 to 5 feet in diameter and 3 to 4 feet high, in which to build the compost pile.

In building the compost pile, add leaves or other clippings and tamp them down. When a packed layer 6 inches deep has accumulated, spread fertilizer (one quart of 5-10-5 or one pint of 10-6-4 per square yard) on top and water the layer well. Repeat the process for additional layers. You may also wish to "ignite" life in the pile by using a biologically active compost starter.

During composting, the most readily de-composed organic constituents are consumed by billions of bacteria, leaving a crumbly product that is relatively stable in the soil and which contains many of the mineral elements needed for plant growth. A properly operating compost pile heats up by bacterial action to 120° to 160° F, a temperature sufficiently high to kill many weed seeds and plant or animal disease organisms. Thus, composting is a clean, safe, and beneficial way to recycle garden waste.

Finished compost can be spread on the garden area 1- to 2-inches deep and forked in. It can be placed on the soil surface around perennial plants—but not directly on top of them—as a mulch in late fall after winter freeze-up, or in early spring. And it can be used to mix with sand and good garden soil for potting plants.

Fertilizers and other amendments. The present trend in the Northeast is toward organic fertilizers. Chemicals produce the desired results in plant growth, but at what cost to life in the soil? Organic fertilizers do not have the precision or strength of the chemicals but they nurture the soil by fostering biological activity. We often hear that excess chemical fertilizer runs off and percolates into the ground water, but this can be said of animal fertilizers as well, if they are not properly dispersed.

The chief plant food elements, whether from chemical or organic sources, are nitrogen (N), phosphoric acid or phosphorus (P), and potash or potassium (K). Any complete fertilizer contains all three, plus very small quantities of such elements as boron and iron, mere traces of which are required for healthy plant growth. Nitrogen, which is essential in initiating new growth, produces the quickest, most easily recognized effects. But unless nitrogen is accompanied by phosphorus and potash, such growth is not normal and may eventually prove injurious to the plant's general health. Working in tandem, these elements should produce the following results:

• Nitrogen: Makes leaf and stem. Promotes

This garden-waste scoop crafted by Fred Ballard, ABOVE, is big enough to do the job, along with a lightweight broom. The scoop is made from half-inch plywood, galvanized screws, leather hinges, and a galvanized metal lip.

Garden hoses, ABOVE, are a necessary, yet not always welcome, sight in an outdoor living room. Here the hose is conveniently coiled and stored in a large ceramic pot, which has a drainage hole broken in the bottom.

Hose guides, ABOVE, can be fashioned of stakes driven into the ground, or purchased ready-made for the purpose, such as this lead fish. Without guidance, the hose is likely to cross over and damage plants along the way.

quick growth, weight and bulk. Gives good color to foliage.

• Phosphorus: Promotes fruits and flowers. Makes strong roots. Ensures crop maturity.

• Potash: Promotes general health of plant and of flowers. Strengthens stems or stalks. Increases size and flavor of fruits.

Together the NPK triumvirate provides the macronutrients. Micronutrients, or trace elements, are also essential and while found to some extent in all living soils, they are likely to be missing from the so-called soil-less mixes used extensively today in commercial horticulture. When you buy a chemical fertilizer, check the label carefully for indications that it contains micronutrients.

Acidity and alkalinity of the soil also affect its fertility. A soil that is well provided with nutrients, but too acidic or too alkaline for the crop being grown, may—in effect—keep the nutrients locked up. A lack of water can have the same effect, since the nutrients are available to plant roots only when they are in solution.

There is no denying the convenience of modern petrochemical fertilizers. They are readily available in many different NPK ratios, each designed for a specific plant or group of plants and growth response. Organic fertilizers, derived from plant and animal materials, have the same chemical properties, but usually in smaller amounts that break down less rapidly. Chemical fertilizers are inherently dead, while those derived from plants and animals team with desirable biological activity.

Animal manures such as horse, cow, and chicken, may be applied to fallow ground in the late fall or winter as top-dressing, around plants and between rows (but take care to keep it from touching stems, roots or other plant parts, which it will burn). By spring this will have broken down sufficiently so that it can be readily cultivated into the soil. At planting time you may work the well-rotted or decomposed animal manure into the planting hole. Here are

the basic facts about manures and some other possibilities for organic additives:

• Cow manure is considered "cold"—slow acting, long lasting—but rich in the nutrients needed by plants. Being wet and heavy, it works ideally to enhance light to medium loam soils. Dried cow manure, which can be purchased in bags, can form the basis for manure "tea," a time-honored booster for potted bulbs such as amaryllis, clivia, crinum and agapanthus. To prepare, drop about two cups of well-rotted manure or the dried product in a 10-quart bucket filled with water, ideally rainwater. Let stand a few days. Dilute to the color of weak tea and apply to moist soil.

• Horse manure is considered a "hot," dry manure that serves to warm up the soil and is especially effective when applied to heavy, cold, clayey earth. The straw litter that usually comes along with horse manure adds to the warming effect.

• Sheep, poultry, and pigeon manures: These "cold" types are best accumulated under cover and kept dry. Lightly dust each day's accumulation with superphosphate (any of various phosphates, such as bone, which has been treated with sulfuric acid to increase its solubility for use as a fertilizer). Apply to any kind of gardening soil at the rate of one-half to three-fourths pound per square yard. Hoe or spade in at cropping time or mix with an equal amount of soil and apply as a top-dressing around established plants.

• Human hair clippings, presuming they are

A bench of wood and painted iron is the focal point for this flower border in the Pennsylvania garden of Mr. and Mrs. J. Liddon Pennock, Jr., that features yellow-and-mahogany Gloriosa daisies, yellow Tagetes filifolia, a refined marigold, along with the blue of globe thistle (Echinops ritro) and chaste-tree (Vitex agnus-castus). To the left is a pink-flowered bergenia, silvery lamb's-ear, and beyond, a potted juniper topiary.

free of dyes or other treatment residues, are a more potent source of nitrogen than animal manures. They may be composted or mixed directly into the earth.

• Green manure: This is the practice of sowing on fallow soil the seed of a quick-growing and leafy plant such as Italian ryegrass, buckwheat, vetch, rye, soy bean, rape, or turnip that will be allowed to grow, then dug into the soil as a source of nitrogen and humus.

• Bone meal: This organic material may be raw (very slow-acting) or, more likely, steamed (less slow-acting). Mix into the hole at planting time, or apply as a side-dressing. A time-honored source of nutrients for all bulbs, tubers, and corms, such as narcissus, dahlia, and crocus. Steamed bone meal is often used to advantage when planting roses. Bone meal contains about 25 percent phosphate and a touch of nitrogen. The NPK rating is 1-12-0. It also contains small amounts of calcium and magnesium. Superphosphate serves about the same purpose as bone meal but does it more quickly, and must be reapplied with greater frequency. Some gardeners apply equal amounts of superphosphate and bone meal at planting time, thus assuring adequate phosphorus over the short term and the long term.

• Dried blood meal contains 5 percent nitrogen and is often used for acid-loving plants such as azaleas, and other rhododendrons, and also for aquatic plants.

• Cottonseed meal, which rates high in nitrogen, is often chosen for fertilizing acid-loving plants in general, such as holly, hibiscus, camellia, and rhododendron.

• Limestone: Quick lime is too "hot" and not recommended for gardening. Dolomite or dolomitic limestone is slow-acting and may be used to "sweeten," which is to say raise the pH level, of an overly acid soil.

• Wood ashes: The ashes from the burning of hardwoods contain up to 5 percent potash,

small amounts of phosphorus, and up to 45 percent calcium. They leach quickly, so store the accumulation of ashes from the fireplace under cover until it can be dispersed as side-dressing in the garden, around such plants as lilac, delphinium, and peony. Do not use the ashes from barbecue briquets as they contain sulfur and heavy metal residues (lead, cadmium) that can be absorbed by plants to deadly effect.

• Coffee grounds: These are excellent as an addition to the compost pile, or as top-dressing around acid-loving plants. They contain 2 percent nitrogen, .32 percent phosphoric acid and .28 percent potash.

Coming to Terms with Pests

The late T. H. Everett, author of the ten-volume *New York Botanical Garden Illustrated Encyclopedia of Gardening*, said the best policy was to plant enough for yourself, your neighbors, the animals, and the insects. In my own studies and applied experiments I have seen proof over and over again that plants growing in healthy soil, which is to say high in biological activity, are stronger and less apt to succumb to stresses of all kinds, insects and air pollution included.

Just in case the disastrous effects of "modern" pesticides have not yet convinced you to give them up, consider these alarming facts:

• Every year millions of pounds of pesticides are applied, yet only .003 percent is estimated to reach its intended target.

• Of any given pesticide, only the active ingredient has been tested and approved by the Environmental Protection Agency (EPA). The inert ingredients have not been tested nor has the possible effect of the particular combination of ingredients. Further, there have been no studies of what happens when two or more pesticides are intentionally or inadvertently combined, either in the spray container, or as comingling particles in the neighborhood air.

• A newsletter published by the Horticultural Society of New York advises, "Alkaline water is bad news for many pesticides. Mix them with water having a pH above 7.0 and you run the risk that the pesticide will quickly degrade in your spray tank or on a treated surface (before the water evaporates). Unfortunately, while pure distilled water has a neutral pH of 7.0, tap water is often alkaline. City water frequently ranges between 9.0 and 9.5 because of water treatment procedures. Some points to remember: The longer the exposure in water, the greater the breakdown. The more dilute the pesticide, the less stable it will be."

• Malathion continues to be recommended as a safe pesticide for a wide range of crops, yet it is said to be reliably stable for only a year. How long had the bottle been on the shelf before you brought it home? More to the point, when did you purchase the bottle of malathion sitting on your shelf of gardening supplies?

• Beware of systemic pesticides designed to be applied directly to the soil. In solution these enter the plant's vascular system, thus rendering it toxic to certain pests. Repeated testing in my garden has produced the same results again and again on a variety of different plants. After the initial application to a plant infested with spider-mites, brown scale, mealybugs, aphids, or white flies, there is an abatement in insect activity and there may be signs of healthy new growth. However, the plant itself inevitably goes into decline and dies unless transplanted to fresh soil that has not been contaminated by a systemic pesticide.

• Findings announced in 1989 from a study on pesticides used in and around the home, conducted by University of California researchers James Grieshop and Martha Stiles, showed that one in four respondents report suffering illness related to pesticide exposure. Two out of every five home pesticide users don't read pesticide labels. One in five admit applying stronger-than-recommended dosages.

More than half don't wear protective clothing when applying pesticides. Pesticide poisonings rank third among all non-drug poisonings at the University's medical center. It would be foolish to think that gardeners in the Northeast are more prudent in these matters than those on the West Coast.

Besides a general trend away from the use of all toxic pesticides, there is also widespread acceptance of integrated pest management (IPM), a wholistic approach that places the treatment of insects and diseases into a framework rather than treating it as an isolated problem. In the heyday of modern chemicals that came into the garden following World War II, gardeners were advised to spray crops weekly whether or not insect populations were sufficient—or indeed even present—to indicate the need. We were also encouraged to use broad-spectrum, kill-everything combinations. Now we follow the dictum of less is more. Insect populations are carefully and regularly monitored. If a crop is threatened, the pesticide used will be as narrowly focused as possible so as to do the job without unnecessarily killing beneficial insects.

One of the most effective, safe, and frugal means of insect control is to prune away and discard the leaves and stems that are heavily infested. Then apply a 0.2 solution of soapy water, which can be made by adding 1 teaspoon liquid dishwashing detergent to 1 quart water. For greatest effectiveness you must be thorough, consistent (spray affected plants weekly until they are clean), and vigilant in your watch for undesirable insects.

The practice of introducing a pest's natural enemies has grown increasingly popular in recent years. The "good" guys can be ordered by mail and may in fact be parasites, predators, or fungi. The principle here is control, not the total kill of a potentially lethal pesticide. Best-known in this category is the ladybug or ladybird beetle of the family *Coccinellidae*. In its most popular configuration the ladybug has black spots on a bright orange or red ground. Other

species are black with red spots, or ashy gray or tan with black spots. One of these can consume fifty aphids in a day, and may also feast on mealybugs, spider-mites, scales, Colorado potato beetles, white flies, weevils, chinch bugs, and rootworms. The larva of the ladybug is flat and warty, black with orange, red, blue, or white markings, and has an appetite for pests similar to that of the adult. One ladybird female can lay up to 1,500 eggs over a period of one to two months. These are orange and stand out on end in clusters of about a dozen on stems, leaves, bark, and in ground debris. Pesticides kill this friendly garden helper, although there are insecticidal soaps available that have been formulated to spare the ladybird and other beneficial insects.

High levels of organic matter in the soil, crop rotation, and the use of genetically resistant plants are also consistently effective in controlling the spread of insect pests and disease. Beginning in the 1940s, for instance, American breeders used a Chinese cucumber as the source for resistance to cucumber mosaic virus. One of the most beautiful and satisfactory cultivars of summer phlox, 'Bright Eyes', is notably mildew-resistant.

"A weed is a plant whose merits have yet to be discovered" is one proverb, another is that a weed is merely a plant out of place. Liberty Hyde Bailey, the patriarchal figure of American horticulture, said that he would much prefer to have that militant weed known politely as burdock growing at his doorstep than lifeless rubble. "Old Free Skin," as his students fondly referred to him, might well have advised to

Cutting gardens like this one in the Quebec kitchen garden of Mr. and Mrs. Francis H. Cabot, with annuals such as larkspur, China aster, and zinnia, can be set out in efficient rows in any convenient spot having a half day or more of sun and well-drained soil. Perennials may be similarly rowed out in any appropriate bed in the yard where cutting the flowers for bouquets will not detract from the landscape.

count the presence of vigorous weeds as a sign of soil well suited to a productive garden.

What I have learned about weeds is that their extrication leads to physical and emotional pain if you think of them as the curse of Adam. If a weed is no more than a plant out of place, can we not be rid of it without anger or guilt? Perhaps its most beneficial role is to be played out in the compost pile, thus converting misplaced energy into a livelier garden.

Tomorrow's weed problems can be partly solved by pulling today's before they go to seed. Remove weeds the day after watering, or rain. This eases the eviction of the weed's entire root system. The only possible excuse I can think of for employing a herbicide—weedkiller —is to rid a property of insidious poison ivy.

Lawns and Ground Covers

Gardens and green carpets go together and, uniting with the blue sky, form a universe that invites our presence. How much green carpet and of what material pose no different questions today than at the beginning of this century, yet answers that are environmentally correct as we approach the year 2000 suggest questions that could not have been asked before the arrival of modern chemicals following World War II. In short order, monoculture lawns have become chemically dependent. Striving always for the picture-perfect lawn, we have lavished it with nitrogen until the grass plants outgrew the system's ability to absorb spent growth. Thatch formed, so that water ran off instead of down and the soil at the surface

A lattice garden house in the Connecticut garden of Lynden and Leigh Miller provides a welcome retreat to escape the midday sun and to have lunch, while contemplating the fruits of one's labors. Inside may also be stored the tools and supplies that are in constant demand, such as stakes, ties, and labels, not to mention packets of seeds, bulbs, and newly arrived plants waiting to be set out into the garden.

turned to hardpan. Fertilizer, too, washed away more than down, and so ever increasing amounts have been applied. Weeds and disease always wait for the opportunistic moment to move in, and so they have, causing our lawns to need ever increasing amounts of herbicides.

The good news is that you can declare peace with your lawn, and possibly reduce its size considerably, thereby gaining valuable space for outdoor living and other more rewarding, less environmentally hazardous pursuits. Encouraging healthy soil is the only way to have a lawn that is by nature healthy. Biologically active products that help achieve this end are available by mail and at local garden centers. Pull the weeds; it is good therapy and a toxin-free environment will foster a life long enough to pull lots of weeds. Use a power mower if you must, but only if a silent push-type is unquestionably inadequate to the task. As a general rule, cut the grass high, no less than 2 inches, and remove no more than an inch at a time. This encourages the grass to proliferate, at once also discouraging sun-loving weeds.

An elegant and increasingly popular choice for carpeting the ground where grass proves difficult to grow is moss. The moss gardens of Japan have given many gardeners in the Northeast a new appreciation for it. The moss seemed to be taking over their increasingly shaded lawns anyway, a byproduct of maturing trees. Fred Ballard saw this happening in front of his house in Philadelphia, and has since turned a frustrating problem into a splendid moss lawn. Here is his program:

1) Watch for signs of moss where you thought you wanted a lawn. "God will tell you."

2) Transplanting moss is hopeless. It can last for up to two years but gradually sloughs away. To encourage moss that is already growing on the site, there is no substitute for meticulous weeding, "on hands and knees, mostly from the first of May to July 15."

3) Sweep with a besom (English twig broom). Fred uses a Japanese bamboo broom,

or a soft American broom might be used. Keep leaves off the moss in winter.

There are many species of moss. Some prosper in dry seasons and will have blue-green color, others when it is wet, and these are predominantly green. If you water regularly you will encourage the water-dependent mosses. If you do not water, the result will be a sparser but tougher moss lawn.

Ground covers other than grass or moss can also be planted for the effect of a green carpet; and it may flower or change leaf colors in season. These are not meant to be walked upon (except in the course of maintenance, which is minimal after they become established). Ground covers traditional in the Northeast—English ivy, myrtle, and pachysandra, for example—have been set out in masses of one kind of plant, a monoculture the same as an all-bluegrass lawn. Another view, expressed in the New American Demonstration Garden at the National Arboretum in Washington, D.C., is to think of masses of any plant, in particular certain hardy herbaceous perennials and ornamental grasses, as ground cover. This frees the gardener from the idea that a ground cover has to be green in all seasons and invites appreciation of numerous plants in all seasons and stages of growth. One major cutting-back in spring, bulb plantings in the fall, and the rest runs practically on automatic. Some perennials suited to planting in large sweeps of a kind, to serve primarily as self-reliant ground cover in the landscape, are astilbe, bergenia, coreopsis, dicentra, hosta, liatris, liriope, rudbeckia, salvia, sedum, and yucca. There are hundreds of ornamental grasses from which to choose, for massing with shrubs or perennials. Part of a lawn might also be converted to a wildflower meadow and the wildflowers encouraged to reseed themselves.

No matter your choice or style of ground cover, nothing about this endeavor is as important as thorough preparation of the planting bed, or individual planting pockets if nothing more ambitious is feasible. There is also no substitute for well-rotted compost in impoverished soil and, in some situations, top-dressing at the beginning of the growing season with 14-14-14 timed-release fertilizer pellets may be advisable until nature can take over.

Trees for Northeastern Gardens

Shade trees are undergoing major changes today, brought about by improved propagation techniques, widespread research to find disease-resistant and pollution-tolerant varieties, and the almost year-round merchandising of up-to-date cultivars in containers.

In the past, we have depended on a few relatively common shade trees, most of which were propagated by seed. If you went to a nursery and asked for, say, a sweet-gum, there was no assurance as to its overall shape, its rate of growth, how it would branch, leaf size and placement on the branches, or whether it would be colorful in autumn. Now you can request a named sweet-gum cultivar, 'Burgundy' or 'Festival', for example, and plant either with complete certainty that your tree will give an outstanding performance year after year.

Such named selections, versus naturally occuring varieties, of shade trees have been around for years, but until recently their propagation was a slow and costly process. They must be propagated vegetatively in order to guarantee that the progeny will be exactly like the superior parent. Today, cuttings begin life under mist propagation systems, each planted in a container in which it will grow to marketable size. After cuttings form roots, they are moved to nursery beds, where the young trees are scientifically fertilized and automatically watered for maximum growth.

A container grown tree can be selected and planted any time the ground can be worked. By contrast, bare-root specimens and balled-and-burlapped trees are usually planted only in early spring or late fall.

Local climate is the first consideration in selecting a shade tree that will perform well over a long period of time. Up-to-date and specific guidance can be gleaned from a botanic garden or arboretum in your region, your local Agricultural Extension Agent, or from many outstanding tree nurseries in the Northeast.

Once shade trees are in place, be conscientious about them whenever any large scale construction projects are planned. Thomas Kowalsick, a horticultural consultant of the Cornell Cooperative Extension in Suffolk County, New York, offers this advice:

• Before construction begins, decide which trees are to be preserved, moved, or cut.

• Erect a sturdy, clearly visible fence around every tree to be saved, at least to the edge of the drip line.

• Allow no changes in the grade of the earth within the drip line. If grade changes are necessary near the tree, construct a dry well, a retaining wall, and an aeration system.

• Designate a single access route for all trucks, a parking area, and an area for fill or building materials.

• Designate a common trench for all utility lines. If it is necessary to go through a tree's root system, have a nursery specialist—not the contractor—excavate.

Shrubs and Evergreens for the Northeast

By one estimate, 90 percent of all landscaping in the United States today relies on only 40-odd species of woody plants, the result being more and more of less and less. This self-inflicted sameness can be escaped by a willingness to venture beyond the most ordinary forsythia, single-flowered lilac, flowering dogwood, and common privet, along with the more usual junipers, yews, and hemlocks. Howard S. Irwin, commenting in a newsletter from Clark Garden, Albertson, Long Island, says that we may fail to do this, ". . . partly out of fear of the unknown and partly because we are a nation of spring-time gardeners. We

buy what we know and recognize in flower and we do so mainly in April and May, as a sort of rite of spring. This pilgrimage to nurseries and garden centers to satisfy a seasonal yen to plant, enhance and rearrange has resulted in the all-too-familiar dazzling show of color from Easter to Memorial Day, followed by green, green and more green. It need not be this way.

"For example, even in winter the wintersweet (*Chimonanthus praecox*) displays its creamy, purple-centered flowers some three-fourths inch across, while in protected corners the glossy green twigs of winter jasmine (*Jasminum nudiflorum*) will on mild days push out red-tipped buds that soon expand into clear yellow long-lasting salvers. Oriental witch-hazels follow in February to March with their weeks-long show of spicily-scented blooms, each with four golden straps arising from a dark reddish purple base. They set the stage for late March and April's forsythia, but why not one of the better-

behaved forms, such as 'Arnold Dwarf', not over 4-feet tall, or creeping forsythia, which grows in tip-rooting arcs less than 2-feet high?

"Or instead of the ordinary thicket-forming lilacs, one of the nonsuckering double-flowered hybrids or perhaps a new yellow-flowered selection. Or, in place of the regrettably disease-prone native flowering dogwood, perhaps the June-flowering Japanese or Kousa dogwood; or, if that lovely dogwood gestalt is essential in May, then the unrelated but similarly pagoda-

A mere formality in the Pennocks' garden, seen through top of ornate metal gate: Dwarf boxwood hedges clipped to inverted V-shape are flanked by grafted blue spruce tree-form standards and, on the left, standards of hardy orange (Poncirus trifoliata). The statue is surrounded by a hexagonal, straight-sided boxwood hedge, with four variegated ivy (Hedera helix cv.) topiaries in Victorian urns. The classic columns form a temple of love in the background, which creates a vista and—from another vantage point—frames another scene.

form doublefile viburnum (*Viburnum plicatum forma tomentosum*)."

For continued summer color in the shrub border, Dr. Irwin suggests purple butterfly bush (*Buddleia davidii*), summer lilac or chaste-tree (*Vitex agnus-castus*), and rose or white crape myrtle (*Lagerstroemia indica*). All three of these shrubs prove root-hardy considerably beyond where the tops live over.

Hedging shrubs infinitely more interesting than the overused privet include a trio of glossy-leaved evergreens: the copiously thorny wintergreen barberry (*Berberis julianae*), evergreen euonymus (*Euonymus fortunei* forms), and Japanese holly (*Ilex crenata* forms); as well as the half-evergreen summer- and fall-flowering glossy abelia (*Abelia × grandiflora*), the deciduous burning-bush (*Euonymus alata*), and jetbead (*Rhodotypos scandens*).

While Dr. Irwin writes from the view of a gardener in Zone 7, there is no lack of interest-

ing woody material for gardens in the Far North. 'Northern gold' forsythia, for example, is exceptional among forsythia cultivars because it produces flowers up to the top of the branches in Ottawa and Morden, whereas other cultivars flower only where they are protected by snow cover. 'Cardinal' dogwood, which has brilliant red branches in winter, and 'Northern Lights' azaleas, all developments from the University of Minnesota, offer just a hint of the exciting possibilities.

All-white gardens rank among the gardener's most sublime endeavors. Here the focal point is a Siamese spirit house, which John H. Whitworth, Jr., purchased for his New York state garden from a handcraft shop in Bangkok. In Thailand virtually every garden has one, to serve as an abode for the spirits that inhabit the land before it is disturbed by human hands. A specimen cypress tree glows golden-green, behind the white flowers of cleome 'Helen Campbell', sweet alyssum, astilbe, and spires of snakeroot (Cimicifuga racemosa).

Conservation through Propagation

One of the most common oversights made by gardeners is to proceed to plant at full-speed without setting up a home nursery first. Newly arrived plants can be coddled here until they can be properly planted in the garden. Ideally, this area should be shielded from prevailing winds and offer a variety of lighting conditions, from shady to sunny. A nursery exposed to full sun may need an area with lattice shading if not a slathouse proper. Holding beds can be framed with railroad ties or rot-resistant wood planks such as 1 × 10s or 2 × 10s. For containerized stock, nothing need be added except a couple inches of gravel for drainage in the bottom. For direct planting or heeling-in of bareroot nursery stock until it can be transplanted permanently to the garden, fill the raised bed with your best mixture of garden loam, peat moss, clean, sharp sand or builder's sand (not from the seashore), and compost.

Here, too, is the place for specially prepared beds, for starting seeds and cuttings. The best insurance against losing a favorite plant is to replicate it and give it to friends. Where rare or endangered species are concerned, the cry of our time is conservation through propagation. Generally speaking, seeds and cuttings root best at a fairly constant temperature around 70° to 72° F. Thereafter, remember that high temperatures combined with low light tend to produce tall, lanky, spindly growth while relatively low temperatures combined with high light produce short, stocky, sturdy growth. Maintaining an evenly moist growing medium is vital to success. One drying-out can spoil the best-laid plans for seeds and cuttings.

Perennial Flower Propagation. Any hardy perennial, one that survives winter freezing and returns year after year, can be dug and divided after it has multiplied so that numerous stems or clumps of leaves rise up from the soil. Those that bloom in spring, iris and peony for example, are usually best not disturbed until late summer or early fall. This is also the preferred season for hemerocallis. Most other perennials can be dug and divided as soon as the soil can be worked in spring.

One of the most rewarding of all gardening projects is starting hardy perennial flowers from seeds. The payoffs include an abundance of growth at low cost and the opportunity to grow species that may not be available from a commercial grower. Here are the basics:

1) Relatively strong, quick-growing seeds can be sown in outdoor seedbeds in the spring and transplanted to the garden in early fall of the first season, or in early spring of the second. These include amsonia, anchusa, baptisia, belamcanda, centaurea, cynoglossum, delphinium, dianthus, gypsophila, hemerocallis, hibiscus, hollyhock, scabiosa, stokesia, and thermopsis. With somewhat greater care it applies also to those species of true lily (*Lilium*) that are suitable for spring sowing, for example *Lilium concolor*, *L. formosanum*, and *L. regale*.

2) For the seedbed, choose a spot sheltered from north winds and where the sun strikes warmly without shade for a good part of the day. A loamy soil that breaks naturally into a loose, friable condition is best; study your soil and amend accordingly with sand, peat moss, or fine, rotted manure.

3) Allow 4 inches between rows in the seedbed, which can be opened by a sowing stick, a thin narrow board with one edge sharpened. Press this into finely prepared soil to the depth required for the seed you are sowing, giving the soil a slight push in one direction to form a tiny ridge at one side of the furrow. After the seed has been scattered along the furrow, covering is merely a matter of pushing the ridge back over the seed with the sowing stick, the row then being firmed down by slight pressure on the same stick.

4) Shading from direct sun may be needed for any seedbed sowings made in late spring or summer. Use cheesecloth or open-weave burlap tacked to a wood frame, or lath snow fenc-

ing. Position the shading device about a foot above the soil, supported by driven stakes.

5) From the time of sowing, it is vital to keep the seedbed soil nicely moist at all times. Apply water gently and slowly, in sufficient quantity to moisten several inches deep.

6) Watch out for weeds in the seedbed and evict them as soon as they can be discerned as such. One of the advantages to sowing in rows is that plants you do not want are likely to be growing at random and can thus be spotted.

Seeds of all perennials can be started in flats or pots, which may be brought along in a sun porch, greenhouse, fluorescent-light garden, or outdoors—on shelves or in a raised planting bed. Primary considerations are the same as for those planted in seedbeds as described above: evenly moist soil, shading from too much hot sun, and prompt removal of weed seedlings.

These perennial seeds are best sown in open-ground beds in late autumn or in flats placed in outside frames through the winter months, for sprouting the following season: *Aconitum napellus, Adonis amurensis, Bocconia cordata, Catananche coerulea,* cimicifuga, helleborus, hosta, *Lobelia cardinalis,* oenothera, peony, and phlox.

Bellis or English daisy, *Viola cornuta,* and pansy are usually sown in frames in late summer, after the heat has broken, or early fall, so that by spring they will be ready to flower.

This group of perennial seeds responds best if sown outdoors early in spring before the sun raises soil temperatures greatly: allium, anthericum, aquilegia, armeria, asphodel, hardy asters, baptisia, callirhoe, clematis, dictamnus, gentian, hardy geranium, geum, heuchera, inula, *Iris kaempferi,* liatris, true lily, penstemon, pyrethrum, thermopsis, and trollius.

The final group of perennial seeds are these that are amenable and adaptable for late spring and summer sowing, and flowering-size seedlings the following year: anchusa, arabis, aubrieta, aurinia, campanula, carnation, centaurea, cynoglossum, delphinium, dianthus, digitalis, dracocephalum, gaillardia, gypsophila, helianthemum, helianthus, hibiscus, hollyhock, lathyrus, linaria, linum, lobelia, nepeta, patrinia, platycodon, poppy, salvia, most scabiosas, stokesia, and scutellaria.

Trees and Shrubs from Seeds

There is a lot of talk currently about the urgent need for reforestation, something we may be inclined to see as being done by others, and in faraway places. One place to begin is at home and one way to do our part is to grow worthwhile trees and shrubs from seeds. Fall is an excellent time to begin. Some can be sown in frames outdoors, others inside in a sunny window or, preferably, in a fluorescent-light garden where uniformly long days can be provided through winter.

The growing of trees and shrubs from seeds is filled with many unknowns. Probably in no other line of plant propagation will you encounter more of nature's tricks. Conditions required for germination can vary even among the species of a single genus. Some tree and shrub seeds have such a hard coating that it needs to be nicked with a file before planting, or another approach is to pour boiling water over the seeds, let stand overnight, then drain and plant. Kinds requiring this treatment before planting include acacia, silktree (*Albizia*), camellia, and honey locust (*Gleditsia*). Kinds requiring this treatment and stratification (see below) are boxwood, red bud (*Cercis*), golden-rain tree (*Koelreuteria*), and juniper.

A majority of tree and shrub seeds need a period of coldness, near freezing, followed by warmth, in order to break dormancy. The natural way to start these is to sow them outdoors in a cold frame in autumn, or into winter as the weather permits. When the soil warms up in the spring, germination begins. You can simulate this period of coolness by a process called "stratification" or "vernalization." To do this, mix the seeds with moist sand and peat moss in a glass jar or plastic container and place in your

olive, spruce, sweet-gum, tulip-tree, and black tupelo (*Nyssa*).

Still another group requires alternating periods of warmth and cold to break dormancy. Left to their own devices outdoors these might not come up for two years. To speed up the process, seeds in this category can be stratified three to five months at room temperature, three to four months cool (33° to 41° F), then planted and kept warm (65° to 72° F). If no seedlings appear in three months or so, place in coolness for three additional months, then return to warmth for germination. Seeds in this category include ash (except *Fraxinus americana*), *Cornus* (except the three previously mentioned species), *Elaeagnus multiflorus*, hawthorn, holly, linden, cotoneaster, yew, juniper, silverbell (*Halesia*), and fringe-tree (*Chionanthus*).

Some woody seeds are best sown as soon as the seeds are ripe, otherwise viability may be lost. These include birch, elm, franklinia, ginkgo, maple varieties (*Acer rubrum* and *A. saccharinum*), poplar, and willow. Also belonging to this category are white alder, catalpa, citrus, photinia, podocarpus, sourwood, and viburnum. Oak, chestnut, and other nut trees in general respond better if their seeds are not allowed to dry out before planting. Camellia seeds ripen from late summer to early fall, de-

refrigerator or somewhere with a temperature range of approximately 33° to 41° F for the specified period of time, then remove and sow.

A four-month stratification period is recommended for buckeye (except *Aesculus parviflora*, which has no dormant period and can be sown when ripe), butternut, flowering cherry, hickory, magnolia, maple, and peach.

Seeds needing a three-month stratification period include apple and crab apple, alder (except *Alnus glutinosa*, to be sown as soon as ripe), white ash (*Fraxinus americana*), beech, birch, boxwood, dogwoods (*Cornus florida*, *C. kousa*, and *C. stolonifera*), fir, golden-rain tree, hackberry, hemlock, privet (*Ligustrum*), black oak, pear, persimmon, pine (highly variable), pyracantha, quince (*Cydonia*), redbud, rose, Russian

Towering deciduous trees shade the Philadelphia moss lawn of Ernesta and Fred Ballard, framed on one side by the house, rhododendrons, and a lacecap hydrangea (Hydrangea macrophylla 'Mariesi'), and on the other by the street, ABOVE. Upkeep consists of pulling weeds and sweeping as necessary to keep the moss surface free of leaves, twigs, or other debris. At Hartwood garden in New Jersey, Japanese spurge (Pachysandra terminalis) flanks a grassy path, RIGHT, in part shade and makes a durable and evergreen ground cover that is set in humus-rich soil and requires almost no maintenance. English ivy may be used similarly, but is more inclined to wander into other areas.

pending on climate and variety, and are best planted at once.

Seeds that are surrounded by a pulp need to have this removed before planting. Soak them in water until the fleshy covering softens, then wash it off; drain and dry the seeds before sowing. Kinds that need this treatment include barberry, holly, magnolia, pyracantha, rose, and viburnum.

Whenever you are ready to plant tree and shrub seeds—either immediately following harvest, after stratification, or after the pulp has been removed and they are dry again—select bulb pans or standard pots of convenient size and fill them with a moist mixture of peat moss and sand in equal parts. Cover small seeds to the depth of their own thickness; cover those the size of a pea and larger to twice the depth of their thickness. After planting, press down on the surface of the soil with the palm of your hand. Set the pots in a basin of water until beads of moisture show at the surface. Remove and allow to drain. Then place inside a plastic bag; position beneath fluorescent lights or in a

sunny window. Watch for signs of germination. When you see a seedling, remove the plastic. Be sure the growing medium never dries out; but also avoid soggy wetness.

If seedlings crowd, transplant to community pots, flats, or individual pots. Seedlings that are small enough to be left in the peat and sand mixture for more than a few weeks will need to be fertilized about once a month with a balanced formula such as 14-14-14 or 20-20-20. Pots and flats of tree and shrub seedlings can be placed outdoors during the summer in a protected place. Be sure the growing medium is kept evenly moist at all times, and this may

Sally Reath's garden work center in Pennsylvania, from left to right: Slathouse (with weeping blue Atlas cedar) provides a place to summer container specimens and display hanging baskets of fuchsias. The walkway leads to cold frames, compost bins, a raised scree for alpines, and storage for clay pots. The doors lead into a potting shed, behind which extends a greenhouse, with a back door leading out to an area of raised planting beds, for container plantings and propagation. The cabinet (foreground right) holds garbage for pickup.

mean twice-daily watering. Seedlings of hardy trees and shrubs may be wintered over in a cold frame, and transplanted to nursery rows for growing on the second spring.

Woody Plants from Cuttings

The chief propagator at the Brooklyn Botanic Garden, Robert Hayes, says that many woody plants can be propagated from cuttings in the summer. The flexibility of the branch is the determining factor. If you can bend it and it snaps, it is hard enough to take as a cutting. "The earlier the better," Bob adds, "as the plant will have more time to establish itself before winter." Kinds to try include azaleas and other rhododendrons, lilac, wiegela, and corylopsis.

If your cutting is too soft, try hardening it by placing in a plastic bag in the refrigerator overnight. Wet the foliage and inflate the bag before sealing. Cuttings that are soft, which is to say wilted, when set into the rooting medium are less likely to grow than those that are turgid with water. Here is the procedure:

1) Prepare a "sweatbox," where the rooting process will occur. Use a wooden crate with a slatted bottom, about 4 to 6 inches deep. Line this with newspaper to contain the rooting medium, which can be composed of equal portions of moistened peat moss and perlite.

2) Take cuttings in early morning, when the leaves and stems are in their most turgid state. Cut a 4- to 8-inch section of the stem just above a node.

3) When you are ready to insert or "stick" the cuttings in the rooting medium, cut them again just below the first node, which is where in most cases rooting will occur. Strip off the leaves halfway up the stem; leave two to three sets. Large leaves may be cut in half, both to save space and to reduce transpiration.

4) Use a rooting hormone, available at your nursery, to promote root formation. Most of these preparations also contain a fungicide that will help prevent rot.

5) Make a hole in the rooting medium with your finger or a pencil, large enough so that the rooting hormone powder will not be removed in the planting process. Insert the cutting to a depth of 1 to 2 inches, so that at least one node is buried. Firm the medium about the base of each cutting with your fingers.

6) Once the cuttings are set, water them in place well. After allowing for drainage, seal the sweatbox in a clear plastic bag, such as from the dry cleaner. Use stakes or bent coat hangers to keep the plastic from touching the cuttings. Place the completed sweatbox in bright light, but never in the sun.

7) After two weeks open the sweatbox, and check that the rooting medium continues to be moist. Cuttings may be rooted after four to six weeks. New leaf growth is a sign that roots have begun. At this stage, gradually open and remove the plastic bag so that fresh air can harden the new plants. If more than one kind of plant is being rooted in the same setup, those which root first can be transplanted, while the others need to be kept covered.

Pot newly rooted cuttings in 3- to 5-inch pots and give them the same sort of care you might give houseplants newly transplanted outdoors. Bob suggests keeping them in a cold frame or other protected spot during the first winter, then planting them in the garden.

Fall or early winter is generally the time to put in cuttings of evergreens. The broadleafs— boxwood, mahonia, pieris, rhododendron— can be put in during September or early October; also easy-to-root conifers such as yew, chamaecyparis, and arborvitae. Fir, pine, and spruce are difficult to root from cuttings, but not impossible. Here are the basics:

1) While a cool greenhouse or protected cold frame is preferable, a sun porch where the

temperature does not fall much below 40° F, or rise much above 60° F, may give satisfactory results. Even if you have only a well-lighted window in a cool room, expect some success.

2) Gather cuttings when the temperature is above freezing. Select healthy young branches bearing a number of shoots. With a sharp knife, remove the shoot and cut down to 4 to 6 inches. Shoots of suitable length can sometimes be pulled off with the heel of the older branch attached and any shreds trimmed off.

3) Treat the cuttings with a root-inducing hormone before inserting in the rooting medium. Numerous products for this purpose are sold at nurseries and garden centers. Take about half a dozen cuttings, dip 1 inch of the butts in water, shake off the surplus, and then dip them in a portion of the hormone powder.

4) Insert cuttings immediately and make sure that the bases are in contact with the rooting medium by pressing down and around with your fingers. Apply water until well soaked. Almost any clean rooting medium can be used for evergreen cuttings. One frequently used recipe is a combination of similar portions of moistened sphagnum peat moss and sand.

5) Heat supplied from below the medium is desirable, although not absolutely necessary. It is generally believed that there is some advantage gained by having the rooting medium five to ten degrees warmer than the air temperature. This can be achieved by using a soil-heating cable that is thermostatically controlled.

6) Fit the pots or flats of cuttings with a transparent superstructure of glass or clear plastic film. This is to maintain a constantly moist atmosphere that is essential to the cuttings.

Evergreen cuttings can also be set to root in autumn in a protected frame outdoors. They should be watered and shaded until winter freeze-up. Mulch generously with pine needles. When warm weather arrives in spring, remove the mulch *gradually.*

One of the safest, surest ways to propagate a woody plant or shrub is by means of layering. For the likes of a lilac, forsythia, cornus, magnolia, witch-hazel, rhododendron, or azalea, this can be accomplished simply by bending a healthy, young branch downward, half breaking or half cutting through the stem. Bury it in moist soil alongside the parent, with a cluster of leaves at the tip pointing up, altogether forming a broad U-shape. A large wire hairpin can be used to secure the layer, or a stone can be laid on top where the branch is buried.

If layering is done any time from spring until late summer, rooting should occur from the break in the stem, so that the following spring it can be severed from the parent and transplanted to a nursery or a permanent location.

Pruning, Staking, Grooming

Perhaps more than any other single activity, pruning shapes the future of a tree or shrub, and by extension, that of the garden. It is not uncommon for the inexperienced gardener to feel queasy at the thought of "hurting" the plant about to be pruned, and there are plenty of insensitive types who chop away while visiting with a neighbor, paying little or no attention to what might be kinder cuts to the plant at hand. Although I had been gardening nearly forty years, pruning did not really make sense to me until I worked a season with the professionals at the Brooklyn Botanic Garden. Reading about pruning is one way to learn, watching a video can be enlightening, but nothing compares to watching over the shoulder of an expert, and then putting into practice what you think you know. Some of the lessons I learned that have helped me feel proficient enough to really enjoy pruning are these:

• Try different types and brands of shears, also called clippers, until you find one or more that feels exactly right for your task.

Slugs are a problem in most Northeast gardens. To protect a hill of germinating pole lima beans in the Ballards' garden, a completely safe way to discourage them is to scatter diatomaceous earth in their path, BELOW LEFT. Diatomaceous earth contains the fossil remains of diatoms (unicellular, aquatic algae), which have hard shells composed mostly of silica. Raised planting beds in the Ballards' small kitchen garden are framed with 1-inch-mesh chicken wire fencing to a height of 18 inches to keep rabbits at bay, BELOW RIGHT. An electrified wire runs around the top perimeter to deter raccoons. House-hold pets—dogs and cats—given free run of an enclosed garden will help scare off squirrels and chipmunks as well, but cats are rarely a friendly gesture toward the birds that are encouraged to visit most gardens. Hummingbirds are especially attracted to flowers that are funnel, tubular, or trumpet shaped, such as these on a late summer-flowering Hosta fortunei at Plum Creek Farm, a Connecticut garden, ABOVE. Hummingbirds are also attracted to orange and red colors, and often hover about lantana and blood milkweed (Asclepias curassavica).

• Keep your shears in a leather holster slung from your belt. The alternative is to buy shears by the dozen since you will never know where a pair is when you need it.

• Pruning shears are meant to cut growth of appropriate size, mostly not more than a half-inch in diameter. They are not the loppers or pruning saws used for large-diameter wood, neither are they pliers, wirecutters, screwdrivers, crowbars, scissors, or trowels.

• Never squeeze the handles of the shears until all your fingers are accounted for. Pruning can be done truly well only if you are in the moment, otherwise, you, the plant, or both will end up maimed. Do not push yourself at pruning time; take it easy.

• Finally, what continues to surprise me about the pruning done at the Brooklyn Botanic Garden is that while there are major seasons, such as cutting back the winter-killed wood on roses in early spring, or the wisteria arbors in winter, some pruning goes on all the time.

My usual "pep-talk" phrases—be consistent, be persistent—are a potential disaster when it comes to pruning. If you know what you are doing, my congratulations. Otherwise, it might be better if you first did your homework. Here are the basics of pruning:

Always prune with a set goal in mind: to control growth, to increase yields, to aid in transplanting, or to improve the general health of the plant. No matter what type of pruning you are doing, remember:

1) The strongest new growth will be made from the topmost buds.

2) Buds that face out or are at the top of a branch or shoot will tend to grow more vigorously than their opposites.

3) New growth will tend to seek sunshine.

4) New growth will likely develop in the direction in which the bud points.

5) Vigorous plants in general need less pruning than weaker plants of the same kind—but the more vigorous parts of the same plant usually need to be pruned more severely than the weaker parts.

6) Any plant, no matter how often pruned, will tend to resume its natural form.

7) There is a limit beyond which pruning defeats its own purposes. If too severe, nature will revolt and then either make an abnormal growth of wood and foliage or quit altogether.

Pruning for transplanting. The top growth is cut back to maintain balance with the root

The butterfly bush (Buddleia davidii) *blooms from summer into early autumn and is an unfailing source of nectar for butterflies like this two-tailed tiger swallowtail and a variety of fascinating smaller moths. These ephemeral creatures will appear in ever increasing numbers in gardens where toxic pesticides are not used. Other favored plants include sedum, rudbeckia, mint, honeysuckle, and morning-glory.*

system, which is reduced in digging. No matter how carefully a tree or a plant is dug up, a large part of the root system is destroyed. Pruning back the top, often from one-fifth to one-third, helps to restore the balance between root and top growth. This lessens or prevents wilting.

Pruning for the health of the plant. The general vigor of a plant can often be maintained —or even improved—by pruning. First remove all the dead wood and the broken branches or stems, then prune away any diseased sections to prevent (or at least check) the spread of the disease; disinfect pruning shears between plants by dipping in denatured alcohol. Remove branches that cross or rub and in general thin out surplus growth at center to admit sun and air. Allow shrubs to assume their natural habit. When growth tangles and crowds, cut out a few of the oldest canes back to the ground.

Clematis in particular prompt a lot of questions about pruning. The large-flowered hybrids need little, except to remove any dead or broken branches in spring. Species that bloom in the spring can be pruned as needed immediately after flowering. Species that bloom in late summer or autumn can be pruned lightly in the spring. One reason clematis have continued to increase in popularity is that they are by nature well-behaved vines. Even if one departs its trellis and starts vining across a neighboring shrub, the effect is more beautiful than harmful.

Wisteria represents another pruning challenge, the usual aim being to control growth and promote bloom. Apart from the possibility that this strong vine might invade your home and literally weaken its structure, gardeners mostly manage to keep it in bounds and blooming. A tree-form wisteria surrounded by a lawn that receives mega-applications of nitrogen is not likely to flower unless the surrounding soil is top-dressed in early fall with a bulb fertilizer such as 3-10-6, a 5-10-5 fertilizer, or steamed bone meal, at the rate of approximately 1 pound, scattered over an area to 5 feet out from the base of the wisteria. (Arrange to have no lawn fertilizer spread over the wisteria's turf.)

Proper pruning is also necessary for wisteria bloom and, like other pruning tasks, becomes a pleasure once you get the hang of it. With the tree form, snip new shoots as soon as three to five leaves have formed, or back to the third, fourth, or fifth leaf when you get to it throughout the growing season. Prune vines the same as soon as the vine reaches the desired height and coverage. This practice will develop spur-like growth and heavy flower production.

Staking and grooming are aspects of gardening that never fail to please me. I realize that there are special varieties that need no staking and whose flowers disappear into thin air, but to be honest, I enjoy bringing order to my garden. Bamboo stakes are my usual choice, preferably homegrown and left in their natural color, but often purchased, pre-dyed dark green. I also use twigs or branches in the English manner of "brushing" and find they get a lot of tidying up done quickly and have a way of blending into the background of nature. Besides green twist-ties, green-dyed jute cord, and green plastic ribbon sold for tying plants to stakes, you can also use strips of stockings, strong fabric, or raffia. The idea is to encircle the stem so that the tie holds it in place but does not strangle; tightly secure the tie about the stake.

Winter protection is an important part of putting the garden to bed in autumn. Standard or tree-form roses need to be wrapped in straw or salt hay, which may in turn be enclosed in burlap; where winter temperatures drop below zero, these grafted plants need to be buried in a trench. Broadleaf evergreens exposed to prevailing winter winds may be given a burlap screen. The trunks of newly planted trees may be wrapped with a product sold for this purpose, also to protect against undue drying by cold winds. Stop active fertilizing by the end of summer, so that growth will have time to harden before winter. An application of a no-nitrogen fertilizer such as 0-6-5 in early fall serves to set flowerbuds and harden wood on such plants as azalea and tree peony. Avoid late pruning as it will foster new growth that will not have time to harden before frost. Finally, all plants will come through winter in better condition if the soil in which they are rooted is well moistened at the time of hard freezing.

Wildlife in the Garden, Pro and Con

During a recent visit to the Day Butterfly Center at Callaway Gardens in Pine Mountain, Georgia, it dawned on me that in all the years I had been advising gardeners on what to plant in order to attract butterflies, not once had there been any mention of caterpillars. Until we learn to recognize and respect this creature in all its ages and stages, from egg to caterpillar to chrysalis, there can be no butterfly on the wing. The most carefully orchestrated habitat with all the right nectar-bearing flowers and juicy leaves for caterpillars will not have butterflies if it is routinely bombarded with poisonous substances.

Some plants favored by butterflies are black-eyed Susan (*Rudbeckia laciniata*), butterfly bush (*Buddleia* species), butterfly milkweed (*Asclepias tuberosa*), purple coneflower (*Echinacea purpurea*), cosmos, Dutchman's-pipe vine (*Aristolochia;* the pipevine swallowtail feeds on only aristolochias), impatiens, lantana, marigold, passion-flower (*Passiflora* species), pentas, sunflower, and zinnia.

At the North Carolina State University Arboretum in Raleigh, director J.C. Raulston has observed that among the 6,000 different plants that grow there, *Abelia chinensis* attracts the largest number of butterflies for the longest period of time, surpassing even the butterfly bush. It produces delightfully fragrant white to pink flowers from June to October, and is hardy to Zone 6, or might be grown as a container plant and wintered over in a sun-porch.

Gophers, moles, chipmunks, rabbits, and squirrels commonly visit gardens in the Northeast. Dogs and cats given free run on a property will discourage other furry visitors, although they themselves can be destructive. Cats often prey on the very birds you wish to encourage

and hardly any dog is immune to a sudden, instinctive urge to dig, more often than not precisely in the middle of your latest planting. Rabbits can be excluded from a garden by surrounding it with 1-inch-mesh chicken wire fitted snugly to the ground and at least 18 inches high. An electrified wire immediately above will further serve to disinvite raccoons from your garden party. Squirrels are particularly annoying when they dig in garden beds and container plantings. If no reasonably aggressive dog or cat is available to police the garden, the placement of 1-inch-mesh chicken wire over the newly planted will prevent digging until roots are established.

Gophers can be routed by opening a hole in the hill with a water hose, then dropping in several seeds of red stock castor bean. The gophers will take the poisonous beans when they come up to close the hole. Mole runs indicate the presence of white grubs in the soil, their chief diet. Killing the grubs requires the use of a pesticide which can be found at any garden center along with other supplies for lawn maintenance. Personally I prefer learning to live with the moles rather than pouring poison on the soil. Dropping pieces of rolled-up Juicy Fruit gum at intervals along the mole run is a folk remedy you might wish to try; supposedly the mole is attracted by the smell but is ill equipped to digest the swallowed gum.

What can I plant that deer will not eat? The straightest answer in my experience is this one by Joan Lee Faust, garden editor of the New York *Times*: "Nothing. No plants are deer proof. Repellent sprays work for a time, but must be sprayed directly on the plants, and repeated after rains. An electrified or high fence tends to be the only solution." John H. Whitworth, Jr., whose garden is in upstate New York, came to the same conclusion after observing that the deer population was swelling at a greater rate than he and all of the rest of nature put together could support. Now his property is framed by a high electrified fence, hardly noticeable to the eyes of human visitors, since the garden itself is so inviting.

(37)

CHAPTER TWO

URBAN GARDENING

When I come up out of the subway and enter the Brooklyn Botanic Garden, the rush of oxygen is exhilarating. When I run in Central Park, especially around the reservoir, there is no denying a sense of euphoria. Large open spaces like these, and the countless other parks and gardens, public and private, make life in the city bearable. Despite pollution, soils that may be overly acidified, compacted, and poorly drained, or rubble-based, sharply drained, and overly alkaline, urban gardeners are succeeding as never before. This chapter is unabashedly based on my experience of urban gardening where I live, but what works for us will serve as well the needs of all urbanized gardeners. To paraphrase the song, if you can garden in New York City, you can garden anywhere.

Secret Urban Gardens

Perhaps least known of urban gardens are those sequestered behind townhouses and high walls. More often than not, these spaces are found rubble-strewn, or supporting straggly old shrubbery that has been starved for light by surrounding buildings and the advancing age of ailanthus trees. Turning this into a garden takes nothing less than goatlike stubbornness, which is not to accuse some of my best friends of being goatlike. It also takes determination, unlimited amounts of money, or resourcefulness —and sometimes courage. People whose apartments overlook your garden may admire it and wave thanks or they may use it as a place to throw trash.

A prime example of this kind of hidden urban garden is that of Hope Hendler, whose tiny backyard, nestled at the feet of towering buildings, brings a touch of France into Manhattan's Upper East Side. When I first interviewed Hope for *House Beautiful* magazine in 1970, she described the space as having been only six years before, "a forgotten parcel of earth, soot-covered, and strewn with debris." The photo-

Hope Hendler's New York City garden was starved for light and strewn with rubble when she began fixing it up some twenty years before this photograph was taken. An Aubusson carpet inspired the design for the formal central bed, with dwarf boxwood hedging. Seasonal flowers in a finely tuned color scheme are planted in the open spaces; lily- and other late-flowering tulips (shown) might be followed by white impatiens or pink begonias. Mirror and antique trellising, salvaged from building sites, adorn the back wall and open up the garden.

graph in this chapter shows the garden in spring two decades later, neatly trimmed, filled with tulips, and looking more beautiful than ever, not unlike its indefatigable owner, who recalls, "The most difficult part was putting in tons of peat moss, topsoil, leaf mold, and builders' sand so that I could dig a decent hole without using a pickax."

A favorite Aubusson carpet inspired the central portion of the garden, with its formal, swirled, and rounded design realized in dwarf boxwood hedging. Seasonal flowers color the inner spaces: tulips in spring, white impatiens or pink begonias in summer, and field chrysanthemums in fall. Winter finds the little garden under a mulch of salt hay and it hardly ever looks prettier than when lightly blanketed with snow. The 2-foot-wide planting beds next to the walls on either side receive the least amount of sun, yet silver-lace vine (*Polygonum aubertii*) forms a graceful backdrop for lush plantings of hardy ferns, white-flowered bleeding-heart, white heuchera (or coral bells), and the spires of snakeroot (*Cimicifuga racemosa*) in late summer. There may also be green-and-white fancyleaf caladiums in warm weather, and numerous hostas having any shade of green or green-and-white leaves.

Part of this garden's on-going success lies in its fundamentally sound design and the clever combining of mirror, trellis, statuary, splashing water, and night lighting. Hope spotted the antique trellis in the garden of a church that was being razed. The mirror behind it was salvaged from an embassy nearby, also being razed. In front of the trellis sit three of the classic Four Seasons statues ("the one depicting Winter is visiting a friend's garden"), around a fountain with splashing water to mask city noise.

Hope's garden has two kinds of furniture, vintage wire found in thrift and antique shops, and, in her words, "The rest is common ordinary French garden furniture which I paint in my own special shade of green every spring."

Community and Volunteer Gardens

Some years ago I got really discouraged with living in the city and thought seriously about leaving. However, when I faced up to what I wanted—which was a sense of community and of being a responsible citizen in that community, with friends and neighbors I cared about —it became clear that all this was possible by changing my attitude, not my address. Participating in the New York Flower Show has been a great outlet for me, and for a time I volunteered my services to install and maintain a container garden of large ivy topiaries at the City of New York's Department of Cultural Affairs. Working on an advisory committee for the Board of Education has given me an opportunity to influence what students in the New York City school system are taught about horticulture, and attending the evening lecture series at the Horticultural Society of New York, which is cosponsored by The New York Botanical Garden, has helped me feel at home in the midst of megalopolis in much the same way my parents do in a small town surrounded by a community of farmers and ranchers.

Apart from private gardening spaces, one of the greatest opportunities for hands-on gardening in the city is to participate in an organized community garden. Barbara Earnest, executive director for New York City's Green Guerillas, says they have four hundred fifty community gardens on their mailing list alone, and that up to twice this number are active within the city's five boroughs. Barbara sees each of these as inherently healthy places where it is convenient for city dwellers to exercise, be outdoors, participate in recreative activities, and relax with other people. "It is a golden opportunity to teach youth, defuse neighborhood tensions, and generate hope, for if you plant a garden, it is a statement of hope for the future." I asked Barbara to comment in response to key words having to do with urban community gardens:

Theft. "It happens but is a relatively minor concern out of maybe twenty other things you have to think about."

Water. "After you have the space, the availability of water is the top priority. Some gardens use fire hydrants, which is legal only with a permit from the city. Best is to be able to attach a hose to a building next door. Otherwise, the solution is to carry the water in buckets from your home."

Soil. "The story goes that the original West Side Community Garden, at 90th and Broadway, was based on ground-up movie theatre. In practice you go in first and remove large debris, paint or other potential toxins, but mostly you leave what is there to form the basis for what you have to have faith will come to be. What is essentially crumbled up old brick makes an alkaline soil base that rapidly drains. The answer is to add tons of humus, which can be from the Christmas tree recycling mulch program, as well as manure hauled from the city stables. This year we have high hopes for a new composting project that will turn kitchen scraps back to the living soil."

Uncertain future. "Permanency for each community garden is a major concern of all technical assistance groups, including the Council for the Environment, the Trust for the Public Land, Cornell Agricultural Extension, and Operation GreenThumb, an agency within the Department of General Services, created when the city realized that city-owned land could be improved while plans for development were under way. An Adjacent Site program seeks to match garden spots with a day-care center, school, social services agency, or an AIDS center, so that the maintenance needs of the garden can serve the needs of each cooperating institution. All of us work to influence builders and architects to plan new buildings with permanent open space, which is what has happened at the West Side Community Garden."

Supplies and plants. "At present we have two hundred fifty active Green Guerillas we can call for technical assistance and help at giveaways, two big ones in spring and fall, and lots of little ones all through the year. We sweep the city for donated plants, seeds, bulbs, trees, soil, containers, and supplies, which we accumulate at a holding area within the Liz Christy Bowery-Houston garden. At the appropriate time we announce a giveaway, which brings members from all over the city with shopping carts, bicycles, cars, and vans. We are the ultimate green recyclers. If there's life in it, we'll see that it gets invested in an ongoing garden."

At the Green Guerillas quarterly meeting held in December, I found a pot-luck supper and camaraderie not all that different from dinner on the ground at my parents' little Baptist church in the country. After a rousing discussion about the contest for best compost recipe scheduled for the spring meeting, we were treated to a slide lecture by the effervescent Lynden Miller, whose designs, installations, and ongoing management of public gardens in Central Park have made her much loved and revered, no doubt destined to be a legend in her own time when she finishes important new gardens behind the New York Public Library, at 42nd Street between Fifth Avenue and the Avenue of the Americas, and a new perennial garden at The New York Botanical Garden.

Mean Streets, Tough Trees

The New York City Street Tree Consortium, a nonprofit organization, was formed in the late 1970s when the city was in a financial crisis and was ill-prepared to finance the Parks Department in taking care of the city's 700,000 street trees. An ad hoc class comprised of a handful of "little old ladies and retirees" has grown into a formalized course that has graduated upwards of 2,000 citizen pruners, each of whom pays a modest fee to learn how to water, mulch, fertilize, and prune the city's precious street trees.

Those who participate run the gamut from blue-collar workers to the very rich. One of the most famous graduates is Frank Field, the television personality and weather forecaster.

A recent class included citizens with these concerns: A need to know about the bugs that were decimating trees near Columbia University. The student will take back what has been learned to the neighborhood block association. Another student came to find answers about worms devouring the tree leaves on a block near Central Park. A landscaper from Queens took the course as a refresher, knowing he would be brought up-to-date on the many changes that occur constantly in this field. Students come, in general, out of a desire to help city trees, many of which routinely have garbage piled around and propped against them, not to mention scuffs, multiple abrasions, and worse from careless drivers.

Graduates not only receive a diploma, they get to shake hands with one of the city's foremost lovers of trees, or so one always hopes, the Parks Commissioner. In addition, they receive an official ID card from the Parks Department that shows they have the right to prune, but only from the ground level, to avoid injury and forestall lawsuits. Anyone caught pruning a city-owned tree without a pruner's ID runs the risk of being arrested.

While rules may vary from city to city, those in force in New York City are an indication: "No person shall deface, write upon, injure, sever, mutilate, kill, or remove from the ground any trees, plants, flowers, shrubs, or other vegetation without permission from the Commissioner. Violators face a possible maximum sentence of 90 days in jail and a $1,000 fine. Citizens who take it upon themselves to destroy or move a tree are fined, usually $150, and ordered to pay for its replacement, which can cost as much as $700 per tree."

Although New York City has one hundred fifty Park Enforcement Police, they have the awesome and impossible task of patrolling all five boroughs. Vigilant strangers do much of

Raised planting beds, annually top-dressed with well-rotted compost produced on the site, hold healthy, productive vegetables, herbs, and flowers for cutting in the Westside Community Garden, New York City, OPPOSITE ABOVE. Roses grow along the chain-link fence. The arbored main entrance leads to a terraced, more formal garden, with beds of flowers and seating for gardeners, neighbors, and friends to rest and visit in formerly vacant lots. This small oasis in front of St. Bartholomew's Episcopal Church, at 50th Street and Park Avenue in New York City, manages to appear country-fresh despite air pollution from car and bus exhaust fumes, OPPOSITE BELOW. Maintained by volunteers, it is seen in summer, with the central bed of red-and green-leaved wax begonias outlined by dwarf boxwood, and the perimeter beds outlined with variegated spider plant (Chlorophytum comosum 'Vittatum'). Lettuce, tomatoes, rhubarb, and strawberries grow in fruit baskets lined with plastic garbage bags on this New York City rooftop, ABOVE. Grapestake fencing shields from the strongest winds and provides a place to tie the tomatoes as they grow taller. Equal portions of soil, sand, sphagnum peat moss, and well-rotted compost produce a relatively lightweight growing medium that also holds moisture and supplies nutrients on a slow-release basis.

the policing and daily call in to report infractions on the rules.

Selecting and Planting City Trees

It is understood universally that we plant trees for future generations, therefore the selection and initial planting merit special considerations. It is primary that the tree be pollution-resistant and that it not have any unfortunate traits, such as dropping junk fruit on the garden. As to planting, the first step is to ascertain the condition of the soil and if any water mains, fuel lines, or telephone wires could impede the digging of an adequate-size hole.

Current favorites among trees that tolerate city conditions are these:

Abies concolor (White fir)
Acer species and varieties (Maple)
Aesculus species and varieties (Horse-chestnut, buckeye)
Betula pendula (European white birch)
Carpinus species and varieties (Hornbeam)
Chionanthus virginicus (Fringe-tree)
Cornus kousa (Japanese dogwood)
  C. mas (Cornelian cherry)
Crataegus species and varieties (Hawthorn, thorn-apple)
Elaeagnus angustifolia (Russian olive)
Euonymus species and varieties (Spindle-tree)
Fraxinus species and varieties (Ash)
Ginkgo biloba (Maidenhair tree)
Gleditsia triacanthos (Honey locust)
Halesia carolina (Carolina silver-bell)
Koelreuteria paniculata (Golden-rain tree)
Magnolia species and varieties
Malus species and varieties, especially crab apple
Oxydendrum arboreum (Sourwood)
Phellodendron species (Cork-tree)
Picea pungens (Colorado spruce)
Prunus serrulata var. 'Kwanzan' (Japanese cherry)
Pyrus calleryana var. 'Bradford' (Bradford ornamental pear)
Quercus phellos (Willow oak)
  Q. rubra (Red oak)
Rhamnus species and varieties (Buckthorn)
Robinia pseudoacacia (Black locust, Yellow locust)
Styrax japonica (Japanese snowbell)
Syringa reticulata (Japanese tree lilac)
Taxus species and varieties (Yew)
Tilia cordata (Small-leaved linden)
Viburnum prunifolium (Blackhaw viburnum)
  V. sieboldii (Siebold viburnum)

The Urban Farmer

The first step if you are going to grow vegetables, herbs, and edible fruits in an urban garden, is to have your soil tested to make sure it does not contain a high level of lead that could become concentrated in food crops. If present, you will likely have no recourse other than to dig out the contaminated earth and replace it with fresh soil, or you may opt instead to do your growing of edible crops in containers. King Louis grew his orangerie in wooden tubs and you can do the same with outdoor space the size of a patio, terrace, balcony, or even an extra-large window box. A half day or more of direct sun is the primary requisite for fruits including dwarf citrus, vegetables, and herbs. The rest is fairly easy. You will need containers, soil, water, and fertilizer. Presumably you will be the gardener, a position in my view better than the king's; he had to delegate this pleasant work to others.

Containers can be baskets lined with polyethylene, boxes built from redwood or cypress, shipping crates, or custom Versailles tubs. Fill with potting soil. Water deeply and often so roots never dry out. Apply fruit or vegetable fertilizer regularly. Here are eleven specific crops uniquely suited to urban food gardens at ground level or in the sky:

Dwarf citrus of all kinds grow well in containers outdoors. Move indoors when frost or colder weather threatens. Plant in a mix of two parts sphagnum peat moss to one part each of sand and packaged potting soil. Fertilize faithfully with 30-10-10 or fish emulsion. Water regularly—whether lime, lemon, kumquat, tangerine, tangelo, orange, or grapefruit, severely dry soil will cause leaf drop—or possibly worse.

Cucumbers like 'Patio-Pik' will climb a trellis if one is provided, or dangle from a hanging basket. Sunny warmth and constantly moist soil make the vines fairly leap, but pity the poor cucumber if you are careless about watering your plants regularly, thoroughly, and consistently.

Eggplant grows well in a peck-size basket (which holds eight quarts of soil) or larger. Warm weather and roots never allowed to be thirsty will keep the plants bearing well until frost. The varieties 'Bianca Ovale' (pure white fruits, best harvested when the size of a hen's egg) and 'Slim Jim' (lavender to purple fruits in clusters, perfect "baby" vegetables that color up while hardly the size of a peanut) are recommended for containers.

Figs that bear edible fruit can be grown in containers outdoors in the same manner as ornamental ficus trees indoors. Use bushel or larger tubs. Fruit follows a long season of sunny warmth, and an abundance of water. Winter over in a cool place, ideally not below 28° F. Prune back by a third or more in spring to increase fruiting.

Lettuce of loosehead or leaf types is easy to grow from seeds or transplants, but it needs the cool weather of spring or fall. Lack of water and too much heat cause it to taste bitter and go to seed. Try several gourmet varieties having different leaf shapes and colors. A surprising amount of harvest can be gotten from a bushel-basket-size container, which might be given over in summer to heat-tolerant New Zealand spinach (*Tetragonia expansa*) as a ground cover for tomatoes or peppers.

Peaches like the dwarf 'Bonanza' can be both ornamental and fruitful in containers the size of a bushel or larger. Use a loamy soil generously enriched with sphagnum peat moss and well-rotted compost or manure. Water freely. Caution: In areas colder than Zone 6 it will be necessary to winter the peach in a protected but cold place, 28° F being the ideal storage temperature. In all cases, move the container in winter to the most protected part of the terrace or rooftop, and take care that the soil is well moistened before winter freeze-up.

Peppers, sweet and hot, thrive in 10-inch pots or baskets, on the ground or in the air. Constantly moist soil, warm weather, sun, and fertilizer nurture an early and long fruiting season. Not to make a pun, but peppers in general are presently a "hot" item among the grow-it-and-cook-it crowd, definitely on the ascendancy as worthy occupants in all kinds of Northeast gardens. Fruit colors may be green, cream, yellow, orange, scarlet, or purple to near black, and a well-grown plant brings joy to any gardener.

Strawberries are surprising troupers in urban containers, including planters, window boxes, and hanging baskets. Allow each plant a minimum of a 10- to 12-inch pot. Keep soil moist. Fertilize every one to two weeks. Provide midday shade if the area tends to be hot, dry, and windy. 'Tristar' is a day-length neutral cultivar and therefore flowers and fruits over the longest season possible. Be sure that soil in containers is moistened through and through before it freezes in late fall or early winter.

Tomatoes that taste like tomatoes are grown by more urban container gardeners than perhaps any other crop. Numerous cherry and pear varieties, red- and yellow-fruited, are suited to boxes and baskets. Upright growers in all tomato colors, from white to yellow, pink, and red, can be staked or espaliered to create a decorative screen or wall cover and a bumper crop. Insert wood trellising in a bushel basket or large container of soil. Tie the main stem to the center pole; save and train the low-

est sucker on either side and tie to left and right poles. Remove all the other suckers as they appear. Water and fertilize the tomato plant faithfully. Warm weather and sun encourage growth.

Zucchini and other summer squash need half-bushel or larger containers. Place outdoors when the weather has become dependably warm. Lots of water may be needed daily in the hottest weather. Pick the fruit when no more than 5- or 6-inches long.

Gardens in the Sky

There are untold rooftops and terraces begging to become urban gardens. It is a special privilege to be able to walk directly outdoors from an apartment or loft, one that usually commands a premium price. I often think that those who have such spaces and do not take advantage of them for gardening ought to trade places with those of us who would.

The most proletarian of gardens in the sky is that of the fire escape, strictly illegal, yet widely used for everything from bonsai to summering houseplants to pots of herbs. To be honest, I've never known a fire-escape gardener to get in trouble with the law, except maybe one or two who've made the news because they were caught growing pot, the source of sisal in Colonial times and known as *Cannabis sativus* to herb botanists.

A primary consideration for gardens in the sky is that the structure be sound, strong enough to hold containers of soil and plantings that will presumably grow heavier by the year if not every instant of the growing season. There is also the matter of drainage and being certain that when it rains or you apply water the excess is not seeping into your neighbor's ceiling. In order to make these determinations, you will likely need to consult with an architect or engineer, or with an experienced, professional, urban landscape specialist. All railings and any enclosing walls must be regularly inspected and no potted plant can ever be set

Window boxes seen from the street, such as these red geraniums in terracotta, photographed in Brooklyn, ABOVE, give pleasure to those inside, and also are an encouraging sign to all who pass—especially welcome on the urban scene. Boston ivy (Parthenocissus tricuspidata) clothes the stone house walls with green in summer, fiery scarlet in autumn, and through winter a delicate tracery of stems. The New York City terrace garden of professional landscape gardener William T. Wheeler, BELOW, wraps around the south and west sides of his apartment. A canvas awning can be lowered against the summer sun. Wood floor decking extends up the side walls for seating and to display plants such as sempervivums (foreground, right), with large pots of ornamental grasses and perennial flowers such as echinacea and rudbeckia next to the wall.

where a gust of wind could topple it to a terrace below, or to the street.

Another reality of gardening in the sky is how you will transport supplies from the street, necessities such as soil, water, containers, and plant materials. Transporting large trees and shrubs from the street to a high-rise terrace or rooftop garden, not to mention containers and huge amounts of planting medium, is no small task. Items that will not fit in the freight elevator of a building must be carried up the steps, or in extreme cases may require a crane to lift them up from the outside. The initial setup invariably involves some hard work and no small investment, yet the rewards will far outweigh whatever difficulties may be encountered along the way.

Plants suited to rooftop gardening, as well as terraces several stories from the ground, must first be tolerant of strong winds, or else they will need to be situated where there is protection from a wall, trellis, or other structure. In no kind of gardening are the microclimates more important than in this situation; a few feet in any direction can mean the difference between life and death or merely so-so performance from a plant. Trees that tolerate city conditions have been previously listed in this

The New York City rooftop garden of Mr. and Mrs. John Burgee reflects his love of architecture and hers of gardening. Watered automatically by a drip irrigation system, large wood planters hold 'Sunburst' locusts, a seedless cultivar of Robinia hispida, with underplantings of green and gray foliage plants and floribunda roses. A rectangular pool holds water-lilies and goldfish. Clematis and hardy ferns grow inside the groined lattice arbor, which leads to a deck with furniture for dining, and lattice fencing for privacy and climbing roses.

chapter; among these, the best for planting in the sky are those having relatively small, pliable branches, and small leaves, that offer less wind resistance, such as Russian olive, honey locust, and Cornelian cherry.

Shrubs suited to rooftops and terraces, and city gardens in general, are these:

Acer palmatum (Japanese maple)
Amelanchier laevis (Serviceberry, shadblow)
Berberis thunbergii (Japanese barberry)
Caragana arborescens (Siberian pea-tree)
Cornus species and varieties (Dogwood)
Euonymus species and varieties (Spindle-tree)
Forsythia species and varieties
Hamamelis species and varieties (Witch-hazel)
Hibiscus syriacus (Shrub althea)
Ilex crenata (Japanese holly)
I. glabra (Inkberry, winterberry)
Juniperus chinensis var. *pfitzeriana* (Pfitzer juniper)
Kerria japonica
Ligustrum species and varieties (Privet)
Lindera benzoin (Spicebush)
Lonicera species and varieties (Honeysuckle)
Magnolia tomentosa (Star magnolia)
Philadelphus coronarius (Mock-orange)
Physocarpus opulifolius (Ninebark)
Pieris species and varieties
Potentilla fruticosa (Cinquefoil)
Prunus subhirtella (Higan cherry)
Pyracantha coccinea (Scarlet firethorn)
Rosa multiflora (Japanese rose)
R. rugosa (Rugosa rose)
R. wichuraiana (Memorial rose)
Spiraea bumalda (Spirea)
S. vanhouttei (Bridalwreath spirea)
Syringa species and varieties (Lilac)
Taxus species and varieties (Yew)
Viburnum species and varieties
Yucca filamentosa (Adam's-needle)

Flowers set to grow in windswept urban gardens require the same durability or protective measures as those in seaside gardens, a discussion of which may be found in Chapter Three. Gardens in the sky are especially needful of shielding from prevailing winds, which in most cases can be provided by trellis-work or fencing, or from a lattice structure that may serve as well as an outdoor living and dining room. Canvas awnings may also serve these various needs.

One of the longest-running high-rise terrace showplaces in New York is that of William T. Wheeler, a landscape designer and gardener by trade, whose private garden in the sky is the best advertisement imaginable for his services. The worth of good design is not always recognized, but here I have seen the beauty and efficiency of simplicity at work for more than a decade, achieved as follows:

The entire terrace, which faces south and west, measures no more than 6 feet wide by 60 feet long. Wood decking extends over the floor and up the interior railing walls, there becoming a 60-foot-long bench that invites the display of seasonal potted plants, sculpture, and also accommodates large numbers of guests at party time. Wood planters, built in the same style as the decking, hold pine trees; the soil surface around them is also covered with decking, again offering a place to sit or display a favorite plant or object.

All major planters and large pots are hooked into an automated drip-irrigation system, comprised of functionally invisible black piping and spaghetti tubing.

All plantings are by nature adapted to a situation that is intensely sunny and often windswept: Pine trees, ornamental grasses, and succulents such as hen-and-chicks sempervivum and sedum.

Canvas awnings can be raised or lowered as dictated by the season and the day's weather.

Containers of leafy seasonal flowering plants, which Bill brings from his garden in the country, are nestled against the outside walls of the building, where there is some measure of protection from burning sun rays and blistering winds. Here, too, English and Boston ivies succeed in clothing the walls, adding to the sense of a leafy, secluded surrounding, that can in fact be spied upon by untold neighbors from similar aeries.

Across Central Park from Bill Wheeler's is the city home of gardener *par excellence* Gwen Burgee and architect John Burgee, Philip Johnson's partner. Although perched atop an apartment building, the living quarters, surrounded as they are by terraces and leafy plantings all around, seem more like a house in the country. A circular stair leads to a rooftop garden that looks out over all of the vastness of the cityscape, yet the architecture and its content could be the model for any earthbound backyard gardener who wants a place to garden that also serves as a series of spaces for outdoor living.

Besides a greenhouse where Gwen grows orchids and clivias and winters over such terrace container plants as bleeding-heart vine (*Clerodendrum thomsoniae*) and rosemary, there is a formal water-lily pool about 2 by 15 feet, built up to the same height as the surrounding raised planting beds. There are pine and deciduous trees, shrubs and evergreens, perennial and annual flowers, a salad and herb garden, all automatically watered by the same type system employed in Bill Wheeler's garden.

My favorite part of the Burgee rooftop is a white-painted trellis structure that serves to enclose and suggest privacy, at once also framing near views and distant vistas. Perhaps not so obvious is that this romantic structure breaks the gusty and high velocity winds that are endemic to this kind of garden site, and creates partly shaded, protected spots where woodland ferns and early spring wildflowers are quite at home. More exposed trellis walls provide the perfect place to train climbing roses intertwined with clematis.

Best Plants for Urban Gardens

Plants for city gardens must be resistant to the types of pollution most common in urban settings—carbon monoxide, sulfuric acid, and others. Some possibilities have been previously listed in this chapter. There are in addition dwarf fruit trees that can be espaliered on any wall exposed to the sun, as well as dwarf rhododendron, and English ivy that can serve to soften the corners and make everything look as though it had always been there. Spring bulbs do well in city gardens, as well as shade-tolerant plants such as impatiens, nicotiana, bedding begonias, and fuchsias. Where a half day or more of sun is available, hardly any urban plant is more satisfactory than an everblooming rose, in almost any size from a miniature under a foot tall to a climber that may cover an entire wall.

Where evergreens are concerned, especially the broadleafs such as holly, rhododendron, and kalmia or mountain laurel, it is important to shower them clean with the hose on a regular basis, unless there is sufficient rainfall to keep them free of the insidious grime that settles on everything outdoors in any urban setting. In the event of protracted drought, city gardeners are often the first to be put on water rationing. If such restrictions occur, it is important to use available water on trees, shrubs, and perennial flowers, since they are not as readily replaced as the annuals. Mulches will also help conserve moisture. It may be better not to fertilize at all under these circumstances, in order not to encourage new growth for which adequate water may not be available.

Despite seemingly overwhelming odds, all kinds of city gardens go on being beautiful and productive oases of oxygen and natural beauty. The only way to lose out is to stay indoors in hiding, something an increasing number of city dwellers are doing in response to street crime and persistent threats of unprovoked violence. Those of us who are able-bodied and strong-minded must not forget we chose to live in the city and that doing whatever we can to build and maintain safe public gardens is a responsible and necessary act, as Barbara Earnest says, a statement about our belief in the future.

(49)

CHAPTER THREE

SEASIDE GARDENING

The Northeast has hundreds of miles of shoreline; if we count the bays and inlets and islands, the total amounts to well over a thousand. Some kind of gardening occurs virtually non-stop from Atlantic City to St. John in New Brunswick and Yarmouth in Nova Scotia. While winter temperatures are much colder only a few miles inland, relatively mild Zones 6 and even 7 prevail in close proximity to the ocean. The cold tides and winds of spring delay the season while the warm ones of autumn extend it. Carl Totemeier, who has retired recently as vice president for horticulture at The New York Botanical Garden, elaborates:

"A gardener on the North Shore of Long Island may have to wait longer to plant tender annuals in the spring than a friend in central New Jersey. But the Long Islander will worry less about early flowering fruit trees being damaged by frost. The water effect retards bloom.

"The South Shore of Long Island may have to wait even longer to plant, but can also expect to have fruit trees flower a bit later and will probably be picking tomatoes later in the fall. A rhododendron can flower a week later on the South Shore than on the North Shore."

Gardens by the sea, whether cultivated or wild, have a special kind of beauty born of endless struggle with the elements. The relentless wind that sculpts a tree can also flatten a tender flower and shift the anchor of its roots to another part of the beach. A friendly sun that chases away the morning mist and reveals flower colors of unmatched brilliance can change by noon to a blazing torch that sears every young leaf and bud. The bracing, salty air that sharpens the fragrance of pine and rosemary may affect other plants as if it were a killing spray. Gardening in this atmosphere can be frustrating but it can also be a success.

One of the most direct routes to a thriving garden by the sea is to encourage the plants that grow naturally in the area. What could be more beautiful than a blanket of indigenous goldenrod spreading to meet the blue sea? Or

Ornamental grasses and yuccas, shown in the monocotyledon border at the Brooklyn Botanic Garden, are valuable, hardy perennial seascape plants. Seen opposite in full late summer–early autumn bloom are Miscanthus sinensis gracillimus *(far left) and* Miscanthus sinensis *(near left), with* Yucca filamentosa *'Gold Sword' (foreground), which sends up panicles of white, bell-shaped, 2-inch flowers in summer, to a height of 6 feet. Hardy yuccas are essentially evergreen. Grasses change seasonally and are carefree except for cutting back in the spring.*

colonies of butterfly weeds sequestered in the dune grasses and hovered over by Monarch butterflies in late summer? On a single dune you may find as many as a dozen or more different plants, and some will be on the seaward slopes, some on the crest, and others on the more protected land side. The native denizens of our coastlines, such as beach grass, bayberry, beach plum, beach pea, and seaside aster, are commonly joined by Japanese black pines and rugosa roses from the Orient, and by such European favorites as the sea buckthorn, Russian olive, and heather.

Seashore Growing Belts

As you study plant life by or near the sea, you will discover where various plants grow. In the parlance of seaside gardening, there are Belt I (fully exposed, with salt in the soil); Belt II (somewhat protected, often by plants in Belt I); and Belt III (well back and protected). These divisions intermingle in subtle ways, but they do provide a basis on which to select plants.

Beach plants recommended for Belt I can grow in the existing sand, but will get off to a faster start if some organic matter is mixed into the planting hole. Those for Belt II can manage in sandy soil, but plants in Belt III need beds of enriched garden soil, to a depth of at least 12 to 18 inches. The best natural protection for plants in Belts II and III is the dune. A "live" one can be stabilized by dense plantings of beach grass, beach pea, and pine (excepting white pine which does not do well by the sea). A natural windbreak of Belt I trees and shrubs is also desirable, and the lee of a house or other building can provide a place for a more protected cultivated garden. A high fence can also be used as a wind buffer, but in an exposed position unusually rigid construction and deep concrete anchoring will be necessary. A slatted fence may be more effective than a solid one, since it breaks the force and velocity of the wind without putting up the resistance of a solid barrier.

Soil Preparation

Your first step, before any planting, is to evaluate the soil. Poor drainage is rarely a problem here, but an insufficiency of humus can almost be taken for granted. Richard Pough, whose gardening success is well known to his neighbors on Martha's Vineyard, says that for twenty years in early fall he has been piling a foot of hay on his vegetable garden. In the spring he parts the hay and does his planting. By the end of summer the hay is mostly gone, having been incorporated into the soil by the elements, earthworms, and biological activity. The hay comes from four acres of sheep pasture, comprised of fescue, *Panicum virgatum*, and andropogon, the latter noteworthy for growing well in soil that is poor and sandy. At mowing time in late summer a haypile is made which, come fall, gets moved to the garden. No fertilizers are used except a "little bit of superphosphate" and, for sweet corn, "a touch of nitrogen." No pesticides of any kind are employed. Richard says he picks slugs by hand and drops them into a jar; when filled it is summarily sent off with the trash.

If your garden by the sea doesn't come with a sheep pasture, Richard suggests buying bales of salt hay. If you have access to the beach, eelgrass and other organic matter washed up after a storm can be collected. Do not actually place salt hay or organic matter collected from the beach in the garden until several rains have washed out the excess salt. Richard notes that despite the constant alkalizing effects of salt, the pH of his garden remains healthfully acidic, presumably the result of organic management.

Richard says that deer are his biggest problem, something he shares with gardeners all over the Northeast. His solution was to erect a 6-foot-high wire fence around the garden, inside the lower stone walls, with a narrow path between. "The fence is essential, otherwise the deer would ruin everything."

Every seaside garden needs a compost pile, the same as those that are landlocked. Make it your golden rule never to throw out any vegetable matter that can be composted. A mechanized compost shredder-grinder can speed the process, especially for small, woody branches and twigs. Any poor, sandy soil can be immediately improved by the addition of as much sphagnum peat moss as you can afford, or of well-rotted compost which can be purchased or begged from a neighbor.

When planting directly in the dunes, first make pockets in the sand, as wide and deep as feasible or appropriate. This sounds easy but in practice the walls of the hole have a way of tumbling in upon themselves. Persist, then line the bottom of the hole with a few sheets of newspaper, the black-and-white part—avoid, at all cost, color inks as they often prove toxic. This layer of paper is to help hold moisture about the roots until they take hold. Mix into the bottom of the hole and fill in around the transplant's rootball with as much rich garden soil, premoistened peat moss, and compost as you can muster. This technique encourages plants to send out roots in the new location. Snow fencing or burlap screens can be erected to shield the newly set plants.

If you are setting larger trees and shrubs into the sand, Judy Glattstein—who has written on the subject of seaside gardening in the Northeast for a handbook published by the Brooklyn Botanic Garden—advises lining the planting hole with an old bushel basket, cardboard box, or jute burlap. She continues, "It is then simpler to put the prepared planting mix around the plant roots. The basket or box helps retain moisture, and stabilizes the plant against the wind—a frequent problem along the shore. Until the plant's roots have spread into the new site, it can be shifted by strong onshore/offshore breezes. (A reason to select smaller material. It will have less surface to act as a sail.) Both box and basket will decay over time. Do *not* use plastic bags, plastic burlap, or other rot-resistant materials."

Best planting times for seashore gardens are usually in spring, early or late in the day, or in cloudy weather, and again in autumn when the earth is warm and conducive to root growth while the air is cooling and preparing the garden for winter. In any season, newly set trees and shrubs will benefit from sprays of an anti-transpirant, also known as anti-desiccant, which gives leaves and stems a transparent coating that helps them retain more moisture. Herbaceous plants, including annual and perennial flowers and herbs, will recover more quickly if shaded the first few days by fruit baskets, cardboard boxes, old window screens, twig-supported cheesecloth, or perhaps a couple of well-placed shingles hammered into the ground on the windward side of the transplant. Remove the coverings late in the day so the fogs and dew of night can rejuvenate leaves. Replace them in the morning before hot sun strikes them directly, until strong growth indicates the end of transplant shock.

Stock of native plants for establishing a garden by the sea can sometimes be transplanted from the wild, but it is usually better to purchase nursery-grown material. The main reason for this is that sand plants by nature send roots deep into the earth. However, if you do decide to transplant, presuming you have the right or permission to take them, most wildlings can be moved in the spring or early fall with a ball of soil around the roots. In the absence of rain, water generously at least twice a week until established. A mulch may be employed to further conserve moisture and stabilize the sandy soil. Organic mulches do their work and gradually disappear as humus, which is what you are always needing more of in a seaside garden. Cobbles or smooth pebbles are also appropriate in this setting and won't require replenishment.

Trees and Shrubs for Belt I

It is not feasible to divide and classify all the best plants to grow in Belts I, II, and III. There are too many variables. However, some with a proven track record in Belt I are suggested here. To learn of other plants suitable for your partic-

ular area, observe those that grow naturally near the ocean in the vicinity of your garden. Visit the gardens of neighbors. Make friends at nurseries or garden centers in your community; they can advise you on—and help you obtain —appropriate stock. If the plant of your choice is not found listed here, chances are it will grow in Belts II or III.

Trees recommended for Belt I planting along northern shores include numerous deciduous types, some of which are noteworthy for fall foliage color, and needle evergreens. Select from these for windbreaks, screening, hedging, for general shading, and as specimens.

Acer platanoides (Norway maple)
   A. pseudoplatanus (Sycamore maple)
Alnus glutinosa (Black alder)
Caragana arborescens (Siberian pea-tree)
Elaeagnus angustifolia (Russian olive)
Fraxinus americana (White ash)
Juniperus chinensis var. *keteleeri* (Keteleer juniper)
   J. virginiana var. 'Canaert' (Canaert juniper)

Picea abies and varieties (Norway spruce)
Pinus thunbergiana and varieties (Japanese black
   pine)
Platanus acerifolia (London plane tree)
Populus alba and varieties (Silver or White
   poplar)
   P. tremula (European aspen)
Prunus serotina (Wild black cherry)
   P. spinosa (Blackthorn)
Quercus ilex (Holly oak)
Robinia pseudoacacia (Black locust, Yellow
   locust)

Calendula, the pot marigold of herbalists, thrives in sandy, humus-enriched, well-drained soil and full sun. This wind-tolerant hardy annual blooms best and longest when nights are cool and days are moderately warm; seed catalogs list cultivars having unusual heat tolerance. Fresh, pesticide-free calendula petals may be enjoyed raw in salads or cooked for color and texture in breads. The more you cut, the more they'll bloom. The photograph was taken in late August at the Cook's Garden in Londonderry, Vermont, several days after the first light frost.

Salix alba (White willow)
   S. caprea (Goat willow)
Taxus baccata and varieties (English yew)
Tilia cordata (Small-leaved linden)

Shrubs recommended for Belt I planting along northern shores include needle and broadleaf evergreens, and an array of deciduous types. In addition to seasonal flowers, some notably fragrant, several have berries or other fruit that is pleasing to the eye and to visiting feathered friends. Again, as with trees, any favored shrub you may not find in this list likely can be grown in Belts II or III. Bear in mind, these shrubs are the hardiest in terms of seaside gardens in general, and can form a front line of defense for those less tolerant.

Amelanchier canadensis (Shadbush, Serviceberry)
Arctostaphylos uva-ursi (Bearberry)
Baccharis halimifolia (Groundsel bush)
Berberis species (Barberry)
Comptonia peregrina (Sweet fern)

Cotoneaster species and varieties
Cytisus species and varieties (Broom)
Halimodendron halodendron (Salt tree)
Hippophae rhamnoides (See buckthorn)
Ilex glabra (Inkberry)
Juniperus species and varieties (Juniper)
Lonicera species and varieties (Honeysuckle)
Myrica pensylvanica (Bayberry)
Pieris japonica (Japanese andromeda)
Pinus mugo var. *mughus* (Mugo pine)
Prunus maritima (Beach plum)
Raphiolepis umbellata (Yedda hawthorn)

Silver-leaved plants in general and many conifers or needle evergreens do well in gardens by the sea. Here the contrasting colors and textures of Artemisia 'Powis Castle' (foreground) and dwarf Scotch pine (Pinus sylvestris 'Nana') are thoughtfully juxtaposed in the Pennsylvania garden of Mrs. J. Pancoast Reath. A recent introduction from the English garden bearing its name, 'Powis Castle' artemisia grows strongly to knee height and requires no staking. The filigreed gray leaves combine beautifully with pink, blue, and pale yellow.

Rhamnus species (Buckthorn)
Rhododendron indicum
   R. mucronatum
Rhus species (Sumac)
Robinia hispida (Rose acacia)
Rosa rugosa (Rugosa rose)
Salix species (Willow)
Shepherdia species (Buffalo berry)
Symphoricarpos orbiculata (Coralberry)
Tamarix species (Tamarisk)

From the preceding list of shrubs for Belt I, *Rosa rugosa* might be singled out for reliable performance in the most stringent of seascape conditions. Plantings of these low-maintenance roses function as dune stabilizers at Robert Moses State Park on Fire Island, for example, where the stiff, very thorny canes serve to keep the waves of beach visitors at bay. Rugosas grow to 6 feet in a single season, and bloom from June to frost. The flowers invariably smell of "true" or "old" roses, and are followed by large, showy red hips that persist into winter, unless you have harvested them to make a delicious jelly. No pruning is needed, except to remove dead wood and to restrict or guide growth, and neither is spraying of pesticides.

Two of the most popular rugosa roses are the white 'Alba' and the magenta-red 'Rubra'. Both have large single flowers that tend to bloom recurrently through a protracted season. There are also hybrid rugosas, such as 'Sir Thomas Lipton', a large, double, snowy white that blooms most heavily in late spring or early summer and again in autumn, and 'Therese Bugnet', a lilac-pink double that is nearly thornless and blooms nonstop, early summer to frost, on wood produced during the previous season.

Roses in general are associated with gardens by the sea, although most will do best with protection, in Belts II or III. The salt air and a growing season that might be characterized as having moist, cool nights, and sunny, dry days suit roses, as well as geraniums and delphiniums, somehow encouraging more flowers and less disease. Roses that receive ample humus in the hole at planting time, and are thereafter side-dressed with well-rotted manure or compost in late fall or early winter, will grow innately stronger and more resistant to insects and diseases than those given short shrift at planting time and thereafter bombarded with chemical fertilizers and pesticides.

Flowers for Belt I

Hardy perennial flowers for Belt I include excellent colonizers, ground covers, and candidates for all kinds of cultivated borders, cottage gardens, and even large containers, such as for deck plantings.

Achillea tomentosa (Woolly yarrow)
Ammophila breviligulata (American beach grass)
Anthemis species and varieties (Chamomile)
Arabis species and varieties (Rock-cress)
Armeria species and varieties (Thrift, Sea pink)
Artemisia stelleriana (Beach wormwood)
   A. 'Powis Castle' (Powis Castle artemisia)
Baptisia australis (False indigo)
Chrysanthemum species and varieties (including
   Shasta daisy, Hardy chrysanthemum)
   C. nipponicum (Montauk daisy)
Coreopsis lanceolata and cultivars (Tickseed)
Eryngium amethystinum (Eryngo)
Euphorbia myrsinites (Spurge)
Gaillardia × *grandiflora* and cultivars (Blanket
   flower)
Glaucium species (Horned poppy, Sea poppy)
Iberis sempervirens (Perennial candytuft)
Lathyrus japonicus (Beach pea, Seaside pea)
   L. littoralis (Beach pea)
Lavandula angustifolia (English lavender)
Liatris species and varieties (Gayfeather,
   Blazing-star)
Lupinus polyphyllus varieties and cultivars
   (Lupine)
Oenothera species and varieties (Evening
   primrose)
Opuntia species (Prickly-pear cactus)
Perovskia atriplicifolia (Russian sage)
Sedum species and varieties (Stonecrop)

Sempervivum species and varieties (Houseleek, Hen-and-chicks)
Solidago species and varieties (Goldenrod)
Stachys byzantina (Lamb's-ears)

There are three plants represented in the preceding list that merit special mention. *Artemisia* 'Powis Castle' has been recently introduced to America from England. The filigreed silvery foliage grows on plants that form compact mounds to 3 feet tall, without the disconcerting habit of splitting apart which often happens with 'Silver Mound', a smaller, grayer, and lacier cultivar. 'Powis Castle' mixes or matches with almost anything, but looks especially beautiful with pink and blue flowers.

Perovskia atriplicifolia, or Russian sage, which is actually from West Pakistan, has been in cultivation a long time but has only recently become familiar as part of the New American Garden, often in combination with plantings of ornamental grasses. Technically a subshrub, it is treated as any herbaceous perennial, and grows 3- to 5-feet tall, becoming a cloud of tiny violet-blue flowers in late summer and early fall. No staking, no deadheading, no pest or disease problems, no need for rich soil. Russian sage may sound like too much of a good thing, but the only questions heard about it are, "What is it?" and, "Where can I buy it?" (The answer to the second question is, from any nursery that specializes in perennials.)

The third herbaceous perennial that merits special attention is *Sedum spectabile* 'Autumn Joy', a recent introduction of the old showy stonecrop that has gained rapid acceptance by gardeners all over the world. 'Autumn Joy' forms symmetrical clumps 18- to 24-inches tall of succulent bluish green leaves that become covered with flowers in late summer or early fall, at first pale pink, then salmon, finally rosy russet. These can be left to ornament the garden through winter, or cut for dried bouquets.

Relatively few annual flowers can take Belt I conditions, yet only steps or a windbreak away, it is possible to have almost anything and everything seen in seed catalogs or at the garden center. Perhaps toughest are these eight, not a dull lot by any means:

Arctotis species and varieties (African daisy)
Calendula officinalis (Pot marigold)
Catharanthus roseus, sometimes sold as Vinca rosea (Madagascar periwinkle)
Echium 'Blue Bedder' (Viper's-bugloss)
Eschscholzia californica and cultivars (California poppy)
Helianthus annuus and varieties (Sunflower)
Lobularia maritima (Sweet alyssum)
Portulaca grandiflora (Rose moss)
P. oleracea cultivars (Flowering purslane)

Of the annuals for Belt I in the list preceding, I single out for discussion the *Echium* 'Blue Bedder', whose parentage seems in question. It is reminiscent of the pasture and fence-row blueweed or blue-devil, *Echium vulgare*, but is never invasive. Hairy, small-leaved plants to 12-inches tall are covered in summer by sky blue flowers. It thrives in soil too sandy and poor for most annuals.

Three other flowers often seen in Belt II and III gardens by the sea are delphiniums, bedding and scented geraniums (species, varieties, and cultivars of *Pelargonium*), and nasturtiums. The bracing air, cooler night temperatures, and abundance of sunny weather in summer help keep delphiniums and geraniums productive and free of the diseases that can decimate them inland in hot, humid weather. Delphiniums require perfect drainage and adequate nutrients; side-dressing with compost in late fall is recommended. Nasturtiums need moisture and coddling in the early stages, but then the sandy soil keeps them lean and flowering instead of growing mostly leaves and few flowers as is their habit in overly rich soil.

Herbs Are Beautiful by the Sea

Plants having hairy or gray leaves often do well in close proximity to the ocean, and this class

includes many herbs. In addition to the previously mentioned achillea, artemisia, lavender, rosemary, Russian sage, and scented geranium, almost any plant classed as a herb is fair game. The greater the exposure to sun and to ocean breezes and winds, the more compact will be the habit of any given plant. Woolly and other creeping thymes (*Thymus* species and varieties) are outstanding for planting in pockets between flagstones. Additional hardy perennial herbs suited to seascaping include *Calamintha grandiflora* (calamint), *Chamaemelum nobile* (fragrant chamomile), *Chrysanthemum balsamita* (costmary or Bible leaf), *Monarda didyma* (beebalm), *Origanum vulgare* 'Aureum' (gold-leaved marjoram), *Phlomis fruticosa* (Jerusalem sage), *Poterium sanguisorba* (salad burnet), *Ruta graveolens* (rue), *Salvia officinalis* and varieties (garden sage), *Santolina chamaecyparissus* (gray-leaved) and *S. virens* (green-leaved), *Stachys byzantina* (lamb's-ears), and *Valeriana officinalis* (garden heliotrope).

There are in addition a host of tender perennial and annual herbs that can be accommodated in seashore gardens, if not in Belt I, with a little shelter. (See also Chapter Four: The Kitchen Garden, and Chapter Eight: Container Gardening.)

Ornamental Grasses

Despite the full-time work done by beach grasses to stabilize the dunes, we are inclined to take them for granted. Most gardens by the sea have some parcel of lawn, but even here we

Echium vulgare 'Blue Bedder', a cultivated form of blueweed, which is widely naturalized in the Northern Hemisphere, has hairy leaves and stems, a trait that often indicates adaptability in close proximity to the ocean. 'Blue Bedder', seen here in the Pennsylvania garden of Sir John Thouron, is a hardy annual that can be sown where it is to grow as soon as the soil can be worked. If given the chance in succeeding years it will self-sow and can be left to grow randomly or selectively transplanted. 'Blue Bedder' blooms over a long season.

are inclined to think of the whole and not the individual grass plants. Beyond these standbys are the ornamental grasses that constitute a distinct and separate class worthy of consideration by all gardeners. Those that form tufts or short clumps to 12-inches tall are more likely to adapt in the most exposed areas, while the medium-to-tall ones may be more at home where there is some protection, yet with breezes that give them graceful movement and restless or soothing, rustling sounds.

Among the short ornamental grasses, to 1-foot tall or less, are:

Alopecurus lanatus (Woolly foxtail)
   A. pratensis 'Aureus' (Yellow foxtail, Meadow foxtail)
Chaseolytrum subaristatum, formerly *Briza aristata* (Quaking grass)
Festuca amethystina 'April Gruen' (Sheep's fescue)
   F. amethystina 'Bronzeglanz' (Bronze sheep's fescue)

F. cinerea superba (Blue fescue)
   F. ovina glauca (Dwarf blue fescue)
Hakonechloa macra 'Aureola' (Golden variegated hakonechloa)
Koeleria glauca (Blue hair grass)

Ornamental grasses in a medium-height range, to 4 or 5 feet, include:

Briza media (Quaking grass)
Calamagrostis × *arundinacea* (Korean reed grass)

The ornamental grasses and hardy perennials associated with the New American Garden are in general suited to gardens near the sea. When massed in colonies of a kind, these tough plants become relatively maintenance-free and offer beauty in form, color, and texture in all seasons. Seen above are blue fescue (Festuca ovina glauca) and feather reed grass (Calamagrostis acutiflora 'Stricta'), with a cloud of silvery blue Russian sage (Perovskia atriplicifolia), in an urban public garden designed by landscape architects Jim Van Sweden and Wolfgang Oehme.

Chasmanthium latifolium (Northern sea oats)
Deschampsia caespitosa and cultivars (Hair grass)
Imperata cylindrica rubra (Japanese bloodgrass)
Molinia caerulea 'Variegata' (Variegated purple
    moor grass)
Oplismenus hirtellus 'Variegatus' (Ribbon grass)
Panicum virgatum 'Rotstrahlbusch' (Red switch
    grass)
Pennisetum alopecuroides (Fountain grass)
  P. orientale (Oriental fountain grass)
Phalaris arundinacea picta (Ribbon grass,
    Gardener's-garters)
Stipa capillata (Feather grass)
  S. pennata (European feather grass)
Themeda triandra 'Japonica' (Japanese themeda)

Taller ornamental grasses, to 6-feet high and
more, include these:

Andropogon gerardii (Big blue stem)
Arundo donax (Giant reed—for Zone 7 or
    warmer)
Calamagrostis acutiflora stricta (Feather reed grass)
Cortaderia selloana 'Rendatleri' (Pink pampas—
    for Zone 7 or warmer)
Deschampsia caespitosa 'Schottland' (Scottish
    tufted hair grass)
Erianthus ravennae (Ravenna grass, Hardy
    pampas—to Zone 6)
Miscanthus sinensis (Eulalia)
  M. sinensis 'Gracillimus' (Maiden grass)
  M. sinensis purpurascens
  M. sinensis 'Variegatus' (Variegated Japanese
    grass)
  M. sinensis 'Zebrinus' (Zebra grass)
Panicum virgatum (Switch-grass)
Stipa gigantea (Giant feather grass)

There are also numerous ornamental grasses
that are annuals. You can start the seeds in a
protected place for transplanting later to the
garden. Look for these in seed catalogs, including such favorites as:

Briza maxima (Quaking grass)
  B. minor (Little quaking grass)
Coix lacryma-jobi (Job's-tears)

Lagurus ovatus (Hare's-tail grass)
Pennisetum setaceum, sometimes sold as *Pennisetum
    rueppeli* (Crimson fountain grass)

Although the pleasures of annual grasses are
not to be overlooked, it is in the hardy perennials where we see a life cycle going on year
after year, each season in turn bringing its rewards. Mostly these grasses can be planted
once and not disturbed again until they have to
be dug and divided, usually after four or five
years. And while the gardener with a compul-
sion for tidiness may chop the frost-bitten
growth to the ground in autumn, it is the habit
of the enlightened to leave the grasses standing
until spring, content to observe their muted
colors in the winter landscape and to witness
the magic that occurs when they are encased
by ice or snow. Soon after being cut back to
the ground in spring, ornamental grasses show
promising new shoots. They look splendid in
full leaf as well as when the inflorescences appear. Fresh or dried, the flowers look beautiful.

Bulbs for Seashore Gardens

Bulbs in general need well-drained conditions,
so the sandy soils that prevail in coastal gardens
are an excellent beginning for having flowers in
any season, winter included. Those that bloom
in early spring benefit in particular from wind
screening. The small or miniature species tulips
originating in Iran, Iraq, and Turkey often persist longer than the larger-flowered hybrids, or
may become permanent colonies in gardens by
the sea that aren't overwatered or fertilized in
summer when the bulbs are dormant.

Ornamental onions belonging to the genus
Allium, including the herb chives, *A. schoenoprasum*, do well in all but the most exposed of
seaside gardens. These bulbs can be planted in
fall or spring and come in many sizes, colors,
and bloom times. With lots of sun, well-
drained soil, and free air movement, they increase annually and are virtually trouble-free. It
is a good idea to cut off the dead flowers before

they go to seed, otherwise the seedlings may crop up uninvited in places where they can become hard-to-evict weeds. If cut just before they are completely open, allium flowers last well in fresh or dried arrangements.

Espaliers by the Sea

Plants in close proximity to the ocean grow shorter and stockier in response to constant shaking from breezes and winds. This can be taken as a blessing by the artist–gardener who enjoys sculpting plants. Besides the previously mentioned hedges and topiary, there are tree-form standards and espaliers in all the classic designs and ones you invent to suit the site. A fully exposed Belt I landscape may not be the place for these activities, but elsewhere, perhaps only a windbreak away. Here is a list that includes some exciting prospects for ornamenting seaside gardens.

Acer palmatum var. *atropurpureum* (Bloodleaf Japanese maple)
  A. p. var. *ornatum* (Spiderleaf Japanese maple)
Caragana arborescens var. *lorbergii* (Lorberg Siberian pea tree)
Cedrus atlantica var. *glauca* (Blue atlas cedar)
Cotoneaster franchetti (Franchet cotoneaster)
  C. horizontalis (Rock cotoneaster)
  C. salicifolia var. *floccosa* (Hardy willowleaf cotoneaster)
Ilex cornuta var. *burfordii* (Burford Chinese holly)
  I. crenata (Japanese holly)
  I. c. var. *convexa* (Convexleaf Japanese holly)
  I.c. var. *hellerii* (Heller Japanese holly)
Juniperus chinensis var. *sargentii* (Sargent juniper)
  J. horizontalis var. *plumosa* (Andorra juniper)
Pinus aristata (Bristlecone pine)
  P. parviflora var. *glauca* (Silver Japanese white pine)

Prunus serrulata var. 'Amanogawa' (Amanogawa flowering cherry)
  P. subhirtella var. *pendula* (Japanese weeping cherry)
Pyracantha coccinea var. *lalandii* (Laland firethorn)
Tamarix pentandra (Five-stamen tamarisk)
Taxus baccata var. *repandens* (Spreading English yew)
  T. cuspidata var. *nana* (Dwarf Japanese yew)
  T. × *media* var. *hicksii* (Hicks yew)
  T. × *m.* var. *wardii* (Ward yew)
Viburnum plicatum (Japanese snowball)
  V. p. var. *tomentosum* (Doublefile viburnum)
  V. prunifolium (Blackhaw viburnum)
  V. sieboldii (Siebold viburnum)

While some may live and work all year by the sea, for most of us these are get-away places where we go to in summer, which we hope we can extend from a month or so before Memorial Day to a couple of months after Labor Day, or to the end of Indian summer. In order not to be wild-eyed and sweaty more than you can appreciate or assimilate, try to be realistic in the amount of gardening to be accomplished in any given season. The voice of experience can be heard when Judy Glattstein advises, "This is not the place to look for instant landscaping solutions. Smaller plants adapt, take hold, and grow more quickly than large, specimen-size plants. Large plants have generally been 'pushed' with extra fertilizer, copious water, and will be slow to adjust to a more spartan regime." Even if money is no object, large trees and shrubs from inland nurseries will suffer wind burn and may blow over—or worse. If you are impatient, try to embrace the wisdom of Aristotle: "He who sees things grow from the beginning will have the best view of them."

CHAPTER FOUR

THE KITCHEN GARDEN

Most of what I know about growing vegetables has come from women, while the husbandry of orchards and machine-planted truck patches has come from men. This division of labor in the production of food is not unique to my experience but rather reflects centuries-old traditions. Throughout the Northeast women of the past have more likely than not overseen the kitchen garden even when they themselves did not actually do the work.

Grandmother McDonald believed in gardening according to the signs of the moon, which she followed in each year's *Farmer's Almanac*. Root crops were planted in the dark sign, those borne above in the light. Grandmother started gardening as a child, helping her parents hoe cotton in Alabama, and persisted into her tenth decade of life.

My earliest memories are of helping my mother in the vegetable garden, a process in which I was included from the arrival of the seed catalogs in winter until autumn when we made a last hasty harvest on the eve of a predicted killing frost. Mama's plot, roughly 50 by 100 feet, was, like Grandmother's, set in a flat, open spot next to a windmill and water tanks for the livestock. Climate modifiers—wind and sun shields—were a necessity for the tender and newly planted, while bottomless tin cans and leaky old pails were sunk into the ground next to crops needing as much moisture as could be captured from often meager rainfall and limited water for irrigation. A few weeks after an April shower, Mama always took me to help her pick lamb's-quarters (*Chenopodium botrys*), greens that grew with wild abandon along the road. When they are young and tender, I find lamb's-quarters superior to spinach and expect any day to find them at my neighborhood Korean greengrocer's.

When I grew up and moved to the suburbs with my wife and three small children, the entire lot was designed for intensive gardening, with food crops interspersed with ornamentals.

Purple sage (Salvia officinalis 'Purpurea') and Viola cornuta 'Princess Blue', growing together in the Pennsylvania garden of Mrs. J. Pancoast Reath, illustrate the beauty of edible gardening. Purple sage is as full of flavor as the plain, and violet flowers add a touch of romance and lemony zest to a salad. Sage is a hardy perennial in a sunny, well-drained site. Once established, violas self-sow, sometimes in unexpected places and colors. Both plants serve well along a path or at the edge of any planting bed where the soil is not annually turned.

Editing a book about espaliering inspired me to train dwarf fruit trees against the backyard fence and tomatoes on trellises that rose from the ground to the eaves of the house. A fig tree grew in a big tub on the patio and a patch of okra with its big yellow mallow flowers proved as decorative as anything I grew in the side yard for cutting. Best of all is that play spaces for the children were fully integrated into these interconnecting outdoor rooms so that we could be together without any restraints on individual pursuits.

Soon after moving permanently to the Northeast in 1967 I met Jacqueline Heriteau, who was then gardening in northwest Connecticut. Born in France, her father a Cordon Bleu chef, my initial reaction was that Jacqui grew vegetables in order to cook, but as we got to know each other, I saw her more wholistic view, that growing, harvesting, preparing, cooking, serving, and dining were all parts of one grand act of living, you might say life as worship. Jacqui's first book, *The How To Grow and Cook It Book of Vegetables, Herbs, Fruits, and Nuts* (published 1969), and subsequent writings, spawned a new genre of books about growing and cooking and a generation of Americans who celebrate wholeness through the act of kitchen gardening. Moreover, the only way to be sure the crops we eat are wholesome and completely free of soil- or airborne toxins is to grow them ourselves.

No vegetable or fruit sold can compare for flavor with homegrown produce. For one thing, only if the tomatoes, corn, or beans are growing in your own garden can you pick them just moments before they are to be cooked and served, and that is how to capture peak flavor and nutrition. Another reason home-garden crops are so much better is that the home gardener can plant those superior but delicate varieties too tender for commerical picking, handling, and long-term storage. Beyond these practical benefits, there is the sheer joy of harvesting food you have chosen, planted, and watched grow in your own garden.

Besides not planting at all, the only way to fail with a food garden is to plant only the commercially adapted varieties that tend to ripen all at once rather than in small, manageable amounts as they are needed over a long season; or to plant only the most popular and commercially available vegetables, and to expect them to be of uniform size and blemish-free, like those seen in television commercials and seed catalogs. Real vegetables often taste better than they look and diversity is to be cherished more than sameness.

There are perhaps as many different kinds of food gardens as there are gardeners, for in no area is there greater opportunity to serve personal tastes. Gone is the strictly utilitarian vegetable garden relegated to the back of the yard. In its stead we think of the food garden as beautiful, not necessarily comprised of food crops alone, and of its upkeep as beneficial therapy. In no other endeavor is it possible at once to exercise the body, rest the mind, and produce food for the table.

Four trends that particularly affect the way we look at food gardening today are:

1) The growing of heritage, nonhybrid varieties, some of which date back a hundred years or more; seeds from these can be saved from year to year.

2.) Seeking out only the best in terms of taste and performance, hybrid or nonhybrid, with an eye for appearance in the garden as well as on the table. Ellen and Shepherd Ogden, whose Londonderry, Vermont, garden was photographed for this book, exemplify this stance. They seek out vegetable varieties from around the world, test them in their own garden and kitchen, and then make seeds of only the best available through a catalog called The Cook's Garden (see Resources).

3.) Eating only raw vegetables, or at most, lightly steamed, is not exactly a new idea among some vegetarians, but Cathy Wilkinson Barash has brought the concept full circle by tying together the growing with the eating.

Cathy, from Cold Spring Harbor, Long Island writes and lectures as a gourmet horticulturist.

4) The idea of food plants as inherently beautiful, and therefore worthy of use in the landscape the same as ornamental plants.

Where to Plant Food Crops

All food plants require well-drained soil and a lot of sunlight. Any spot will do for vegetables, herbs, fruit plants, and nut trees as long as these two needs are met. A Southern slope that offers protection from North winds is an excellent site, and if your soil happens to be a sandy loam that warms quickly in spring, the situation could be just about ideal. Avoid steep slopes where soil will erode and really low spots where late and early frosts settle. Keep food plants away from airless corners where pests and diseases prosper; also avoid any site that is shaded by trees and shrubs for they will rob the light, water, and nutrients required to grow vegetables. If you can, locate food crops near your water supply and toolshed.

Preparing the soil. To get good crops from vegetables and other food crops, the soil must have three properties: good structure, high fertility, and a correct pH.

Structure refers to the composition of the soil. The good garden loam everyone talks about is usually a combination of one third each soil, sand, and humus. Soil contains nutrients; sand allows air and water to penetrate the soil; humus retains moisture, which plants need on two counts: one, they need moisture, and two, their nutrients are absorbed through water.

Fertility has to do with nutrients available to plants. Many of the nutrients plants require are already part of the soil. Others you may add. However, unless the soil is in correct pH balance, nutrients may get locked up so they are unavailable to plants.

Ideal soils for most vegetables and fruits are between pH 6.0 and 6.8. Most cultivated soils in the Northeast are in this range. However, if yours is not, the acidity, or lack of it, can lock up vital nutrients. Ground dolomitic limestone is an additive that "sweetens" soil, and ammonium sulfate is one of the additives proposed when soil is too "sweet" or alkaline.

Digging a new garden. If your soil has never been turned before—the fall before, if possible, or as early in the spring as the soil can be worked—strip away the sod on top (grassy growth and its roots), and turn the soil to a depth of 12 to 18 inches. Break soil clods before returning them to the earth. (A rototiller —which digs and fluffs the soil—is a blessing for when the garden needs to be dug brand new.)

Once the soil has been dug or rototilled, it is time to dig in additives—manures, fertilizers, acidifiers, or sweeteners. If you are liming, apply before fertilizing. Wait a few days between the stages if there is time. If you have precious compost to add to the garden, dig it in only when and where you will actually plant.

Preparation for sowing. To keep everything trim and tidy, plant rows so that they will be straight and evenly spaced. A few big plants— cabbage, for instance, and tomatoes—need more space between the rows than most others. The average space between rows is 12 inches for small things, like radishes, 18 inches for medium things, like bush snap beans, 24 inches for larger things like green peppers, and 36 inches for big things, like tomatoes.

To keep rows straight, attach a cord to two pointed pegs or stakes about 12- to 16-inches tall. Poke the pegs into the soil at each end of a row, and pull the cord taut. Make sure the line is straight before you start to plant, and plant under the cord.

Before sowing, do some strategic planning to keep tall crops from shading out the low ones and to make the most of your space. Interplant rapid-growing varieties—such as beets or radishes—between slower-growing vegetables— such as cabbage or corn. The rapid growers will push above the soil line and be ready for har-

vesting before slower types start shading them.

Rotate your crops for the best garden yield and to protect against insects. Different types of vegetables use different soil elements and attract different insects. Root crops, heavy in their use of potash and phosphorus, should be followed by leaf crops or legumes such as peas or beans, which need less of these elements.

How to sow seed. Once the cord and its pegs are in place and a furrow drawn, go down the row dropping seeds carefully at spaced intervals, according to the specific directions on each packet. With the back of a rake, tamp the seeds into the soil lightly or tamp them into place with your hands.

Thinning. Seeds planted outdoors require thinning as soon as the row shows signs of crowding. Remove the weakest plants, leaving space for the strongest to develop.

As root vegetables grow (carrots, for instance, and turnips and beets), thin by remov-

Dwarf myrtle (Myrtus communis 'Microphylla') *trained as a double sphere topiary spends winters in a solar-heated greenhouse at Logee's in Connecticut,* ABOVE LEFT. *This plant is approximately ten years old and spends summers outdoors. Growing along with it are a host of scented geraniums, tree-form standards of laurel or bay* (Laurus nobilis), *and numerous younger myrtles in various stages of training. Herbs and scented plants enhance the overall experience of kitchen gardening outdoors for the duration of frost-free weather. There are scores of different scented geraniums (species and varieties of* Pelargonium), *varying in habit from trailing, as in 'Apple' and 'Nutmeg', to small but stiffly upright, as in lemon 'Prince Rupert Variegated', to the big, bold, upright bushes of 'Old-fashioned Rose'. They can be used in all kinds of containers, or as edgers or fillers in beds. A variety of lettuces not only make a more interesting salad, they look beautiful in the garden as well,* ABOVE RIGHT. *Here, more than a dozen different varieties of green and red loosehead grow in one small wedge-shaped bed at the Cook's Garden in Londonderry, Vermont. The photograph was taken in late August, following the first frost. In warmer regions of the Northeast, sowings of lettuce in late summer yield harvest until November.*

ing the largest, not the weakest, leaving the smaller plants to develop. The bigger the thinned-out plant, the more baby carrot or beet or lettuce you'll have to eat. Since thinned-out corn and cabbage isn't edible, you remove the weakest, not the strongest, of these.

Watering. Vegetable gardens need watering, a good soaking, about once a week. If the sky doesn't open up and do it, you must. There are many watering devices on the market. The soakers are the best, since they keep leaves dry, and do little to encourage diseases. (See also Chapter Six: Water in the Garden.)

Weeds and mulching. Mulch—compost, salt hay, licorice root—is great for keeping weeds down, but many gardeners prefer to apply it after the seedlings are up and thriving. Mulch keeps heat from the soil, as well as moisture in the soil, so when the weather is still cool, mulch may hold seedlings back by keeping heat from them. For the first days and

weeks after planting, weeding by walking down the garden row with a rake or a hoe—disturbing the soil just enough to uproot those tiny beginning weeds—is easy. If you let them get a few inches higher, however, ease goes.

Once the seedlings are prospering, a mulch several inches deep keeps the weeds at bay, holds moisture in the soil, and is beneficial in several other ways. It keeps weed seeds from

The New York state kitchen garden of John H. Whitworth, Jr., stands in a clearing in full sun and is securely fenced against deer and other animals. Planting beds along the outside perimeter hold carefree perennials, including Sedum spectabile *'Autumn Joy', the tall yellow-flowered Jerusalem artichoke (*Helianthus tuberosus*), black-eyed Susan (*Rudbeckia hirta*), and old-fashioned tall single-flowered hollyhocks. Beds inside for tomatoes, peppers, cucumbers, and sweet basil are laid out more formally, with dwarf marigolds neatly edging bark-mulched paths.*

landing on the soil, for instance. The underside of the mulch decays, adding humus to next year's garden.

Seed Frames and Cold Frames

Seed frames and cold frames are essentially the same thing, a bottomless glass- or plastic-covered box set in the soil, heated by the sun, and intended for raising seedlings.

A cold frame is a relatively simple structure that extends the growing season into early spring or very late fall. It is particularly useful for starting slow-to-germinate herbs, such as rosemary and lavender, and early vegetables. Seeds can go into a cold frame several weeks, four to six at least, before they can go into the open ground.

The soil inside the frame must be dug well, as garden soil, to a depth of 6 inches, and well supplied with humus and nutrients. Beneath the 6 inches should be layers of similar depth, one each of sand, straw, and gravel.

Plant a cold frame much the same as you do the garden, except sow the seeds much closer together. During the day, especially when it is warm, the sash should be raised 4 to 6 or 8 inches, to let air in and to let excess moisture out. Water the cold frame when the soil surface shows signs of dryness. Water in the morning; watering inside the frame at night could encourage damping off.

Vegetable Planting Schedule

Vegetables divide into two groups according to whether they are cold-hardy or cold-tender. Here is a suggested planting schedule; numbers indicate days from planting until harvest.

Very hardy; plant four to six weeks before frost-free date: broccoli (70–150), cabbage (65–110), garlic (95–105), lettuce (45–50), onions (90–130), peas (58–75), potato (90–120), spinach (35–45), and turnips (42–55).

Hardy; plant two to four weeks before frost-free date: beets (55–80), carrots (60–85), chard (45–55), mustard (45–60), parsnips (110–130), and radish (23–30).

Not cold-hardy; plant on frost-free date: beans, snap (45–72), corn, popping (95–105), corn, sweet (65–90), okra (55–60), squash (50–60), and tomato (65–90).

Requiring hot weather; plant one week or more after frost-free date: beans, lima (65–78), cucumber (55–75), eggplant (70–85), melons (80–95), peppers (62–80), pumpkin (110–120), and sweet potato (120–150).

Medium heat-tolerant (good for summer planting): beans, all (45–72), chard (45–55), corn, sweet (65–90), and squash (50–60).

Hardy plants for late summer or fall planting (except in the far North), six to eight weeks before first fall freeze: beets (55–60), collards (70–80), kale (55–70), lettuce (45–50), mustard (45–60), spinach (35–45), and turnips (42–55).

Gardening with Orchard Fruits

The orchard fruits, including apple, apricot, pear, peach, plum, and cherry, come in a variety of sizes and habits, from dwarf to standard, and may in some instances take the place of the more usual ornamental shrubs and trees in the landscape. Perfect fruit is not possible without a yearly spraying program. This can be achieved through the use of environmentally safe products designed for this purpose.

Pruning and training fruit trees is one of my favorite gardening activities, one that summons fond memories of Grandfather King and a strong association with my father, now in the early part of his ninth decade and still an active pruner. It helps to read books on the subject, but nothing beats watching the job being done well firsthand, then having a go yourself.

Cross-pollination is an important factor in the yield from orchard fruits. Most apples and pears require cross-pollination to set fruit. So do most plums. Most peaches and nectarines are self-pollinators, but not all. Sour cherries, the cherries so good in pies, are self-pollinators, but most varieties of sweet cherries are not. Species that require cross-pollination are those that will not produce fruit unless pollen from a suitable other variety is carried by insects or the elements to the flowers of the species requiring pollination.

Berries and Brambles

Blackberries in general do well in milder sections of the Northeast; the cultivar 'Darrow' is hardy to the warmer parts of Zone 4. The red and black raspberries thrive even in colder Canadian zones. All three fruits require garden loam well supplied with humus, well drained, and with a pH between 5.5 and 6.5. Avoid the fertilizers high in nitrogen; they produce lots of leaves, fewer berries. Training and pruning raspberries can get as complicated as you like; I favor Ernesta Ballard's system: Cut everbearing raspberries to 12 inches after frost in the fall. They will bloom sparingly and fruit the following spring and summer, but heavily in September and October when the delectable fruits are most appreciated.

Blueberries are easy on the gardener, providing the soil is really acid, with a pH between 4.4 and 5.1. If your soil tends to be alkaline, you can grow them by adding two parts acid peat to one part garden loam and establishing the plants in barrels or boxed trenches, but it is a lot of work. Blueberries are among the plants requiring cross-pollination, but this is easy to achieve since any two varieties will cross-pollinate each other. The only pruning needed is the removal of excessive small growth and dead branches or twigs in the spring of each year.

There are almost as many different strawberries as there are tomatoes. It may take several tries to get the one cultivar or combination of cultivars, such as early, midseason, and late, that performs well in your conditions and yields fruit that measures up to your taste buds. In standard runner-bearing strawberries there are those that bear primarily in June and those that are everbearing.

Grapevines and Hardy Kiwi

Grapes will grow on poor soils where not too many other fruit plants will flourish. The rather sour 'Concord', excellent for jellies and once the only grape possible for Northeastern home gardens, is being replaced by numerous newer cultivars of table grapes that are sweet and delicious.

Situate grapes in a very sunny, well-drained location in soil well supplied with humus. Set the plants 8- to 10-feet apart and plant in early spring while the ground is still moist. Plant as you would a small tree. Training will depend on your garden space and whether you are growing vineyard-style or up and over an arbor or other garden structure. Grapes will produce the second or third year after planting and will go on producing for decades. A few cultivars require cross-pollination, but most do not. Mulch to keep the ground free of weeds and to preserve moisture. Water the plants when they begin to set fruit. In early spring, fertilize by top-dressing with compost or a purchased fertilizer recommended for fruit-bearing plants.

The hardy kiwi, *Actinidia arguta*, makes an excellent deciduous vine for training on an arbor or trellis structure, and bears clusters of 1-inch fruits that ripen in early fall. Unlike the larger, fuzzy-skinned commercial kiwi (*A. chinensis*), these have a smooth, thin skin and can be eaten out of hand the same as a table grape. To my taste, the hardy kiwi is superior, and the plant itself is useful in general landscaping, cold-hardy to about 20° below 0° F. Be sure to order at least one male to assure pollination for up to four females planted in fairly close proximity.

Dwarf apples are espaliered in the classic palmette verrier pattern on a sunny brick wall of John H. Whitworth's New York state home, OPPOSITE ABOVE. Strategically placed galvanized concrete nails serve as tie points for training the branches. The increased warmth of this microclimate results in an earlier harvest, not to mention the ornamental effect of the trees in all seasons. At the Cook's Garden, OPPOSITE BELOW, in Londonderry, Vermont, Ellen and Shepherd Ogden grow and test vegetables from all over the world, critically judging garden performance and eating qualities. Here are rows of onions for winter, Italian parsley, and edible-pod peas, with pole beans in the background, and cutting flowers such as zinnias, cosmos, calendula, and larkspur in abundance. This young knot garden outside the dining room of Mr. and Mrs. Francis H. Cabot in Quebec, ABOVE, consists entirely of naturally dwarf plants that will mature beautifully with a minimum of clipping. They include dwarf boxwood, dwarf red-leaved barberry, and dwarf variegated euonymus. The spaces between are mulched with pebbles, sand, and fine bark chips in muted but contrasting earth colors. Despite the intricate appearance of such a parterre, once established, it requires less maintenance than a "perfect" lawn having similar dimensions. Hence, in a space measuring 12-feet square, a simple knot is satisfying when viewed at ground level, or from second-story windows. Woolly-leaved mother-of-thyme (Thymus praecox arcticus), here established on the flagstone terrace at Plum Creek Farm, a private garden in northwest Connecticut, RIGHT, can be stepped on occasionally with no noticeable effect other than giving off a pleasant scent. Different creeping thymes smell variously of camphor, caraway, lavender, lemon, and pine.

Growing Nuts for Shade and Bounty

Although some of the best nuts can be grown in home orchards only in milder regions of the country, there are many excellent new cultivars that will succeed in the cooler climates of the Northeast, among them butternuts, filberts, and some new paper-shell pecans, black walnuts, and hickory. Select named varieties or grafted trees since these bear in two or three years instead of the five to ten years required by many of the self-rooted types. Cross-pollination seems to produce higher yields in most nut species, so plant two varieties of whatever type you choose.

Allow the nuts to fully mature on the tree and to fall to the ground of themselves. Gather the nuts as soon as possible after they have fallen. This is easier if old sheets have been spread under the branches. Husk the nuts and spread them in their shells on screens in thin layers. Allow them to dry for several days before storing.

The butternut is just about the hardiest of the northern climate species. It belongs to the walnut family and is a native tree from New Brunswick to Arkansas. The trees reach to about 75-feet tall at maturity and thrive in rich

soils and near stream banks. Although butternut shells can be very hard to crack, some of the new varieties offered by catalogs have thinner shells. A beautiful, long-lived tree, the butternut is self-pollinating.

The chestnuts that grew wild in America in the days of the pioneers have been wiped out by a blight that has attacked the trees since the turn of the century. However, in the home garden they can be successfully replaced by the Chinese chestnut (*Castanea mollissima*). Smaller and less hardy than the native species, Chinese chestnuts succeed where peach trees thrive. They reach to about 40 feet at maturity, yield nuts that are a little smaller than the American and European species and require cross-pollination. Named varieties have been bred to be even more blight-resistant than the original Chinese chestnut.

The walnuts are perhaps the most generally popular of all the nuts and among the most beautiful of nut trees. The English walnut, which originally came from Persia, is the walnut whose crop is sold commercially. It is a close relative of the winter-hardy black walnut (which pioneers named the "white walnut"). Walnuts reach to 100-feet tall at maturity and grow well in sections where peaches succeed. Several new varieties are hardier than the peach, among them the much advertised Carpathian walnut (*Juglans regia*) from Poland, a smaller tree that grows to about 50 feet. Walnuts succeed in rich, well-drained soils, but should not be fertilized too heavily in cooler regions.

The heart nut, or Japanese walnut (*Juglans ailanthifolia*), is considered to have better shelling qualities than the Carpathian variety and produces an excellent nut meat. Often called the Japanese walnut, it is not quite as hardy as the Carpathian. Black walnuts are hardier than English walnuts, but are in danger in areas where winters can go below 20° below 0° F. Some of the cultivated varieties are improved and are worth trying if wild black walnuts grow in your climate. Walnuts must be cross-pollinated, so

plant two varieties. When the nuts fall, gather and husk at once, then wash the shells, air-dry them, and layer on screens in a dark, airy room to dry further.

The filberts and the hazelnuts belong to the same genus, and distinctions between the two are so minor as to cause a lot of confusion. The true filbert of Southeastern Europe has oblong nuts in long husks. The hazelnuts have roundish nuts in short husks. Popularly, the two names are synonymous. Improved hybrid forms now offered generally succeed where peaches are hardy. They are small, pretty trees that fit well into suburban landscapes and will succeed as far south as southern Pennsylvania. Plant them in a rich, well-drained soil and give them protection from north winds. Plant two or more filbert trees to ensure a high yield, but they need not be of different varieties.

The pecans are primarily trees for southern growers, although some varieties, such as 'Hardy' and 'Hican' (a cross between shellbark hickory and pecan) have been developed which will produce nuts north of Washington, D.C., into Zone 5. The flavor of pecans is much improved if the nuts are stored in a mesh bag in a dry, airy place for two weeks after harvesting. The pecans grow to as much as 120 feet at maturity and require lots of space all around. They will begin to produce when the trees are six to eight years old.

Herbs and Flowers

The idea of the kitchen garden readily expands to include herbs and rows of flowers for cutting. Annual herbs, such as basil, parsley, and summer savory, can be direct-sown or set out as transplants, in short rows or as edgers for taller crops. Perennial herbs, such as thyme, tarragon, sage, and the many mints, require their own permanent bed or garden spot.

Annual herbs from seeds or transplants: Anise (*Pimpinella anisum*), basil (*Ocimum basilicum*), borage (*Borago officinalis*), caraway (*Carum carvi*), chervil (*Anthriscus cerefolium*), cilantro or coriander (*Coriandrum sativum*), dill (*Anethum graveolens*), sweet fennel (*Foeniculum vulgare*), sweet marjoram (*Origanum majorana* or *Majorana hortensis*), parsley (*Petroselinum crispum*), and summer savory (*Satureja hortensis*).

Perennial herbs from seeds or transplants: Lemon balm (*Melissa officinalis*), salad burnet (*Sanguisorba officinalis*), catnip (*Nepeta cataria*), chamomile (*Anthemis nobilis*), chives (*Allium schoenoprasum*), garlic (*Allium sativum*), horehound (*Marrubium vulgare*), hyssop (*Hyssopus officinalis*), lavender (*Lavandula angustifolia* and *L. spica*), lovage (*Levisticum officinale*), oregano (*Origanum vulgare*), peppermint (*Mentha piperita*), rosemary (*Rosmarinus officinalis*), sage (*Salvia officinalis*), winter savory (*Satureja montana*), sorrel (*Rumex acetosa*), spearmint (*Mentha spicata*), and culinary thyme (*Thymus vulgaris*).

Perennial herbs from started plants: Sweet bay (*Laurus nobilis*) can be started from seeds but they are rarely available. Rooted cuttings and established plants or tree-form standards are sold by herb growers. Sweet bay makes an exceptionally good houseplant in any sunny window, or it can be summered outdoors in half to full sun. Bring inside before frost. Ginger (*Zingiber officinale*) can be started from the roots that are available all year from greengrocers; it makes an excellent container specimen, indoors or out, but cannot withstand freezing. Cover the roots with one inch of soil; keep warm, moist, and in a half day or more of sun. True French tarragon (*Artemisia dracunculus*) is available only through vegetative propagation.

Rosemary is not normally winter-hardy in gardens of the Northeast, but containerized specimens are easily kept over winter in a sunny, cool window. An exception is a recent introduction by the U.S.D.A., *R. officinalis* 'Arp', which is winter-hardy at least to Zone 6 without any special protection other than that afforded by a well-drained site.

Herbs in general thrive in conditions approximating the Mediterranean climate, which is to say sunny, warm, and on the dry side in summer. A well-drained site is imperative, with tolerably lean soil, having a slightly acid to slightly alkaline pH of 6.5 to 7.5. Leafy types such as chervil, parsley, and sorrel can get by on half sun and will do better in nicely moist soil.

Homegrown herbs can be harvested and used fresh or dried. When this year's crop is ready, begin to use it; use leftovers from the previous season as potpourri, or for simmering in a big pot of water to scent the house. Sage and rosemary are especially effective in cleaning up stale air and lavender never fails to impart country freshness.

Freshly cut bunches of the most popular kitchen herbs are available every month of the year in the Northeast. If you believe as I do that living foods cooked little if at all are the most healthful, these are a welcome alternative to any dried product. Another possibility is to finely chop fresh herb clippings and keep them in the deep freeze part of the refrigerator until they are needed for a meal. Kinds such as parsley, cilantro, chives, rosemary, and sage respond well to this treatment, and can be kept in individual freezer bags or plastic containers. Basil is better processed into pesto sauce, which can then be frozen.

Flowers for cutting aren't always available in sufficient quantity from borders in the garden proper, so it makes sense to organize favorite bouquet makers into the efficient rows or raised beds of the kitchen garden. We take for granted there will be annuals such as China-aster, cosmos, marigold, and zinnia, but if some rows or beds can be permanent, there can be perennials such as liatris, summer phlox, platycodon, and Shasta daisy, not to mention that flower arranger's favorite, Queen Anne's-lace (*Daucus carota*), which can be annual (flowers the first season) or biennial (basal, carrotlike leaves the first season, bolting, upright habit and flowers the second). Gladiolus, dahlias from tubers, and tuberose are also popular for cutting gardens, along with numerous ornamental grasses, both annual and perennial.

CHAPTER FIVE

NATURALIZED GARDENS

When I asked Mary How about her friends, the Duncan Pitneys, and their gardening efforts in New Jersey, especially the walk behind a gazebo that is pictured opposite, with its ferns and wildflowers in dappled shade, these words and phrases came tumbling out: "Extremely private. Peaceful repose. Not terribly organized. Kathy puts in things she particularly likes— wildflowers that mean something to her. Gentle and sensitive. Not for design purposes or color *per se*. Some transplanted from friends' gardens. A small statue." My impression of the Pitneys in the same garden was that they had purposefully discarded any notions of imposing themselves. Instead, they had let nature suggest what to plant and where to mow a path wide enough to accommodate numerous strollers. A primary reason for any naturalized garden may be the gardener's need for a place to escape the inevitably rigid schedules imposed by life.

Naturalized gardens can be in sun or shade or in-between. Watch the site; the quality of light and duration will suggest the plants most likely to succeed with the least human assistance. Many shade plants just happen to be native or naturalized to the Northeast. Fortunately, the idea of the naturalized garden is no more applicable than in city yards, especially

those to the sides and back that may receive little if any direct sun.

Since the idea of naturalized gardens is to follow Mother Nature's lead, how does one decide which to encourage and which to banish as weeds? There is no concise answer, except to say we will probably know when the time comes. Over the years I have watched my friend Larry Power consistently save certain plants—trees, shrubs, vines, ferns, wildflowers —and get rid of others from his property in northwest Connecticut until his naturalized and carefully edited garden now encompasses many acres; yet most of the work is achieved by the use of a tractor mower, string-line trimmer, and chain saw.

Seen here in the shimmery light of a showery afternoon in late May, the New Jersey naturalized garden of Duncan and Kathy Pitney is sited between a white lattice gazebo and copse of trees on one side and the high brick wall of an old garden on the other. Dogwoods haze a pink and white canopy over woods phlox (Phlox divaricata) and bugle (Ajuga reptans), hardy ferns, rhododendrons, and the distinctively lobed leaves of Kirengeshoma palmata, which has yellow blooms in summer; to the left are ferns, summer snowflake (Leucojum aestivum), and mock-orange (Philadelphus).

Encouraging Meadow Gardens

More than twenty years ago on an earlier property he owned in New York State, Larry hit upon the idea of lightly tilling a small field in spring and then broadcasting a variety of wildflower seeds. The Iceland poppies were superb, and also bachelor's-buttons, larkspur, white and yellow daisies, and several different dianthus. This idea has since blossomed into a distinct expression of naturalized gardening, the meadow garden, something that can be played out literally in a meadow the size of a small field, with or without sheep, or within a small patch of ground where an island of naturalness is surrounded by a clipped lawn.

In our modern times, "meadows" come packaged in cans. I won't insult your intelligence by saying to read the labels, but not all such products are created equal. A mixture selected specifically for the climate of the Northeast will be more likely to fulfill your dreams of a flowery, romantic meadow, than a one-size-fits-all blend. The usual policy is to plant both annuals and perennials in the first season, so that the annuals will give flowers while the perennials are establishing strong constitutions for the future. The more effort you make in preparing the field before planting, the more likely you will have an abundant germination. There is also an element of luck involved, with the weather, and maybe whether or not you did the right thing in the right sign of the moon. Each year's and each season's meadow garden will make its own unique expression. Paths can be mown so as to avoid cutting any desired crop until it has successfully flowered and ripened seeds, then the cutting can serve to disburse the seeds, along with the chopped stems and leaves that fall to the earth and soon become living humus.

If by chance you have a meadow but are undecided about its gardening merits, spend a season getting acquainted with what is growing there already. Chances are you will discover numerous plants that are naturally beautiful and might be seen in an even better light if given some encouragement, such as mowing or cutting off encroaching weeds. Some of my happiest moments have been spent tramping through meadows in the Northeast, finding flowers, berries, grasses, or sedges that could decorate the dining table and thus bring the experience of the meadow up close to my family and guests.

Having been entertained by all life in meadows, including insects and wild and domesticated animals, it came as something of a jolt to hear that in some parts of the country a parcel of earth destined to become a meadow garden is routinely prepared by first being treated with a herbicide to kill all existing vegetation. I can't speak for the Midwest, where I heard this treatment recommended, but it seems riskier and more radical than could be justified in the Northeast, considering the plant life that occurs naturally in meadowlands.

Naturalized gardens invite the use of native as well as naturalized plants, the difference having to do with the country of origin. Natives have originated in your homeland, while naturalized plants have been brought in, on purpose or not, and have become established to the point of behaving as if they were natives. Trouble arises when a naturalized plant grows too well and begins to upset the ecological balance. This has happened with purple loosestrife (*Lythrum salicaria*), an Old World herbaceous perennial that is now banned in some states.

Woodland Gardens

One of the most readily achieved naturalized gardens is a wooded area that can be enjoyed as it is, and then gradually improved or at least enhanced, after you have gotten to know the land and have a sense of what goes on there in all seasons. With government officials and environmentalists advocating the planting of millions and millions of trees before the dawn of the twenty-first century, we seem destined to have increasing numbers of woodland gardens.

If the woodland contains many evergreens, there may not be enough light at the ground level for anything other than running pine, Indian pipe, partridge berry, and Christmas fern. Deciduous trees allow more direct sun to reach the soil in spring and permit establishing colonies of early flowering wild flowers such as spring beauty, May-apple, Dutchman's-breeches, woods phlox, Virginia bluebell, and cowslip.

Often the first thing that needs doing in a woodland garden is to go in and remove weed trees, all dead growth, and to open up paths. As you can, discern which are the primary trees (tall shade trees), the secondary (smaller—often flowering—types, which grow in the understory beneath primary), or even expendable (weedy ones, those that crowd more desirable specimens, or ones that block a view), and then set about pruning up those you are definitely going to keep. As you thin away underbrush, the chosen trees will become stronger and more symmetrically shaped.

In case you are planting some smaller flowering trees as part of a woodland garden, here are some American natives that might serve as alternatives to the serviceable and widely planted Bradford ornamental pear, *Pyrus calleryana*, not to mention the more usual Oriental magnolias, flowering cherries, and crab apples. All these range in height from 20 to 40 feet; light needs and tolerance are indicated as sun or shade:

Amelanchier arborea: Downy serviceberry; sun/shade
Asimina triloba: Pawpaw; sun/shade
Cercis canadensis: Eastern redbud; sun/shade
Chionanthus virginicus: Fringe-tree; sun/shade
Cornus alternifolia: Pagoda dogwood; sun/shade
Crataegus viridis: Green hawthorn; sun
Franklinia alatamaha: Franklinia; sun/shade
Halesia tetraptera: Carolina silverbell; sun/shade
Magnolia virginiana: Sweet-bay; sun/shade
Oxydendrum arboreum: Sourwood; sun/shade

• • •

Arborist Bob Hyland, writing in a recent publication from the Brooklyn Botanic Garden, notes that pawpaw (*Asimina triloba*) can be planted alone or in small groups, and that ". . . a grove of pawpaws is used effectively to define the edge of a parking lot at the Scott Arboretum on the Swarthmore College campus in Pennsylvania." Suggested companion plants include native summer- and fall-blooming perennials such as New England aster (*Aster novae-angliae*), Michaelmas daisy (*Aster* cultivars), goldenrod (*Solidago* species), ironweed (*Vernonia noveboracensis*), and Joe-Pye weed (*Eupatorium purpureum*).

Redbud (*Cercis canadensis*) looks especially well underplanted with Siberian squills (*Scilla sibirica*), lungwort (*Pulmonaria* species), moss pinks (*Phlox subulata* cultivars), or periwinkle (*Vinca minor*).

Fringe-tree (*Chionanthus virginicus*) gives its white flowers at the same time as tall bearded iris and looks well in the company of Siberian iris and field poppies (*Papaver rhoeas*).

Franklinia, which has white flowers in summer, combines well with late-blooming ground covers such as white lily turf (*Liriope muscari* 'Monroe White') or the blue autumn leadwort (*Ceratostigma plumbaginoides*). Other landscape combinations suggested for franklinia are variegated carpet bugleweed (*Ajuga reptans* 'Burgundy Glow') or late-blooming hostas (*Hosta* 'Ginko Craig' or *H. plantaginea*).

Halesia, with its white or, rarely, pink bell flowers in the spring, combines exceedingly well with a ground-covering colony of native foamflower (*Tiarella cordifolia*) that blooms at the same time.

Sourwood, with its spectacular fall foliage color, never fails to look well in the company of summer- and fall-blooming perennials such as New England aster (*Aster novae-angliae*), daylily (*Hemerocallis* cultivars), black-eyed Susan (*Rudbeckia hirta*), and fall-blooming sunflower (*Helianthus* × *multiflorus* 'Flore-Pleno'). Hyland notes that ornamental grasses are also ideal companions for sourwoods, especially varie-

gated miscanthus (*Miscanthus sinensis* 'Variegatus') and feather reed grass (*Calamagrostis acutiflora* 'Stricta').

One of my favorite aspects of the woodland garden is that it invites taking a walk, often very early or late in the season when other parts of the garden have not yet awakened or have been tucked away for winter. It may be feasible to have some azaleas, rhododendrons, or mountain laurel (*Kalmia latifolia*), strategically placed so as to allow the path to wind and curve and disappear. Install a well-drained walking surface such as pine needles or bark mulch. It is also nice to find a place to sit at some distant point along the trail—or even a gazebo or summer house.

If the woodland garden path can be lighted at night, so much the better. Uplights can give drama to specimen trees, especially the white-barked birches, and small down lights will show up seasonal flowers and the path itself.

One of the nicest things about a woodland walk is that you can pick up a tray of mosses, lichens, tiny ferns, sedges, bits of this and that, and turn it into a miniature garden that can be enjoyed for several weeks in a bright cool place indoors. Such an arrangement can be used as a table centerpiece and will be especially appreciated when brought to a city dwelling. Twice daily misting will help keep everything fresh, along with bright light and temperatures on the cool side, around 60°–65° F.

Large rock outcroppings have inspired and guided the development of the Leonard J. Buck Garden in Far Hills, New Jersey, since it began as a private garden in the late 1930s. Now open to the public and supervised by preeminent plantsman Barry R. Yinger for the Somerset County Park Commission, this completely naturalized 33-acre wooded stream valley serves as a model for ecologically sensitive plantings that include alpines, dwarf or prostrate conifers and shrubs, sedums and sempervivums, azaleas and rhododendrons, and the Foster hardy fern collection.

Wildflowers for Naturalizing

There are four sources for stocking the garden with wildflowers:

1) Seeds that you collect or purchase;

2) cuttings or divisions;

3) plants from nurseries specializing in native material; and

4) plants from the wild.

The last source is tricky, may not be legal, may not be horticulturally practicable, and may be better avoided unless the property is your own or you are one step ahead of a developer's bulldozer. The best procedure is first to become a member of the New England Wild Flower Preservation Society (see Resources) and to visit when possible its Garden in the Woods, located in Framingham, Massachusetts. If you are transferring wildflowers from their native haunts, dig up as much of the sprawled-out root system as possible, and take with the roots a good quantity of the moist soil the plants are accustomed to. Transplant spring wildflowers in the fall; late-summer and fall bloomers in the spring.

While we may think of wildflowers as belonging in the ground of country gardens, they take nicely to shaded, moist situations in the city, and some of the tougher ones do well in containers, in sun or shade, depending on in-

The old rock garden at the Brooklyn Botanic Garden has been newly refurbished, increased in size, and turned into a boulder garden more in keeping with the original site. Seen here in mid-spring are pink and white azaleas, white candytuft (Iberis sempervirens), Spanish bluebells (Endymion hispanicus), forget-me-not (Myosotis species), and in the foreground a yellow intermediate bearded iris. For the person who loves flowers, treasures can be found in this garden almost daily, beginning with snow-defying species crocus, winter aconite, snowflakes, and Siberian squills.

dividual plant needs. I have had surprisingly good luck transplanting from open fields and woodlands, mature and flowering plants of *Achillea millefolium*, sweet-fern, and a host of clump-forming native grasses and sedges that look attractive when potted. Dig very early in the day, immediately pot up, water generously, and keep in a shaded spot until roots become established, about four or five days.

The following lists give a selection of wildflowers that are common to the woodlands and fields of the Northeast. They are grouped according to the individual needs for soil pH, from very acid, to neutral, to indifferent. Following the botanical and common names for each species is its light need, expressed as sun, sun/shade (mostly sun, some shade tolerated), shade/sun (mostly shade, some sun tolerated), and shade.

Very acid soil:
Arctostaphylos uva-ursi: Bearberry; sun
Calla palustris: Wild calla, water-arum; sun/shade
Chiogenes hispidula: Creeping snowberry; sun/shade
Clintonia borealis: Bluebeads, bead-lily; shade
Clintonia uniflora: Queen-cup; shade
Coptis groenlandica: Goldthread; shade
Cornus canadensis: Bunchberry; sun/shade
Cypripedium acaule: Pink lady's-slipper; shade
Epigaea repens: Trailing arbutus; shade
Galax aphylla: Galax; shade
Potentilla flabellifolia: Fan-leaf cinquefoil; sun
Potentilla tridentata: Wine-leaf potentilla; sun
Rhexia virginica: Meadow beauty; sun
Sarracenia purpurea: Common pitcher plant; sun
Shortia galacifolia: Oconee-bells; shade
Trientalis borealis: American starflower; shade
Trillium undulatum: Painted trillium; shade

Medium acid soil:
Arisaema triphyllum: Jack-in-the-pulpit; sun/shade
Asarum canadense, A. caudatum: Wild ginger; sun/shade

Aster cordifolius: Blue wood aster; sun
Aster spectabilis: Seaside aster; sun
Corydalis sempervirens: Pale corydalis; sun/shade
Disporum hookeri: Fairybells; shade
Erythronium americanum: Dogtooth violet, adder's-tongue; shade/sun
Gaultheria procumbens: Checkerberry, wintergreen; shade
Goodyera pubescens: Rattlesnake-plantain; shade
Mitchella repens: Partridge-berry; shade
Sagittaria latifolia: Common arrowhead; sun
Tiarella cordifolia: Foamflower; shade
Trillium erectum: Purple trillium; shade
Uvularia sessilifolia: Strawbell, wild-oats; shade
Viola pedata: Birdfoot violet; sun
Viola priceana: Confederate violet; shade/sun

Slightly acid soil:
Actaea pachypoda: White baneberry; shade/sun
Actaea rubra: Red baneberry; shade/sun
Caulophyllum thalictroides: Blue cohosh; shade
Chelone glabra: Pink turtlehead; shade/sun
Claytonia virginica: Spring beauty; shade
Cypripedium calceolus pubescens: Yellow lady's-slipper; shade
Cypripedium candidum: Small white lady's-slipper; shade
Cypripedium montanum: Mountain lady's-slipper; shade
Gentiana clausa: Closed gentian, bottle gentian; shade/sun
Heuchera americana: Alum root; shade/sun
Heuchera sanguinea: Coral-bells; shade/sun
Houstonia caerulea: Bluets; shade/sun
Iris cristata: Crested dwarf iris; sun/shade
Iris missouriensis: Rocky Mountain iris; sun/shade
Iris prismatica: Slender blue flag, cubeseed iris; sun
Iris pseudacorus: Yellow flag; sun
Lilium superbum: Turk's-cap lily; sun/shade
Lobelia siphilitica: Big blue lobelia; sun/shade
Lupinus argenteus: Bluebonnet; sun
Lupinus perennis: Wild lupine; sun
Polemonium caeruleum: Jacob's-ladder; shade
Polygonatum biflorum: Solomon's seal; shade
Pyrola elliptica: Shinleaf; shade

Sanguinaria canadensis: Bloodrood; shade
Smilacina racemosa: False Solomon's-seal, false spikenard; shade
Smilacina stellata: Starry false Solomon's-seal; shade
Solidago sempervirens: Seaside goldenrod; sun

Slightly acid to neutral soil:
Anemonella thalictroides: Rue-anemone; shade/sun
Aquilegia canadensis: Wild columbine; sun/shade
Caltha palustris: Marsh-marigold, cowslip; sun/shade
Camassia scilloides: Wild-hyacinth; sun
Campanula rotundifolia: Harebell, bluebells-of-Scotland; sun/shade
Claytonia rosea: Spring beauty; shade
Dodecatheon cusicki: Rose shooting-star; shade
Dodecatheon meadia: Shooting-star; shade
Dodecatheon pulchellum: Prairie shooting-star; shade
Hibiscus moscheutos: Swamp-mallow, common rose-mallow; sun
Jeffersonia diphylla: Twinleaf; shade
Lilium canadense: Canada lily; sun/shade
Lobelia cardinalis: Cardinal-flower; sun/shade
Mertensia virginica: Virginia bluebells; shade
Mitella diphylla: Bishop's-cap, common mitrewort; shade
Monarda didyma: Scarlet bee balm; sun
Myosotis scorpioides: Wild forget-me-not; shade/sun
Phlox bifida: Sand phlox; sun
Phlox divaricata: Wild sweet William; shade
Senecio aureus: Golden ragwort, golden groundsel; shade/sun
Silene caroliniana: Wild-pink; shade/sun
Trillium grandiflorum: White trillium, snow trillium; shade
Uvularia grandiflora: Large bellwort, merrybells; shade
Viola blanda: Sweet white violet; shade/sun
Viola pubescens: Downy yellow violet; shade/sun

Neutral soil:
Callirhoe involucrata: Low poppy-mallow; sun
Corydalis aurea: Golden corydalis; shade/sun

Cypripedium reginae: Showy lady's-slipper; shade
Dicentra chrysantha: Golden eardrops; shade
Dicentra cucullaria: Dutchman's-breeches; shade
Hepatica americana: Hepatica; shade
Linaria canadense: Oldfield toadflax; sun

Any soil:
Anemone canadensis: Canada anemone, meadow anemone; shade/sun
Asclepias tuberosa: Butterfly-weed; sun
Aster cordifolius: Blue wood aster; sun
Aster novae-angliae: New England aster; sun
Cimicifuga racemosa: Black snakeroot, cohosh bugbane; shade/sun
Erigeron glaucus: Beach-aster, seaside-daisy; sun
Eupatorium coelestinum: Mistflower; sun
Eupatorium purpureum: Joe-Pye weed; sun
Filipendula rubra: Queen-of-the-prairie; sun
Geranium maculatum: Wild geranium, crane's-bill; shade/sun
Geranium robertianum: Herb robert; shade/sun
Hypoxis hirsuta: Yellow star-grass; sun
Inula helenium: Elecampane; sun
Maianthemum canadense: Wild lily-of-the-valley; shade
Monarda fistulosa: Wild bergamot, horse-mint; sun
Monardella odoratissima: Pennyroyal; sun
Penstemon centrathifolius: Scarlet bugler; sun
Penstemon grandiflorus: Shell-leaf penstemon; sun
Podophyllum peltatum: May-apple; shade
Rudbeckia hirta: Black-eyed Susan; sun
Sanguisorba canadensis: Canadian burnet; shade
Silene californica: Indian-pink; shade/sun
Silene virginica: Fire-pink catchfly; shade/sun
Verbena hastata: Blue vervain; sun
Vernonia noveboracensis: New York ironweed; sun

Ferns for Naturalized Gardens

Hardly any group of plants is as generally useful to the wild and naturalized garden as the hardy ferns. Some are native, others escapees from other continents that have become naturalized. We are blessed with an abundance in the Northeast, a few of the most attractive and

easily grown species being listed below, with their soil preferences. The four listed under any soil are the tallest and need plenty of room and rich, moist soil.

Slightly acid soil:
Dryopteris filix-mas var. *cristata:* Crested male-fern; shade/sun
Dryopteris marginalis: Evergreen wood fern, marginal shield fern; shade/sun
Dryopteris noveboracensis: New York fern; shade/sun

Medium acid soil:
Athyrium filix-femina: Lady fern; shade
Dennstaedtia punctilobula: Hay-scented fern; shade

Slightly acid to neutral soil:
Adiantum pedatum: Maidenhair fern; shade/sun
Polystichum acrostichoides: Christmas fern; shade

Any soil:
Matteuccia struthiopteris pensylvanica: Ostrich fern; shade/sun
Osmunda cinnamomea: Cinnamon fern; sun/shade
Osmunda claytoniana: Interrupted fern; shade
Osmunda regalis: Royal fern; shade/sun

Take Advantage of Boggy Sites

Soil that is poorly drained, whether in full sun or part shade, can be appropriated as is for bog gardening. Presumably the ground is wet if not to some degree inundated most of the year save possibly toward the end of summer, and may or may not be part of a water garden proper; see also Chapter Six: Water in the Garden. Likely places for bog gardens are low-lying, naturally wet ground, and the banksides of ponds, lakes, and streams. Kinds that can march right down and into the water, to a depth of 12 inches or more, include:

Eleocharis tuberosa: Chinese water-chestnut; sun/shade

Pontederia cordata: Pickerel rush; sun/shade

Sagittaria species: Sagittaria; sun/shade

Typha angustifolia: Narrow-leaved cattail; sun/shade

Typha latifolia: Cattail; sun/shade

Typha laxmannii: Graceful cattail; sun/shade

Bog plants that need wet soil and can stand in up to 6 inches of water include:

Acorus calamus: Sweet flag; sun/shade

Acorus calamus variegata: Variegated sweet flag; sun/shade

Equisetum hyemale: Horsetail; sun/shade

Iris 'Clyde Redmond': Clyde Redmond iris; sun/shade

Iris 'Dixie Deb': Dixie Deb iris; sun/shade

Iris fulva: Red iris; sun/shade

Iris kaempferi: Japanese iris; sun/shade

Iris pseudacorus: Yellow water iris; sun/shade

The water course garden of Mr. and Mrs. Frances H. Cabot in Quebec, OPPOSITE, occurs between tall hedges of thuja, a series of rectangular pools, channels, and small waterfalls that gradually step down the gentle slope. The pools are filled with water-lilies. Decorative rhubarbs (Rheum palmatum and its cultivar 'Atrosanguineum') border both ends of the course, which is fed from a dolphin at its source, with the water ultimately running into a lake. Field flowers with shallow, fibrous root systems, such as common white yarrow (Achillea millefolium) and goldenrod (Solidago species), along with clump-forming grasses, ABOVE LEFT, can be dug in the cool of the day, immediately potted, and watered well, for a nearly instant naturalistic effect up close. Magnolia vine (Schisandra chinensis), seen draping a fence in the New Jersey garden of Barry R. Yinger, ABOVE RIGHT, is twining and deciduous, to a height of 25 feet. Fragrant flowers are followed by showy orange-red berries in late summer. Formerly allied with the magnolias, this outstanding hardy vine (USDA Zone 5) is now classified as Schisandraceae.

Iris sibirica: Siberian iris; sun/shade
Iris versicolor: Blue iris; sun/shade
Orontium aquaticum: Golden club; shade/sun
Peltandra virginica: Water arum; sun/shade
Rodgersia podophylla: Rodgersia; shade/sun
Sagittaria latifolia: Arrowhead; sun/shade
Saururus cernuus: Lizard's-tail; sun/shade

My experience of bog gardens in the Northeast is that there will be plants growing there already that are worthy of encouragement and others to be dealt with as weeds. If the soil dries out a little from mid to late summer, Japanese and Siberian iris do splendidly, as well as narcissus, eupatorium, lysimachia, lythrum, astilbe, and aconite. Species of *Primula* that thrive on moist to wet banksides, often next to running water in the spring, include some of the loveliest: *P. beesiana, P. denticulata,* and *P. florindae.* There will also be hardy ferns, grasses such as the giant reed, *Arundo donax,* and in many cases a host of sedges, grass-like plants in an amazing variety of sizes and leaf colors. All you need to enjoy this kind of garden is rubber boots to your knees, at least until you can set down stepping-stones in strategic spots. The rest amounts to encouraging only what you like until all else is overcome.

Rock and Boulder Gardens

It is no secret that when the glacier receded, it left rocks and boulders strewn all over the Northeast. These can be found as is or put together in such a way as to be naturalized gardens with style and content dictated by the rocks and the site on which they appear or are arranged. The better the rock garden, the easier it looks, which feeds the notion that this kind of naturalized planting is easily achieved and requires no maintenance. I suppose it is possible to put together some rocks and a few plants and be done with it, but the most minimal of spaces and rock gardens deserves careful, educated treatment. The bible on this subject originated in the Northeast: *Rock Gar-*

dening by H. Lincoln Foster. Get a copy and read every word. It is not often you will have such a golden opportunity to be taught by a master gardener in your own region of the country. There is also an American Rock Garden Society (see Resources); membership is suggested so that you may learn from the Society publication, attend meetings, make friends having a shared special interest, and exchange seeds and plants.

The complexity of the subject is concisely spelled out in this paragraph by James Fanning, found in Volume 13 of the *Good Housekeeping Illustrated Encyclopedia of Gardening* (New York; 1972):

"Basically, a rock garden is a miniature or partly artificial mountain; a rock skeleton or core, having on its surface pockets of soil, areas of bare rock on which nothing but lichens can grow, projecting points of weathered stone, drifts of loose-packed pebbles or hard-packed clay to walk on and, at the bottom where the slope's natural drainage collects, a swamp, pond, or spring where the real moisture-lovers among plants feel at home."

When siting a rock garden, Jim says to ask, "Will it look as though it belongs here?" If your ground is flat, the answer will probably be in the negative, unless ". . . the contour of a large area can be changed from flat to undulating." A rather sharp change in level is the natural feature one looks for in siting a rock garden. This may be a break or change in grade between two relatively flat areas, a slope falling away from a ridge or high point, or ground sloping upward from a valley or low point.

An ideal siting for a rock garden in the Northeast is a ridge running Northeast–Southwest. The slope facing Southeast gets maximum sunshine the year round, while it avoids the summer baking that a Southern or Southwestern exposure would have to take. The slope facing Northwest is protected from the winter sunshine that many plants dislike, yet gets its full share of light in the summer.

Sloping ground in the Northeast will have its

rocks, either on the surface or close to it, and these provide the key to the whole arrangement of any garden made on that piece of ground. Stone broken up by weather fractures along lines that follow a definite pattern according to the type of stone involved. These fracture lines run at right angles to each other, so that in breaking down, the parent stone divides into rectangular or cubic fragments.

The direction of the greatest amount of cracking or fissuring in a piece of stone shows its layers, or strata, which always run approximately parallel to each other, whether horizontally, vertically, or at any other angle. These lines of stratification must be very carefully considered when you rearrange the rocks on a slope or bring in new rocks, because all strata must run the same way for a natural effect. If, for example, one of the features of the slope is an outcropping that shows strong vertical markings, a chunk of rock bearing strong horizontal markings will look out of place.

Nature itself piles up helter-skelter heaps of rock in a variety of types and sizes. Nature can be improved upon by rearranging the chunks so that they look as though they belonged together. Sometimes only a very slight shift is needed to make two odd-looking pieces of stone nestle together as if they were chips off the same ledge. Other chunks are so awkwardly shaped that the best place for them is buried far underground or used as underpinning for pieces that make a better show.

As a general rule, the principle of "square cleavage" applies here: Stones with sharp, clearly defined edges and square corners not only tend to stay where they are put, but look at home jutting out of a slope, as though nature had placed them there. Rounded stones, on the other hand, not only refuse to stay in place on a slope but look at home only on flatter ground, where they would naturally end up after being rolled about and ground down by the river or glacier that left them there.

Rock walls with planting pockets are popular throughout the Northeast, and give a chance to grow favorite rock plants without the complications implicit in building a full-fledged rock garden. Some plants that will do well in a rock wall pocket facing the sun are *Achillea tomentosa*, *Aurinia saxatilis*, *Cerastium tomentosum* (snow-in-summer), *Gypsophila repens*, *Iberis sempervirens* (candytuft), *Nepeta mussinii*, *Phlox subulata*, *Ceratostigma plumbaginoides*, *Chrysogonum virginianum* (green-and-gold), *Corydalis lutea*, and a large number of different species, varieties, and cultivars belonging to the hardy succulent genera *Sedum* and *Sempervivum*.

Plants that will take the shaded side of a rock wall include maidenhair fern, ajuga, *Aquilegia akitensis*, *Campanula carpatica*, *Dicentra eximia*, heuchera or coral-bells, and *Hutchinsia alpina* (tiny-leaved, mat-forming, with white flowers mostly in spring).

Nature Is the Best Teacher

Darrel G. Morrison, landscape architect and dean of the School of Environmental Design at the University of Georgia, Athens, says his experiences have convinced him of two things: 1) There is great value in studying natural landscapes and native plants in the field, where one can hear, see, smell, touch, and even taste them; and 2) the natural landscapes for study and enjoyment are more critical than ever as more and more of our land is "developed." A garden that is truly "naturalized" will be comprised of plant communities or associations of plants that frequently occur together under specific environmental conditions within a particular region. There will be about this an order and a visual harmony, resulting from the fitness of the plants to that environment.

CHAPTER SIX

WATER IN THE GARDEN

Water in the garden is life, pure and simple, and the Northeast, by comparison to the rest of the country and the world for that matter, is blessed with a relative abundance. We also have our share of ground-water pollution and periods of protracted drought that in the last five years have raised water consciousness throughout the region. Old-fashioned Yankee frugality is the order of the day; with any luck at all, there will continue to be an ample supply of water for plant and animal life in the Northeast well into the third millennium.

A top priority, no matter where you are going to garden, is the availability of water and its quality. Is the water drinkable? Chances are it is, if from a municipal supply which must be treated, but if it is from your own well there is no way to know except through regular expert testing. The giardiasis associated with other countries is on the rapid increase in North America, owing to the overuse of streams and ponds and the surrounding ground for human and other animal waste.

California-based water watchdog Robert Kourik, writing in a 1990 issue of *Garbage* magazine, asks us to look at this from a different perspective. The provocative question he raises is why do we use water for flushing the toilet that has been made potable through costly treatment? Further, why are we using bathroom systems that require eight or nine gallons of water per flush when units are available that require only two or three? Kourik also points out that so-called "gray" water, from showering and bathing, and washing the dishes and the clothes, is wasted down the drain when it might be used productively in the garden.

Serious issues of supply and quality aside, running water is a great convenience, if not a necessity, in most gardens and outdoor rooms, such as terraces or patios. Provisions for it and any electrical wiring and outlets are ideally made and implemented before plantings are installed. Since hoses longer than 50 feet—for

When the stream is full, the reflection of this bridge in the Quebec garden of Mr. and Mrs. Francis H. Cabot forms a moon circle. Copied from a bridge in Seven Star Park in Kweilin, China, the topography of the undulating site dictated its realization here as a dragon moon bridge. The view is across poplar-lined rustic fencing for field and pasture, to the stables and barn. Stream-side plantings are completely natural, with many berried shrubs, vines, and trees that form a thicket to nourish and protect wildlife and birds.

(87)

some, 25 feet will be sufficient—are inclined to unwieldiness, a few appropriately placed spigots can be much more efficient and may themselves be decorative elements—shaped in the form of a bird or small animal.

Water Gardens for Pleasure

Hardly five hundred years ago ultimate pleasure gardens were created in the relentlessly hot and parched Far East by Mogul explorers who had come from a mountainous and watered land of orchards and fields and green forever, or so it must have seemed. These Mogul and Ottoman gardens were oases with a serenity that must have been palpable. The ordered designs formalized into four divisions representing air, earth, fire, and water. Water coursed through straight canals, bubbled and splashed from fountains, and rose in jet mists. Pavilions raised on platforms proffered shade while captive breezes wed droplets of moisture to effect evaporative cooling.

Despite the relative coolness and pervasive greenness of the Northeast, water in the landscape is no less appealing as a symbol of oasis. Splashing fountains and waterfalls can be soothing even as they mask sounds from the outside world. Pervasive noise from traffic can be further obscured by leafy, vine-covered walls, tall hedges, and canopies of trees. These elements together invite birds and help achieve a sense of natural order even when situated in a chaotic cityscape.

Building Your Water Garden

Garden pools are simple to maintain, assuming they are ecologically balanced, and easy enough to build. Fiberglass pools in a variety of sizes and shapes, including round, rectangle, kidney, and assorted amoebic free-forms, are available from water-garden specialists, along with a host of accessories and plumbing supplies designed to suit the unique needs of every situation. An old bathtub, even a plastic wading pool can be set into the ground and landscaped to make a reflecting pool or a small water garden. Make sure the sides are level or the water will appear to run uphill. Formal, larger pools are constructed, as swimming pools are, of concrete or stone masonry and usually are designed and installed by professionals.

Design and location. The pool can be formal or informal. Choice of design and materials is usually dictated by the landscape. A naturalized landscape might look too wild if a formal water garden were set nearby; a formal landscape might lose some of its style if a rough little woodland pool appeared in its midst. Symmetrical shapes are most often associated with formality; a circular, oval, rectangular, or square shape creates an element of formality and looks best when made of materials such as concrete and edged with brick, marble, or concrete. An informal pool can be developed from a precast container such as the tub or a wading pool previously suggested, edged with stones set into concrete, or it can be built from concrete in a free-form shape and edged with stones or pebbles.

Depth. The depth of a garden pool generally is between 2 inches and 2 feet. A 2-inch pool is a reflecting pool and probably will not be suited to the growing of aquatic plants, but it is sufficiently deep to reflect light—just as effective, for this purpose, as a deeper pool would be. A pool 12 inches deep holds enough water to allow fish and many water plants, presuming that it is large enough not to overheat in hot weather; water that habitually overheats because of small size, shallow depth, and lack of oxygen is likely to become overgrown with algae and entirely unattractive. A 2-foot-deep pool is required for some of the very large-rooted water plants and some water-lilies.

Drainage. If you are planning to build the pool yourself keep in mind that water will be required to fill it (and to keep it filled), and that it will occasionally be necessary to empty it. Small bathtub or play pool installations may be filled and drained by hose, but more ambitious installations will require underground pipes to fill the pool and to keep up with water lost by evaporation. Drains to empty the pool are generally located on the bottom, to one side.

The easiest way to provide drainage for a pool is to excavate the ground beneath it an extra 12 inches, fill this excavation with coarse gravel or crushed stone, and install a drain pipe in it. This drainage layer must be tamped down very firmly before the concrete is poured. If you are building on a slope, however, it may be just as easy to extend a one-inch drain pipe from the pool outlet to a low run-off point.

The drain pipe in the pool should be 1 to 2 inches in diameter and of brass. (Do not use copper; it reacts with pool water and may render it toxic to plant and animal life.) Wire the drain pipe into place before the concrete is poured. The pipe may be cut off on the underside of the pool so that it drains directly into a gravel bed, or it may be connected with a long run-off pipe. Into the top of the drain, screw a vertical standby pipe extending just above the water level. If the pool is overfilled or flooded by rain, the standby pipe will empty the excess water down the drain. In winter, when the pool is to be drained, simply unscrew the standby pipe from the drain.

Construction. The usual cement mixture for pools is one part cement, two parts sand, and three parts half-inch gravel. Before the concrete is poured, the floor of the excavation should be lined with 6 inches of stones or gravel, and forms of wood or metal should be constructed to hold enough concrete to make the floor and walls 6 inches thick. Pour the pond floor first and the walls right after, so that the two are firmly joined. In dry weather, and depending on the humidity, concrete usually sets up enough over a 48-hour period so that the forms for the walls may be removed. A thin coat of finer cement mix may be applied to give a more attractive finish, or the whole may be rubbed with a stone or a brick to even out the rough spots. The new concrete will require ten to twenty days to cure and during this period should be kept moist by covering it with a tarpaulin that is given an occasional light soaking with water. If the pool is to have a stone coping (surround), this is cemented into place after the walls have been poured and the forms removed.

Curing the pool. Before planting, the pool must be cured; that is, rid of the alkaline salts that water leaches from the cement. Fill the pool to the brim with water four times; allow the water to rest there four days each time, then empty it completely. At the fifth filling, the pool should be ready for planting.

Planting Your Water Garden

Presumably, water-lilies and possibly the exotic lotus will be the stars of your water garden. Breeders have made vast improvements in the natural species, and today's spectacular hybrids have as much, if not more, stamina than the originals. Success with them depends on providing sun, rich soil, and water. There is no hoeing, no weeding, no watering (other than to keep the pool or pond supplied). The right combination of hardy and tropical water-lilies can give you blooms from early May until late fall.

Hardy water-lilies are perennials that live outdoors, even when ice covers the pool or pond in winter (they are dormant from fall frost until spring). Most hardies produce smooth-edged pads which float on the surface of the water, supporting blooms in fabulous shades of yellow, pink, orange, and red. There are even sunset shades, or changeables, that turn three different shades of color in three successive days of bloom. Colors range from creamy yellow to apricot, salmon and rose to orange copper and bronze.

In Northeast gardens, tropical water-lilies are annuals that require replanting each year. However, they grow taller (6 to 18 inches above the surface of the water) and wider (with flowers the size of a dinner plate) than the hardies. The tropicals also bloom in a wider vari-

ety of colors, including exquisite shades of blue and green, royal purple, pale lavenders, bright and delicate pinks, dark reds, vivid yellows, and pristine whites. They are intensely fragrant, with a sweet, sensual odor that will permeate the whole garden. They make excellent cut flowers.

Tropicals offer 24 hours of bloom, as there are both day- and night-blooming varieties. Day-bloomers open in the forenoon and close as dusk approaches. The night-blooming varieties prefer the cool hours; they open at dusk and remain open until about noon the following day.

To plant hardy water-lilies, you will need movable containers, ideally 18 inches in diameter. Wood tubs, buckets, and half-barrels are fine, as long as they have never contained soil and are clean. Miniatures do well in 6-inch pots. Planters are available in various sizes from water-garden specialists.

The soil needs to be well fertilized, containing some clay, but no sand, peat moss, or rotted wood. Beware of substances toxic to fish, such as dehydrated manure or commercial fertilizer with insecticides. For each 20- to 30-quart bucket planter mix ½ pound of water-lily fertilizer (10-10-10 is fine) or an equal amount of bone meal.

To plant your pond or pool, fill the container with soil, saturate the soil with water, make a depression, and plant the lily tuber at a 45° angle against the side of the planter, with the crown of the plant out of the soil. Lower the container gently into the pool, to a point where the water-lily leaves float comfortably. Ideally, the planter should have 6 to 8 inches of water over the soil line. Place the container at the proper height using bricks or stones to create a pedestal. If the pool is shallow, use a shallower planter, but do not have less than 4 inches of water over the soil line.

Hardy varieties can be planted in midspring, after the forsythia has finished, at about the time herbaceous peonies are up and showing strong new growth shoots. Tropicals should be set out each summer at about the same time as tomatoes. Lift, prune, and repot hardy water-lilies every three or four years. Be careful not to plant more than half the garden pool, otherwise it will appear crowded and the effect of the lily-pads floating on the water surface will be lost. Hardy types come in three different growth sizes; tropical lilies are generally larger.

All tropicals need special care in cold weather. They can be carried through winter in buckets of soil and water in any space that does not freeze. Many gardeners buy new stock of the tropicals every year, in order to avoid the trouble of wintering inside. Although hardy water-lilies can withstand freezing, if they are in shallow pools, especially in the far North, it is wise to winter them as if they were tropicals.

The leaves of water flag (Iris pseudacorus), OPPOSITE, *appear in the foreground, growing at the edge of a pond, with water clover* (Marsilea quadrifolia) *floating on the surface, at the Leonard J. Buck Garden in Far Hills, New Jersey. Water flag offers a profusion of yellow flowers in early summer and quickly colonizes. Japanese iris* (Iris kaempferi) *thrives along the sunny to half-sunny banks of ponds, as here at Plum Creek Farm in northwest Connecticut,* ABOVE LEFT, *next to streams, and in areas of the garden that tend to be wet or boggy early in the season but may dry out toward the end of summer, after flowering finishes. Hardy white water-lilies are featured in an oval pool recessed into the lawn of the Quebec white garden of Mr. and Mrs. Francis H. Cabot,* ABOVE RIGHT. *Steps in the distance are planted with alpines and rock plants, and lead out to the tapis vert, a long green lawn that constitutes the main axis of the garden. The white garden includes lilies, primulas, peonies, lilacs, and mock-orange.*

To provide lilies with plenty of nutrients each year, make a sort of vitamin pill of bone meal and clay and thrust it into the soil, next to the roots of the plant, in spring. Or buy a commercial fertilizer tablet to be used in a ratio suggested by the dealer. Feeding should be completed by September. Your water-lilies will be fine for the rest of the season.

You are attempting to re-create a delicate balance of nature in an artificial pool, so do not overlook the importance of border and incidental pool greenery. Submerged, oxygenating aquatic plants and grasses hold algae in check, and provide a bed for fish larvae. Water-lilies and other surface plants provide a cover for the pond and help maintain a cool temperature. Suggested additional surface plants (most are inexpensive annuals), which are available from specialists, are duckweed, salvinia, water-poppy, water-hyacinth, and water-snowflake.

Suggested compatible, submerged plants are anacharis (ditch moss or water thyme; species of *Elodea*), *Cabomba caroliniana* (Washington grass), *Hippuris vulgaris* (mare's-tail), and species of *Vallisneria* (eel grass or channel grass).

Border plants are beautiful and most beneficial to waterfowl life, and provide a natural backdrop to a languid pool. Appropriate varieties are *Sagittaria* (arrowhead), *Menyanthes* (bogbean), *Scirpus* (bulrush), *Typha* (cattail), *Cyperus papyrus* (Egyptian paper plant), *Butomus umbellatus* (flowering rush), *Iris pseudacorus, I. kaempferi* (iris), *Pontederia cordata* (pickerel-weed), *Thalia* (water-canna), *Nasturtium officinale* (watercress), species of *Alisma* (water plantain), and species of *Zizania* (the wild rice plant). Combine them to create an effect typical of natural pond sites.

Miniature Water Gardens

Growing water gardens indoors, or outside in containers no bigger than a sawed-off whiskey barrel, has great appeal, especially for city and high-rise apartment dwellers, and aquarium fans. Once established, most are carefree and —provided not too much water evaporates— able to thrive alone. If you have a greenhouse or an enclosed garden room, such as a sun porch, a more ambitious built-in pool is possible, with a trickling waterfall or splashing fountain. At its very simplest, a water garden can be a shallow basin containing an inch or two of water, some polished stones, a pot of dwarf cyperus, and colorful petals or blossoms that float on the surface. Tiny duckweed floating either in the teacup pond of a terrarium, or around a flower arrangement that rises from the center of a large shallow bowl, makes a charming miniature water garden.

A free-standing tub garden needs to hold at least 4 gallons and be sealed. If you use olive, whiskey, or wine half-barrels, line with a 4- × 5-feet sheet of heavy plastic sheeting, and secure at the edges. Move the tub into position. Fill it halfway with growing medium, set the plants, then fill with water. Or, set the plants to grow in individual submerged pots. Three parts good topsoil to one part thoroughly rotted cow manure is the ideal soil mix; a heavy clay is also satisfactory. Do not use swamp muck, woods soil, peat moss, or sand. No soil is needed for floaters such as water-hyacinth and water-lettuce. These beautiful and vigorous aquatics have been banned in Texas and other states in the South, but they offer no threat in regions where temperatures regularly fall below freezing. Mosquito fish (*Gambusia*) and guppies are recommended for small tubs, but goldfish or koi are not. Additional aquatics having special appeal in small water gardens—any one of which can be rooted in a 5-inch pot of soil— are marsilea or aquatic fern, which has four-leaf "clover" leaves that float or rise slightly above the water surface; primrose creeper; parrot feather; and any of numerous kinds of sagittaria or arrowhead. Dwarf or pygmy water-lilies are best for tubs and water-hawthorn makes an excellent companion.

Here are some quick and easy put-togethers that can get you into aquatic gardening in a hurry:

• Find a shallow, waterproof container: a ceramic birdbath is excellent; a large clay pot or saucer marked on the bottom as being waterproof, or a plastic one will do. Add clear water, and float a summer flower—a flamboyant hibiscus or tuberous begonia—on the surface. A few polished stones might be included to give the pool itself color.

• A slightly more ambitious project is to find a naturally hollow stone that will hold a quart or more of water. A very large seashell, such as a conch, can also be turned into a natural basin for water in the garden.

• In a waterproof bowl, arrange some plants that thrive when their roots are left standing in water as an attractive, natural abstraction of the streamside in a bog garden. *Acorus gramineus pusillus* (dwarf water iris) is one such plant. Another is the *Cyperus alternifolius*, the umbrella plant, which comes in several sizes, from 12-inches tall to several feet. Finish with pebbles, small stones, and hummocks of green woods moss.

Hardy aquatic plants for pools and ponds
Anacharis canadensis (Water weed)
Hydrocotyle ranunculoides (Wate-pennywort)
Lemna species and varieties (Duckweed)
Myriophyllum proserpinacoides (Parrot's feather,
    Water feather)
Nelumbo species and varieties (Lotus)
Nuphar species and varieties (Yellow pond-lily)
Nymphaea species and varieties that are hardy
    (Water-lily)
Pontederia cordata (Pickerel-weed)
Sagittaria latifolia (Arrowhead)
Stratiotes aloides (Water soldier)
Typha species and varieties (Cattail)
Utricularia cornuta (Horned bladderwort)
    U. purpurea (Purple bladderwort)
Zizania aquatica (Wild rice)

Aquatic plants that tolerate summer shade
Aponogeton distachyus (Cape pondweed, Water-
    hawthorn)

Cabomba caroliniana (Fish-grass, Washington
    plant)
Cyperus alternifolius (Umbrella plant)
    C. haspan var. *viviparus* (Pygmy papyrus)
    C. papyrus (Papyrus)
Marsilea species (Petterwort, Water clover)
Myriophyllum proserpinacoides (Parrot's feather,
    Water feather)
    M. verticullatum (Water-milfoil)
Pistia stratiotes (Water-lettuce)
Pontederia cordata (Pickerel-weed)
Salvinia rotundifolia

Aquatic plants tender to cold weather
Aponogeton distachyus (Cape pondweed, Water-
    hawthorn)
Azolla caroliniana
Cabomba caroliniana (Fish-grass, Washington
    plant)
Ceratopteris pteridoides (Water fern, Floating fern)
Cyperus alternifolius (Umbrella plant)
    C. haspan var. *viviparus* (Pygmy papyrus)
    C. papyrus (Papyrus)
Eichhornia crassipes (Water-hyacinth)
Hydrocleys nymphoides (Water-poppy)
Limnocharis flava
Nymphaea, tropical varieties (Water-lily)
Nymphoides indicum (Water-snowflake)
Pistia stratiotes (Water-lettuce)
Salvinia rotundifolia
Thalia dealbata (Water-canna)
Vallisneria spiralis (Eel-grass)
Victoria species and varieties (Queen Victoria
    water-lily, Water platter)

Bog plants with decorative flowers or foliage
(The abbreviation "SH" following the common
    name indicates a bog plant that tolerates
    summer shade)
Acorus calamus (Sweet flag)
Adiantum pedatum (American maidenhair fern)
    SH
Andromeda glaucophylla (Downy andromeda)
    A. polifolia (Bog-rosemary)
Aruncus sylvester (Goat's-beard) SH
Arundo donax (Giant reed)

Calla palustris (Wild calla, Water-arum)
Calopogon pulchellus (Grass-pink orchid) SH
Caltha palustris (Marsh-marigold) SH
Chelone obliqua (Turtlehead) SH
Cypripedium calceolus (Lady's-slipper) SH
   C. reginae (Showy lady's-slipper) SH
Erythronium americanum (Common fawn-lily)
Gentiana cinita (Fringed gentian)
Habenaria species and varieties (Fringed or rein
    orchids) SH
Helonias bullata (Swamp-pink) SH
Irish dichotoma (Vesper iris)
   I. laevigata (Rabbitear iris)
   I. kaempferi (Japanese iris)
   I. pseudacorus (Yellow flag)
Kalmia polifolia (Swamp-laurel) SH
Ligularia clivorum (Golden-ray) SH
Lilium canadense (Canada lily) SH
Lobelia cardinalis (Cardinal flower) SH
Lythrum salicaria 'Morden's Pink' (Sterile purple
    loosestrife)

Menyanthes trifoliata (Bogbean) SH
Myosotis sylvatica (Forget-me-not) SH
Parnassia species (Grass-of-Parnassus)
Pinguicula vulgaris (Butterwort, Bog-violet) SH
Pogonia ophioglossoides (Rose pogonia) SH
Pontederia cordata (Pickerel-weed) SH
Primula pulverulenta (Silverdust primrose) SH
Rhexia virginica (meadow-beauty)
Sagittaria latifolia (Arrowhead)
Sarracenia species (Pitcher-plant) SH
Spiranthes species (Ladies'-tresses) SH

The dipping pool in the Pennsylvania garden of Mr. and Mrs. J. Liddon Pennock, Jr., looks like a garden pool that fits into the landscape plan, yet it also functions as a pleasant place to cool off on a warm day. The paving and the pool color were played down to avoid drawing attention, while lush plantings and stylized topiaries, with a pink-flowering 'Alice du Pont' mandevilla, bring a delightful sense of secluded privacy to this very personal garden nestled in a 10- by 14-foot corner of a much larger formal space.

Thalictrum polygamum (Meadow-rue) SH
Typha species (Cattail)
Ultricularia cornuta (Horned bladderwort)
Woodwardia species (Chain fern) SH

Ponds for People and Wildlife

If you have a body of water, even as small as 4 feet in diameter, and a few square yards of land with minimum vegetation, you can create a miniature refuge for a pair of ducks, some neighborly songbirds, or a myriad of other small forms of wildlife. This kind of pool or small-size pond can be constructed, cured, and stocked with waterfowl in four to six weeks. Everything you will need is available from water-garden specialists (see Resources).

A pond large enough to accommodate swimmers, floats, and perhaps a rowboat, requires a sizable piece of land—at least a quarter-acre—and some money for development.

To save money, you can design and build your water-garden environment yourself. But this can be an enormous undertaking, so you might consider hiring a professional landscape architect and a contractor to do the work. To start you off in the right direction, free information is available from county agricultural agents, soil-conservation specialists, state-game departments, or a local nature center.

Where to begin? Charles D. Webster, president of the Horticultural Society of New York,

The shallow reflecting pool in the Quebec garden of Mr. and Mrs. Francis H. Cabot reflects the western skies and sunsets and is bounded by terraces planted with alpines. White pots with dwarf conifers frame the view across the tapis vert, with the rock retaining wall of the white garden (see also page 91) seen to the right. Small basins holding no more than two quarts of water can be used effectively to reflect the sky and on occasion to float a flower; these can be ready-made of concrete, a hollowed-out rock, or a large sea shell.

whose haven for waterfowl on Long Island has inspired many gardeners to follow suit, says, "It is wise to plan the water portion of your garden first, in order to design a setting that will make the best use of your landscape. Take advantage of existing plantings and underground water sources. Avoid any area with a lot of trees or steep slopes. To attract wildlife, look for a secluded spot."

Before you start digging, have a soil-smart person assess your property and help you select a pond site that will hold water and provide for safe overflow run-off. Local Soil and Water Conservation District offices usually perform this service for free. Generally, clay soils are best. Sandy soils have a high seepage rate. Beware of limestone or gypsum, which drain too quickly. Also check state and local laws before you make definite plans; some states require approval of designs and construction permits.

How deep should your pond be? If your primary interest is to harbor waterfowl, it need not be deeper than 6 feet. Begin construction in early summer, or whenever the ground is workable. Even if you choose not to do the work yourself, be aware of the three usual techniques of pond construction, which follow.

You can build a pond by impounding water behind a small earthen dam, by excavating a pit on level land, or by a combination of both, depending on the topography of your property. The water-fill can come from rainfall run-off, a spring, or other underground water source.

An embankment, or dam-created pond is appropriate for land with a wide, flat reservoir area (to hold maximum amount of water) and a narrow valley on one end for a damsite. When you build the dam, make sure it is large, stable, and in proportion to your reservoir area. For example, for a dam 10-feet high, the Soil Conservation Service recommends a width of 8 feet; 11- to 15-feet high, 10-feet wide; 15- to 20-feet high, 12-feet wide. You will also need to install a pipe spillway through the dam, to prevent flooding during protracted heavy rains.

An excavated pond is easier to build. On level or nearly level land it is also the only kind that is economically possible. Specially designed spillways are not necessary, but there should be about a 2 percent slope on the pond floor from one end to the other, so excess water can "spill" naturally over the lowest side of the pond. The shoreline should be deep—with a slope of 3-feet horizontal to 1-foot vertical—to discourage weeds and mosquito infestation. When excavating, make sure that the soil bulldozed from the site won't backwash into the finished pond. Spread it over a wide area and seed it with grass.

When your pond is completed, plant the edges with grasses and shrubs to hold the soil and reduce siltation. Such border plants will provide an attractive frame for your languid pool, not to mention a source of food and refuge for your intended waterfowl. Select a variety of flora, and blend plantings to create an edge effect typical of natural water margins.

Your new pond-basin will fill up naturally in anything from a few hours to a few weeks, depending on the source of water and the season. You will need to stock the water with fish, in order to best re-create the delicate ecological balance of a natural pond environment. Fish 3- to 4-inches long are a good size. Make sure you do not buy aquarium species. Members of the goldfish family, such as fantails, comets, Chinese moors, shubunkins, and calicos—with names as interesting as their varied shapes and sizes—are generally recommended for any size pond. They are winter-hardy, but some provision must be made to keep the water supply from freezing over entirely, otherwise the goldfish will suffocate.

Also appropriate are colorful, iridescent, Japanese koi. These remarkable fish can be trained to eat from your hand or to jump through hoops suspended over the water. Breeding will occur every spring and summer. You can expect six to twelve new fish every season.

You are now ready to add waterfowl. Domestic varieties of ducks, geese, and swans that are recommended for the home garden are generally disease-free and hardy for all regions of the Northeast. They should be purchased at the end of the summer or in the fall, when the animals are mature and hardy enough for winter weather.

The first year it is often best to start a collection with a single pair of ducks—one male and one female. The two most common varieties for garden ponds are the mallard and the North American wood duck, the latter being the best known and most beautiful of the species. The courtship display of ducks is a spectacular show to watch. The males promenade in front of the females, whistling and grunting, while ruffling their feathers and tossing their heads. They are polygamous, and pair for only a season.

Ducks feed on seeds, tubers, and other plant parts, insects and other invertebrates. Supplement this natural diet with poultry pellets; provide them generously during the winter when herbaceous plants have died back. If the entire pond freezes over, it will be necessary to keep a hole cracked in the ice—so the ducks have water and so that oxygen can reach the fish.

For a larger pond (at least 30 feet in diameter), *Anser anser*, the domestic graylag goose, is long-lived in captivity—twenty to thirty years—and highly compatible with ducks. A pair of male and female geese costs well under a hundred dollars, not a bad price considering they will do the weeding and mow the grass. Geese are grazers and always need to be provided with plenty of green fodder, such as kale and lettuce, in addition to commercial feed.

Contrary to ducks, geese are monogamous, forming life-lasting bonds, and breeding once a year. The male will strongly defend the nesting territory during a 30-day incubation period. However, other than during nesting, geese are highly gregarious.

One creature that will truly add enchantment to your pond is *Cygnus olor*, the domestic mute swan. With its long neck and elegantly posed wings, it will evoke storybook visions as it glides majestically over your pond.

Swans are most at home on the water, swimming in flocks and feeding on aquatic plants. They will only venture awkwardly onto land to feed occasionally and once a year to nest. Swans are somewhat territorial; their mating is monogamous.

Unless you have an extraordinarily large pond and enough vegetation, buy only two swans, a female and a male, for your garden. Swans do not like to compete with other waterfowl for food and space. Generally you will need a ⅛-acre pond for a pair of either ducks, geese, or swans and at least a ¼-acre for pairs of all three.

The basic survival needs of waterfowl are food, water, shelter, and a place to reproduce. If you follow some general guidelines, you can create a habitat that will meet the requirements of a variety of these animals. Chuck Webster summarizes his experience, "You should provide a feeding box to make sure waterfowl have enough to eat all year. Fill it with cracked corn, grain, or commercial feed pellets for poultry. Keep it clean and full at all times.

"You may want to provide an enclosure for your animals, particularly if there are possible predators around. This is also a good idea for the first year; it will encourage your new brood to stay put. A 10- by 12-foot by 7-foot area is ample for one pair of ducks; double the length and width for two swans. All you will need for construction is a wood frame and enough half-inch chicken wire to cover it. Include some plantings inside the enclosure, such as grasses and low shrubs, to provide warmth, shade, and protection for the young. And of course set out a basin of water for drinking and bathing.

"If your pond freezes over in the winter, a more substantial shelter is a must. A simple wood shed about half the sizes mentioned for the chicken-wire enclosures will keep your brood warm and content."

CHAPTER SEVEN

COTTAGE AND DOORYARD GARDENS

New England's dooryard garden may be old England's cottage garden, but the similarities fade today in the Northeast as we embrace new ideas about the use of native plants and water conservation through Xeriscaping and the use of ornamental grasses and hardy perennials as exemplified by the work of landscape architects Wolfgang Oehme and James Van Sweden. Two additional influences, the concept of the food garden as beautiful (see Chapter Four) and the active cultivation of wild and meadow flowers (see Chapter Five), can also come into play in what may be finally thought of as the new American cottage garden.

Cottage gardening began with the English working class, to provide food for the household and herbs for medicinal purposes. There were fruit trees, but not too many lest they shade out the crops that occupied every square foot of space. In time, though, flowers began to appear, some no doubt planted by birds, others from seeds blown, tracked, or purposely carried home from the manor garden. Eventually the plants that were innately beautiful,

with pretty or fragrant flowers or leaves, came to occupy the front, or doorway, garden, while the more utilitarian vegetables and herbs were relegated to the back.

Such gardens frequently displayed the considerable skills of a gardener-by-trade who might specialize in topiary, espalier, or a particular flower, such as the rose. All additions came through the generosity of the manor or of one neighbor with another, sharing cuttings, divisions, offsets, seeds, and bulbs. Entryways were typically arbored with climbing roses, clematis, or honeysuckle. Bare walls, too, were clothed with these or other upwardly mobile

Mr. and Mrs. James Porter's garden in New Jersey, designed by landscape architect Sieglinde Anderson, is about thirty steps from a back porch and is made deer- and rabbit-proof by cedar wood and hardware cloth fencing. Mown grass paths surround raised planting beds for candlestick flowering tobacco (Nicotiana sylvestris), Rudbeckia fulgida 'Goldsturm', and marigolds and zinnias for cutting, herbs (especially basils), and vegetables (with an accent on tomatoes).

plants that readily took to trellising—sociable climbers, you might be inclined to call them.

Implicit in the cottage garden idea is a refreshing freedom from hard-and-fast rules. Early in this century the English painter and gardener Gertrude Jekyll wrote many observations on color and design in the garden, but deftly put it all in perspective with this thought: A blue garden needn't be all blue, merely beautiful.

Despite the "anything-goes" premise, visual pleasure can be enhanced by the development of a color scheme. Read Faber Birren on color and study the color wheel until it becomes second nature. Then you are ready to go out and start practicing. Remember, opposites on the wheel attract. And if something clashes at bloom time, don't fret. Just get out your planting tools and transplant what offends; or cut the blossoms for bouquets and remember to transplant later.

And so it is that our new American cottage garden needn't be all things to all people but rather our own personal statement, a place we adore being in and where the mind runs free even as we pursue our workaday lives. Start with the most basic of plans, based on measurements and other useful observations about the site, such as placement of trees or other existing plantings, structures, paths, and steps.

The original cottage gardens were laid out in simple beds that allowed access from all sides. Cultivated soil was stepped on as little as possible so as to avoid compaction. Paths were made of gravel, pebbles, or stepping stones. Today we may opt instead for brick, flagstones, or clipped grass.

Initial soil preparation is the single most important step toward a garden that will be abundantly productive for the least amount of work. It is basic that the area be well drained. Then dig out the soil to a depth of 12 to 18 inches. Add a layer several inches deep of well-rotted manure or compost. As you return the soil to the bed, remove sticks, stones, weeds, and loose roots. Each spring add a generous dusting of steamed bone meal or dolomitic limestone. In the fall or early winter, after a killing frost, you may add a top dressing of well-rotted compost, taking care to pile it over the root areas of perennials and any woody plants, but not over the crowns.

As you proceed with planting, remember that masses of one thing, one color, one texture have the greatest impact. Set out established perennial flowers and herbs. Sow seeds of vegetables, annual herbs, and flowers, as many as possible where they are to grow. In time you will be able to fashion little nursery plots within the beds, with established plants offering shade and protection for the newly arrived.

Your goal in all this is to have so many desirable plants, there is no room left for weeds. Along the way it helps to cultivate any exposed surface soil. This needs to be done several times in the season, to prevent a rock-hard crust from forming and also to discourage weeds from taking a deep hold. Mulching may reduce the need for cultivation but it was not generally practiced in the English cottage garden.

Although it is conceivable that a cottage garden might consist entirely of hardy herbaceous perennials, or of annuals alone, it will be more likely a mixture. Some things will return year after year, from the roots or from self-sown seedlings. Vintage tall single-flowered hollyhocks readily reseed so that seedlings grow strong and bloom in the second year even though the parent clumps may die out or be short-lived. The same holds true for foxgloves, while delphiniums usually die out after a season or two and need to be replaced by established seedlings or nursery-grown transplants.

Although in conventional gardens, especially borders, we are always trying to get tall plants at the back and ground carpeters at the front, in a cottage garden all that really matters is that each plant be healthy and productive. And while we're breaking from tradition, nothing says your new American cottage garden can't have the color scheme of your dreams. Let it be as romantic as you can possibly arrange.

There is in the very germ of the idea a reassuring sense of family, of roots, of comforting security and self-reliance.

Jekyll was adamant that collections of plants don't necessarily a garden make. "They are like portions of paints set out upon a palette," she wrote. Jekyll first saw the garden as picturesque —to be seen as a painting—then as gardenesque—the unfolding experience of colors, shapes, and textures as one moved along.

Fragrance in the Garden

Fragrance is inextricably linked with all notions, romantic and otherwise, of cottage and dooryard gardens. Be aware, however, that plants whose names are synonymous with fragrance are not necessarily fragrant and that what is experienced by one person as intoxicating may be repugnant to another. A common misconception is that all the old roses were highly scented, and the new ones are not. It is true that in the early twentieth-century breeders bred out the perfume, the notion being that women did not want flowers in the house that competed with the fragrance they wore or, when arranged in a bouquet on the dining table, could interfere with taste. Today, sweet-smelling roses are back in vogue and from a historical perspective any given new rose introduction is more likely to survive the test of time if it is delightfully fragrant.

Before you plant for fragrance, take a nose test of the plants you are considering, if possible. Not every lilac is fragrant and in the case of mock-orange, plants appearing in every other way to be exactly the same may or may not have scent. Fragrance is also not to be taken for granted in honeysuckle, jasmine, daphne, viburnum, magnolia, or flowering tobacco. Indeed, it is even possible to have marigolds with scentless leaves, a blessing, some may say, while others think it a terrible idea.

Although too much of a good thing can be wonderful where fragrance is concerned, both in the garden and in the house, the idea of less is more plays better over the long haul. Since what we smell influences how we feel, some strategic planning makes sense. Make a list of fragrant plants, including trees, shrubs, vines, groundcovers, flowers, and herbs, and their season or month of appearance. This will allow you to mix or match plantings so that something to delight the nose always awaits your next visit to the garden. At the Brooklyn Botanic Garden there is communal rejoicing when the witch-hazels bloom in February and in the waning days of autumn I can't resist picking up some of the fallen fruits from hardy orange and quince which, when brought into my office, give off a delicious aroma that brings visitors from near and far.

Year-in and year-out I am a devotee of lavender and rosemary. To me, they belong in every cottage garden, indoors and out. Although we take for granted that lavender is put with the bed linens to make them smell good, the other side of the coin is that for hundreds of years it has been thought that smelling lavender was beneficial, at once bracing and calming, an inducement to sound sleep and only the most pleasant of dreams. In the earliest English cottage gardens, beds were often edged with lavender; there, weather permitting, freshly laundered linens were spread out to dry on the fragrant hedges. English lavender plants need cold in winter, and don't make good houseplants, but there are other lavenders, notably *Lavandula dentata* and *L. stoechas*, that will thrive through the cold months in a sunny, cool window garden. The essence of lavender is readily brought into our homes in potpourri, essential oil, scented candles, and drawer liners.

Not all rosemarys are created equal as to habit, cold hardiness, flower color—or scent. Some, 'Rex' for example, grow stiffly upright, while others, like 'Prostrata', have lax stems. Hardiest is 'Arp', a recent introduction from the USDA that can withstand 0° F (Zone 6) or even colder. It has the shrubby, compact habit of everyday rosemary, *Rosmarinus officinalis*. Rosemary flower color varies from quite blue to

lavender-blue, pale pink, and white. The needlelike leaves vary from bluish gray to green and may smell indisputably of rosemary but also of sage or pine. Except 'Arp', all rosemarys need summering outdoors and wintering over in a sunny window, ideally on the cool side. Some will bloom there and when the sun is volatilizing the leaf oils, the room will smell delightful. 'Prostrata', and ordinary rosemarys for that matter, can be readily trained into wreaths, using a circle of wire (which can be bent from a clothes hanger) anchored in the pot on either side with a bamboo stake and twist ties. These can vary in size from 3 or 4 inches in diameter up to 20 inches and more; larger ones can be based on a purchased wire wreath form or on a dried vine wreath. Miniature espaliers in all the classic designs can be trained on trellises fashioned from small pieces of bamboo or twigs; secure the joints with green twist ties or pieces of raffia.

The Subject Is Roses

If we embrace the New American Gardening Ethic, does it mean we can't have roses because they are labor-intensive and can't succeed without harmful pesticides? Happily, the answer is no. The truly old roses that remain in cultivation are quite able to fend for themselves, otherwise how would they have survived the centuries? Even better news is a new race of roses from English breeder David Austin that look scrumptiously "old," yet are everblooming, come in many colors, and can survive 30° F. They are marketed in this country by Wayside Gardens (see Resources).

Surely there will always be great hybrid tea and grandiflora roses, bearing such enticing names as 'Peace', 'Mr. Lincoln', 'Perfume Delight', and 'Double Delight', not to mention the apricot peach-and-pink 'Elizabeth Scholtz' and the big, bold, glowing orange 'Cary Grant', but the trend in rose breeding seems to be toward less upkeep and more blooms. The miniatures, treated as a curiosity until recently, have

A rock outcropping in the Connecticut garden of Lynden and Leigh Miller, OPPOSITE ABOVE, *is the focus for naturalized campanulas; at center is the peachleaf bellflower* (Campanula persicifolia); *to the right, is common bluebell* (C. rotundifolia) *as well as a large pot of pink verbena, surrounded by prostrate juniper, Boston ivy, and Ajuga 'Burgundy Glow'. Under a crab apple tree beyond, are large clumps of Lythrum 'Morden's Pink' and miscanthus and other grasses. Another rock outcropping at the Swiss Inn, Londonderry, Vermont,* OPPOSITE BELOW, *inspires a planting of vivid pink 'Sensation' cosmos and orange-scarlet geraniums. In the distance are naturalized black-eyed Susans, Rudbeckia hirta.* ABOVE, *next to a post and finial in the Miller Garden in Connecticut—and left to right—are red-leaved barberry, Scotch thistle* (Onopordum acanthium), *clary Salvia sclarea turkestaniana (behind Siberian iris foliage), vervain* (Verbena bonariensis), *and beyond—at the front edge of the border—the lacy gray of Artemisia 'Silver Mound' and the ornamental grass Helictotrichon sempervirens.*

proven hardier and more useful in the landscape than anyone might have imagined. Since they grow on their own roots, there is little chance of total winterkill and no incidence of unwelcome suckers from the understock used in grafted roses. There are microminis suited to the tiniest of gardens and larger—but still miniature—roses that can become shrubs as high as a garden wall or climbers to the top of first story windows. Some develop a cascading habit which can be exploited for use in hanging containers or as ground covers with rocks.

In the past, cottage gardeners shared choice roses by digging and removing offsets from those growing on their own roots, or they rooted cuttings. Here is the procedure.

1) Take hardwood cuttings in autumn, when the leaves are falling and the wood has had all summer to ripen. Select mature, one-year-old wood, the thickness of a pencil or more, about 6 inches long; cut to a growth bud at both top and bottom.

2) Remove any remaining leaves before placing the cutting straight into the ground to a depth of half its length, in a sheltered, warm part of the garden. If the soil is heavy, add some clean, sharp sand in the bottom of the trench, mixed with some moist peat moss. It will also help to dip the bottom of the cutting in rooting hormone powder before planting. Alternatively, you can place rose cuttings directly into a pot containing equal parts sand and moist peat, then situate in a cold frame, cold sun porch, or greenhouse.

3) By early spring these cuttings will start to root and then grow into small bushes in the ensuing season. By fall they can be transplanted to a permanent position.

Roses and clematis get on splendidly whether in bloom together or at separate times. A vigorous shrub rose that gives a burst of bloom in late spring, 'Harison's Yellow' for instance, can serve as the support for one of the more refined climbing clematis that blooms in summer or autumn. Since clematis roots need a cool run but the plants need sun, smaller shrub and bush roses can shade the ground while the clematis vines are carried upward by tying them to a wall or trellis. If you have an arbor, it might support an everblooming climbing rose such as 'New Dawn', an old favorite for its profusion of pale pink flowers, intertwined with a clematis that blooms all summer, like the blue-purple Clematis × jackmanii or the large-flowered white C. henryi.

I am personally fond of the abundant sweet autumn clematis, known until recently as Clematis paniculata and now as C. maximowicziana. It appears clambering on fences and into the trees in cultivated and wild gardens throughout the Northeast. Give this hardy vine humus-rich, moist, well-drained soil and lots of sun and it will fairly leap from the ground. I wouldn't encourage it to grow over anything else lest the host be smothered. The nicest clematis I have seen in cultivation are in C.Z. Guest's kitchen garden in Old Westbury, Long Island. Hers stand at four corners where brick paths cross, each trained on a teepee formed by four 6-foot-tall wood stakes (sold for tomatoes at the neighborhood garden center), hammered into the ground on a 24-inch square, drawn together and nailed at the top, then painted dark green. A young clematis was set at the base of each stake, in early spring. By autumn of the second year they were spectacular in bloom, followed by the silken frosted seedheads that persist into winter.

More Fragrant Vines

Besides roses and clematis, here are some more vines that fit into the cottage garden tradition:

Wild riverbank grape, Vitis riparia, yields fabled scent when it blooms in early summer. The fruit is of no consequence (except to the birds) but in the right setting this can be a welcome garden dweller. Another possibility is the frost grape, *V. vulpina*, which has Boston ivy–like leaves and sweet blossoms.

Dutch honeysuckle, *Lonicera pericylmenum* var. *belgica*, yields cream-brushed rose flowers all summer. And yes, they are definitely sweet-smelling, as are those of the autumn honeysuckle, a variety derived from the same species and called *serotina*, which has purple blooms.

Silver-lace vine, *Polygonum aubertii*, is a lusty grower that manages to thrive even in windswept places. It is often successful for cottage gardens in the sky, on rooftops and balconies, where lesser vines would perish. This plant even succeeds in shaded, soot-darkened city gardens. The vines offer a graceful green drapery in summer that becomes snowed over with lacy white flowers in early fall, these succeeded by seed clusters that readily identify this vine's membership in the buckwheat family. There are also a host of other polygonums that range in size from mat-forming miniatures to the towering Japanese bamboo, *P. cuspidatum*, which shoots up from the ground in spring to 6 feet or more by summer. Japanese bamboo is iron-hardy and not usually recommended for small gardens unless the roots can be contained by deep-set curbs. Any of several small polygonums inevitably pop up in cottage gardens and may be rigorously pulled as weeds or allowed to remain in the proper company of selected and invited plants.

Annual moonflower or moonvine, *Calonyction aculeatum*, is deliciously scented at night and also looks beautiful in moonlight. This summer-blooming vine, which looks marvelous intertwined with 'Heavenly Blue' morning glories, can, like they, be started from seeds in the spring, for blooms in a matter of weeks. Sunlight, warmth, and plenty of water will speed the seedlings to rapid maturity, and keep the vines blooming until the end of the season.

Silvery Leaves and Pinks

Dianthus, including the carnations, but especially those known as pinks, have occupied an important role in cottage gardens from early on. I know several gardeners who travel the world in hopes of finding some treasure presumed lost to cultivation. The Logees in Connecticut have recently brought back 'Dad's Favorite'—according to their catalog, "An old-fashioned cinnamon pink with nearly white flowers adorned with a dark maroon central eye and maroon edging. One of the famed picotee pinks."—and 'Pretty Dottie'—". . . old-fashioned picotee form with white flowers enhanced by dark maroon spots in the petals. Very compact growth."

Pinks do especially well in full sun in well-drained soil rich in limestone. They can take wind and drought once established, but soggy, acid soil is anathema. Besides the waves of clove- or cinnamon-scented flowers, often beguilingly eyed in a contrasting color, I am fond of those that form spriggy mats of blue-gray leaves. There is hardly a day in the year when these cannot be appreciated, except possibly when they are snuggled under a blanket of snow, or when a deep-rooted grass has penetrated the pinks' territory; it has to be evicted, but how without devastating the dianthus plant? Persist. Stop to smell the flowers. Persist some more. The only thing not allowed in the cottage garden is frustration.

Pinks and dianthus are eminently collectible. There is even a bible on the subject, which can be found in the libraries of botanical gardens, arboreta, and horticultural societies. It is called *Dianthus*, by Liberty Hyde Bailey, who is sometimes referred to as the great father figure of American horticulture.

Besides the gray foliage of pinks, other plants having silvery leaves are welcome in the cottage garden. Not only do their color and texture complement flowers of all colors, their ghostly appearance at night or in moonlight is an added appeal, at least to me. Lacy *Artemisia* 'Powis Castle' is outstanding and does not break apart at the center as is the inclination of 'Silver Mound'. I vote also for annual dusty millers, lamb's-ear, and *Lychnis coronaria*.

Old Violets Are New Again

Nearly a hundred years ago the Logee family did a thriving business growing sweet English violets as cut flowers for the Boston market. Today's burgeoning cut flower business has passed the shy violet by, but not the Logees or a host of other avid collectors. All the old violets are still in circulation, along with some that can be out-and-out weeds. Violets are widely dispersed in the Northeast; whether or not yours is a weed depends on how you feel.

The true sweet violet is *Viola odorata*, also known as the florist or English violet. Its dusty pink–flowered variety *rosea* is said to be even sweeter. Legendary Parma violets are available in at least three cultivars: 'Lady Hume Campbell' (double blue), 'Marie Louise' (double, dark lavender), and 'Swanley White' (double white with a hint of pale blue).

At least two other violas are welcomed in most cottage gardens: the garden viola and the pansy. Best known as a viola is the Johnny-jump-up, *Viola tricolor*, which figures in the parentage of the modern, large-flowered pansy. The other violas, with flowers larger than a Johnny-jump-up, but smaller (usually) than a pansy, belong to the species *cornuta*. Johnny-jump-ups scatter their seeds with abandon and have a way of showing up in surprising places but are hardly ever doomed to weeddom. Breeders have been working on heat tolerance in pansies and as a consequence it is not unusual for these formerly spring flowers to persist into the autumn months.

Bulbs for Cottage Gardens

Spring bulbs grace nearly every dooryard and cottage garden. The hopeful act of burying them in the warm earth in the fall is as important to me as the blooms that follow. If the path to spring is through winter, let it be bordered by drifts and gatherings of crocus, snowdrops, squills, and, of course, the Big Three: tulips, daffodils and other narcissus, and hyacinths. English bluebells, *Endymion non-scriptus*, also available in white and pink, bloom toward the end of the season. Since the leaves of all these bulbs must be left to mature until they turn brown in summer, it's wise to interplant perennials and annuals whose leaves will hide those of the bulbs.

Summer-flowering bulbs have no finer representative than the hardy lily, available in species and hybrids of all sizes from 15 inches to several feet tall, in almost all colors except blue, and flowering variously for several weeks at a time beginning in late spring and continuing to early fall. Plant them in humus-rich, well-drained, moist soil, with a half day or more of sun, and the bulbs will increase yearly, along with the number of stems and flowers.

Another summer bulb that can be planted once for an investment that will continue to return in greater numbers is the hardy begonia, *Begonia grandis*, known until recently as *B. evansiana*. It has burgundy-backed olive-green leaves, which grow to 3 feet tall, with a profusion of showy pink flowers in late summer and fall. There is also a variety with white flowers. This begonia has the unusual habit of developing bulbils in the leaf axils, and these can be removed before frost, or picked up from the ground, and established elsewhere in the garden or shared with others. It is hardy to 0° F, or in colder regions if well mulched.

The cormous *Crocosmia* 'Lucifer' also seems to belong here as it sends up fountains of grassy leaves in spring, reminiscent of the more graceful species of gladiolus, followed by an extravagant display of flame red flowers held on wiry stems, freesia-style. With heavy mulching 'Lucifer' survives temperatures to below 0° F and will gradually increase until it must be divided after three or four years.

Hardy lycoris, *Lycoris squamigera*, grows leaves in spring, then dies down for a spell before

Opium poppies (Papaver somniferum), OPPOSITE, *in the garden of Anne, Gordon, and Nellie Thorne in Vermont have become true folk plants, since you can't buy seeds but must get them from a friend's garden. They produce an unbelievable number of flowers and seeds. In the background are Klondyke cosmos* (Cosmos sulphureus); *in the foreground right is 'Helen Campbell' cleome, also a prolific bloomer and producer of seeds. Seeds of all these sturdy annuals can be saved from year to year, and some may appear as volunteers. The small-flowered* Crocus chrysanthus, BELOW, *native in Bulgaria to Asia Minor, bloom at the first hint of spring, often through a crust of melting snow. These, which have become naturalized along a berm that surrounds the Brooklyn Botanic Garden, illustrate one of the fundamentals of cottage gardening: Plants that self-sow or volunteer tend to move themselves to fresh soil, thereby maintaining vigor. Crocus can be set free even in grass areas, provided the grass is not cut low before the crocus leaves ripen in late spring or early summer.*

sending up naked stalks crowned by lilac-pink flowers in late summer. It is often found in old gardens, all but forgotten except for the surprising and sudden appearance of the flowers. The bulbs are hardy in the ground to below 0° F and can survive greater cold if well mulched.

The better-known bulbs of summer—tuberous begonia, canna, dahlia, and gladiolus—are frost-tender and require lifting before frost in autumn and winter storage in a dry, cool, dark place. Because of this annual planting, lifting, and storage, they are somewhat labor-intensive. On the other hand, who can judge the worth of sweat as compared to that of any of these flowers?

Perennial Flowers and Grasses

Although dooryard and cottage gardens may be a mixture of many different kinds of plants, the mainstays can be perennial flowers and ornamental grasses that bring long-term satisfaction in return for relatively little maintenance. Star performers among flowers include peony, hosta, daylily, Siberian iris, achillea, columbine, Japanese anemone, hardy aster, campanula, coreopsis, dicentra, echinacea, cimicifuga, and true geranium. There are also heuchera, lamium, liatris, lythrum, monarda, oenothera, summer phlox, astilbe—and a host of other candidates.

Some of these can be started from seeds, others from friends' gardens. I am especially fond of hardy perennials that will grow from seed to bloom in the first year; seed catalogs usually include this information. The blackberry lily, for example, has black seeds the size of buckshot that sprout quickly when sown indoors in late winter, soon forming attractive fans of irislike leaves. Set outdoors in tomato planting weather, they burgeon, sending up wiry stems to 3 or 4 feet, crowned daily by a fresh supply of pale orange, red-spotted flowers that are followed by large green pods that dry and furl open to reveal row on row of shiny

black seeds, quite resembling a big blackberry.

No class of plants has gained more notoriety in recent years than the ornamental grasses. There are annuals, but the hardy perennials are more carefree. Leaf color of ornamental grasses varies from plain green to green with white or yellow striping or crossbanding, to an array of blue, red, rose, and golden colors. Size and habit of ornamental grasses vary as well. For a more detailed discussion, see Chapter Three: Seaside Gardening.

Annual and Biennial Flowers

The habit of self-sowing is important for cottage-garden annual and biennial flowers. True, they may not always return next year exactly where you had them before, but nature's way can be serendipitous. As an example, shiso or perilla, a relative of basil and mint, has purplish olive-green leaves that are intricately quilted and veined. They have an extraordinary sheen in the late summer light. Seedlings that appear where you do not want them can be easily pulled and added to the compost pile, or coddled and shared with a friend, in the tradition of the true cottage gardener.

Self-seeding flowers and herbs constitute welcome cottage garden dwellers for the very impreciseness of their sow-and-grow cycle, here one year, over there the next. This mixing up benefits both soil and plants, in that the same crop tends not to grow in exactly the same place year after year. Add to shiso or perilla these happy returns: starry blue-flowered borage, coriander or Chinese parsley, dill, Iceland and Flanders' Field poppies, nicotiana —especially the tall candlestick *Nicotiana sylvestris;* which bears unbelievable numbers of jasmine-scented white flowers right up to frost—hollyhock, linaria, Johnny-jump-up viola, calendula or pot-marigold, cosmos, alyssum, coreopsis and calliopsis, foxglove digitalis, sweet rocket hesperis, and gilia or ipomopsis. Basil and nasturtium are examples of annuals whose seeds can't survive winters in the Northeast.

Cottage Gardens on Display

Two of the finest examples of gardens that embrace the abundant beauty of the old-fashioned cottage garden, along with the most up-to-date influences of Xeriscaping and the New American Garden, exist today in New York's Central Park. They may be found at the Conservatory Garden, located at 105th Street and Fifth Avenue, and at the Central Park Zoo, behind the Arsenal at 68th Street and Fifth Avenue. Both have been created and are maintained under the direction of Lynden Miller.

Another inspiration is the countryside garden of Sir John Thouron, located in Unionville, Pennsylvania, not far from Longwood Gardens at Kennett Square. Although not open to the public in the strictest sense, Sir John has been most generous in permitting busloads of garden lovers to visit, by special arrangement of course. I was able to go there as part of a week-long course in perennials given through the Education Department at Longwood Gardens. Sir John's garden, like those of Lynden Miller, is based from the beginning on deep soil cultivation and the addition of large amounts of well-rotted manure and compost. Little or no fertilizing is done. Hardy perennials and ornamental grasses play major roles, while self-sowing annuals and biennials fill in, often in surprising if supporting roles.

Although it is not located strictly in the geographic area we have chosen to represent the Northeast, there is one other public garden I hope you will visit as a source of knowledge and inspiration for your cottage garden. It is the New American Garden maintained—actually there is remarkably little maintenance—at the U.S. National Arboretum in Washington, D.C. Designed and installed at the request of the Arboretum's director, Dr. Henry Marc Cathey, by Washington- and Baltimore-based landscape architects Wolfgang Oehme and James Van Sweden, this model garden is based on Cathey's vision for what America's front yards could be instead of the cookie-cutter sameness that prevails. He has proposed a New American Gardening Ethic that promotes the use of native plants and exchanges high-upkeep and chemically dependent lawns for low-up-keep, pest-free gardens.

Two of the finest private gardens in the cottage style which I have recently encountered are at Hartwood in New Jersey, illustrated elsewhere in this book, and at Stonecrop, the Cold Spring, New York, property of Anne and Frank Cabot. Hartwood's cottage garden is relatively small, not much bigger in dimensions than the adjoining Edwardian-style conservatory and the adjacent living room, reached through French doors. With creeping thymes chinking between the stepping stones, twig furniture beckoning, and a flowering tobacco that had chosen to sow-and-grow itself under a round metal table, I never wanted to leave. And, oh yes, there were hollyhocks and climbing roses that carried one's eyes to the sky. Perfection.

The cottage garden at Stonecrop is perhaps larger than the Cabots' entire house and is itself divided into several roomlike spaces. What most impressed me was the ordered abundance of so many different flowers and that there was not one bare spot or anything remotely resembling a weed. Caroline Burgess, the English gardener largely responsible, says that when she first came to America everyone seemed intent on telling her all of the things that couldn't be done and couldn't be grown here. Mostly she's proven them wrong and done it first by deeply cultivating and enriching the soil and second by not being afraid to take risks. Pesticides stronger than insecticidal soap, herbicides, and chemical fertilizers have no place in the cottage gardens of Stonecrop.

CHAPTER EIGHT

CONTAINER GARDENING

Gardening in containers bridges the gap between full-fledged outdoor gardening and the garden that is exclusively indoors. We may associate the practice with the terrace and patio living that has become increasingly popular in the last half of the twentieth century, but it has deep roots in history. Cleopatra had potted roses on her barge and Louis the Sun King expanded the idea into an orangerie that thrives today at Versailles. The practice is not for the privileged classes alone, for in fact some of the most extraordinary container plantings rise from salvaged or "found" planters—tin cans, plastic pails, wood shipping crates, fruit baskets. In this chapter we will explore some of the possibilities as they apply in myriad ways to virtually every gardener in the Northeast who has space outdoors for so much as a pot, a hanging basket, or a window box.

Summering Houseplants Outdoors

Summering houseplants outdoors is one way to think of container gardening. Except some of the hairy-leaved gesneriads, such as African violets and florist gloxinias, which are ill-prepared to be rained upon, most indoor plants can benefit from a summer spent outdoors. Move them into open air when the weather is settled and warm, in spring or early summer. Bring them back indoors well ahead of the cold weather. They need the same care as other plants in the garden.

Provide routine pruning, spraying with insecticidal soap to prevent insect damage, watering in the absence of sufficient rainfall, and feeding every two weeks, or more frequently, of soluble fertilizer. It is easier to care for potted plants being summered outdoors if they are grouped together in one or two places rather than scattered over the garden. Besides, massing pots or plants of a kind, or in complementary groupings, has a way of turning less into more.

This porch garden of a weekend house in Connecticut features container plantings with deep saucers so that when they are watered well on Sunday evenings and left standing in some water, there will be ample moisture to sustain them until the following Friday night or Saturday morning. Wax and tuberous begonias, Cape primroses, impatiens, and gloxinias grow in shady, more protected recesses, while an ivy topiary sphere, nasturtium, and dwarf dahlia receive more sun. The house and furniture are built of American chestnut.

Any location that receives protection from whipping winds and hard rains can be decorated with container plants. My preference is a porch that affords protection, yet allows enough sunlight to encourage vigorous leaf and flower production. Trelliswork can be added to protect against too much wind or hot sun.

For those of us who want to be outdoors as much as possible, the porch is a wonderful compromise for family and friends who may be more indoorsy by nature. Porch gardening and living apply similarly to the apartment terrace, bearing in mind the higher up you are, the greater will be the need for trelliswork or some other means of wind control.

Other places you might consider for houseplants, and find them especially enjoyable in warm, frost-free weather, are near entranceways, on steps, terraces, patios, walks, landing strips by driveways, the tops of walls, sun decks, and rooftop gardens. Many will thrive in the summer under large trees, heavy-foliaged shrubs, or beneath groups of perennials such as daylilies and hostas. Some do well in hanging baskets, window boxes, and large planters.

Perhaps most important in all this is to sink small pots to the rims in moist peat moss or garden soil. Or unpot little plants and grow them community-style in one large pot. The trouble with little pots outdoors is that they dry out too quickly and the roots get too hot to grow. There is also the wind factor—the slightest top-heaviness means a toppled plant.

Another primary consideration is the need to harden houseplants so that they will be able to withstand full exposure in the outdoors. Place them first on a cool porch, under trees and shrubs, or beneath overhanging eaves for about a week. This gives them time to harden or stiffen their stems, and to firm up foliage. In this respect, they are not that different from us: Houseplants have to acquire their sun "tans" gradually, otherwise leaves will be burned, possibly beyond recovery. Cool-tolerant types from temperate climates can go out first, as

soon as danger of hard freezing is past. The subtropicals can follow around Mother's Day, or when the peonies are up and budded, and finally the tropicals, which can go out at tomato-planting time. This routine is reversed at the end of the season; start bringing in tropicals when night temperatures drop to 50° F, followed by subtropicals, then the temperate types before hard frost.

Window-Box Gardening

A window box is a great place to garden when you have no garden. Of course, you could do volunteer work in a public garden or community beautification effort, but there is nothing quite like having your own piece of ground— even if it is decidedly confined.

If you live in an apartment building, check first to be sure that window boxes are allowed on the outside. If they are, see to it that each is securely anchored to a wall, sill, or window frame. Metal or wood brackets can be used, often in combination with hook-and-eye screws at either end that fasten into the window frame or house wall. A good basic size is 6-inches wide by 6-inches deep by almost any length; all things considered, bigger is better when the subject is window boxes.

At planting time, add one inch of pebbles or gravel in the bottom of each box for drainage, then proceed. Use a growing medium composed of two parts packaged all-purpose potting soil to one each of sphagnum peat moss, clean, sharp sand, and well-rotted compost or leaf mold.

For maximum pleasure from a window box, treat it as a little garden, a place to grow the most interesting, rewarding plants imaginable. Be adventuresome. Geraniums, petunias, and trailing vinca make a great combination for a box outdoors in sun, but they are mere hints of the possibilities. Why not also your favorite herbs, dwarf vegetables, strawberries, and more unusual annual flowers such as hybrid portulaca (rose-moss), flowering tobacco or nicotiana (especially one of the dwarf bedding cultivars), plumed and crested celosias, and arctotis daisies? Or a collection of desert cacti and other succulents? Or miniature roses?

In partial to full shade outdoors, the usual choices for window boxes are impatiens, tuberous begonias, and fuchsias. Consider also blue or white browallia; torenia, or wishbone flower; gesneriads such as achimenes, aeschynanthus (lipstick vine), columnea, and the succulent *Streptocarpus saxorum* cultivars that are sometimes known botanically as *Streptocarpella*; bromeliads; and unusual begonias such as rex, rhizomatous, and cane types.

Some additional plants that are favorites of mine for window boxes—or any container planting for that matter—are dwarf carnation, gerbera, heliotrope, and nasturtium. A recent addition to this repertoire is a dwarf bush morning glory, the delightfully blue-flowered and profuse *Evolvulus glomeratus*, which is becoming widespread in Sun Belt horticulture, known by the name of 'Blue Daze'. Two old and related plants from the mint family also come to mind, coleus and plectranthus. Fancy-leaved coleus and *Plectranthus australis*, or Swedish-ivy, are ubiquitous. Less known but definitely worth growing are the more succulent species from both genera, such as *Coleus pentherii* and *Plectranthus prostrata*, that have aromatic foliage or the delightful habit of bursting into a season of showy flowers, as in *Coleus thyrsoideus* and *Plectranthus behrii*.

Some gardeners plant window boxes once in the spring and consider the job done for the duration of that growing season. Another approach is to treat the window-box garden as evolutionary from season to season. Early spring might bring pansies and violas, primroses, crocus, and miniature narcissus. As each of these finishes it is removed, to be immediately replaced by something just coming into flower. By fall there might be dwarf asters, field mums or chrysanthemums, and French mari-

golds in all their glory. In winter the box might hold dwarf conifers—be sure the rootballs are saturated with water before the winter freeze-up, otherwise winter burn (if not kill) will be inevitable—or cut evergreen branches stuck into the moist soil before it has frozen.

If there is a secret to success with window-box gardening, it is to be generous: Prepare the basic planting medium well. Employ lots of plants for immediate effect. Water freely and consistently, so that roots never become so dry that leaves and growing tips wilt. Apply fertilizer at half strength every week, at fourth strength with every watering, or use timed-release fertilizer pellets. Promptly remove discolored leaves and spent flowers. When a plant finishes, replace it immediately. The more you put into a window-box garden, the more it will give back.

Whiskey-Barrel Gardens

A by-product of the distilling industry, sawed-off whiskey barrels are available and reasonably priced at garden centers and nurseries. They look especially nice in more rustic settings, are strong, durable, and hold enough soil to accommodate a dwarf fruit tree or tree-form standard, such as a rose or grafted conifer. The ground in a whiskey barrel can be gardened intensely, the same as in a window box.

If the weight of a sawed-off whiskey barrel filled with planting medium constitutes a problem, you can add a bottom layer of peanut-size plastic foam pellets equal to a third or more of the height of the planter. Or start with coarse perlite—a two-bushel bag of it weighs next to nothing. For the growing medium, use the same mix recommended for window boxes. It is also a good idea to fit a layer of burlap or similar coarse material over the lightweight filler before topping with soil; this will reduce the loss of soil particles into the perlite and facilitate replacing the upper layer in succeeding seasons.

Hanging Container Gardens

Plants that naturally trail, creep, cascade, or climb are ideal choices for hanging baskets, urns and other pedestal containers, as well as window boxes and other planters. Hanging baskets can be suspended from hooks installed in overhanging eaves, from tree branches and porch ceilings. Some arbors are built solely for them. Brackets can be mounted on walls, fences, and posts. Other than hanging them so they are absolutely secure, the main problem with basket plantings outdoors is how to protect them from too much exposure to hot, dry winds. Baskets outdoors in full sun may need to be watered every day in summer.

To hang a planter from a tree branch, always use screw eyes or hooks. Don't tie wire around the branch, because it will hurt the tree even if you use protective padding.

Most hanging-garden plants do well in a growing medium of equal parts packaged potting soil, vermiculite, perlite, and sphagnum peat moss. For a lean mix (for cacti and other succulents), add one part sand. For a rich mix (for gesneriads, aroids, such as caladium and philodendron, and begonias), add one or two parts well-rotted leaf mold, compost, or sphagnum peat moss.

Line open baskets—wire or wood slats—with unmilled sphagnum moss or florist's sheet moss before adding the potting mix. Use a sin-

Container plantings such as these bonsai are displayed throughout the Philadelphia garden of Ernesta and Fred Ballard. An apple tree espaliered as a single cordon serves as a dramatic backdrop, with totems for climbing vegetables in the adjoining kitchen garden, and a small greenhouse that is used all year for propagation and in winter as a cold but frost-free storage spot for temperate and subtropical container plants. Just outside the greenhouse door, a large clay pot standing in a deep saucer of water is filled with watercress.

gle layer of moss, about 1-inch thick if the slats fit tightly together, a 2- to 3-inch layer for more open wire, plastic, or wood-slat containers.

After planting in a moss-lined basket, immerse the basket in a pail or sink full of water until the water bubbles up onto the surface of the soil. Let the basket drain before hanging.

Pinch off the growing tips of hanging plants occasionally in order to get full, many-branched plants. This is especially important in spring and early summer.

Keep hanging-garden soil in a range between wet and moist during the summer months to assure best growth. If the soil is allowed to dry out to the extent that the plant wilts, the leaf tips will die, flower buds may fail to develop, and older leaves may dry up prematurely.

Remember: The more porous the container, the more water the plant will need. (Plastic containers are least porous; moss-lined baskets are most porous; clay pots are in-between.)

Utilitarian plastic hanging pots can be camouflaged by sponge painting in several shades of green. Unglazed clay pots are relatively heavy and require extra watering because of moisture lost by transpiration through the walls, a process that is beneficial for its cooling effect on the roots.

To keep new flowers coming on everblooming species such as sweet alyssum, phlox, and petunia, snip off spent blooms and any signs of developing seedpods regularly. Before leaving

A winter garden at the back of the Ballards' property, on direct axis from windows in the house, stands open and mostly empty in summer. Come cold weather, the space will be filled with large container specimens of citrus, camellia, ficus, sweet bay, and jasmine; only enough heat is provided to prevent frostbite. The Blue Atlas cedar bonsai in a large blue glazed pot stands on a small white iron lacework table, and spends winters in a holding pit along with other temperate bonsai, where a minimum temperature of 28° F can be maintained.

on a one- or two-week vacation, cut back most open flowers as well. This way blooms will be starting rather than finishing when you return.

Among the most beautiful flowering hanging baskets seen outdoors in the Northeast are tuberous begonias of the cascade type, summer-into-winter-blooming campanulas represented by *Campanula elatines, C. fragilis,* and *C. isophylla,* fuchsias, pelargoniums represented by the ivy-leaf and cascade geraniums, and cascade petunias. All of these do best in moderate day temperatures, up to 75° F, and cooler nights, to about 50° F.

Among my favorites for hanging baskets are prostrate rosemary, *Rosmarinus officinalis* 'Prostratus', any of the trailing sedums, and scented pelargoniums that cascade, such as apple and nutmeg geranium. Creeping thymes, dwarf bush basils, and parsley also take well to the air, not to mention bush-type zucchini, patio cucumbers, cherry tomatoes, Japanese gourmet eggplants, and a host of peppers.

The Philadelphia School

The venerable Philadelphia Spring Flower Show and its sponsor, the Pennsylvania Horticultural Society, have had a major impact on container gardening in the Northeast. In the same way that watching the Olympics stirs the spirit of the athlete in all of us, a sure way to get hooked on container gardening is to observe the prize-winning plants displayed in the amateur horticulture classes at the Philadelphia Spring Flower Show. Prime movers in this arena for several decades have been Mr. and Mrs. Frederic L. Ballard, Mrs. J. Pancoast Reath, and J. Liddon Pennock, Jr.

The Ballards, Fred and Ernesta, have gardened together for so long that each knows by instinct the strengths and weaknesses of the other. The casual observer might easily mistake their low-key manner and drop-dead results as having been achieved automatically or with the help of a small army of paid professionals.

The Ballards' garden would be beautiful with-

out container plantings; with them, it is an extraordinary experience. Hundreds of pots and other containers have been collected from all over the world. Each plant, from smallest to largest, youngest to oldest, is matched to its container, considering both horticultural needs and esthetics. Ernesta's early interest in the art of training plants introduced Fred to bonsai, a pursuit that keeps him constantly "snipping, wiring, tucking, and raking," except when he is working on behalf of the National Bonsai Foundation. Together they work to carefully apply the principles of bonsai to virtually every plant on the property, including towering old trees, which are treated as individuals and with the utmost respect.

The Ballards' property is blessed with numerous walls, ledges, steps, terraces, and a grape arbor that serve for growing and showing their collection of bonsai and other trained container plants. In winter these are dispatched to a variety of places: Besides window gardens all through the house, a large sunny entry hall, and a bank of fluorescent lights in the basement, there is a very small cool greenhouse, a cold frame for temperate-climate bonsai, and a cold but frost-free winter garden, or orangerie.

Considering the great variety of plants grown by the Ballards in containers, it may come also as a surprise that everything is potted in the same mix and is fertilized regularly with only one NPK formula, 30-10-10. A small but apparently mighty compost pile behind the modest kitchen garden is their "secret." Grass in one small formal garden is cut weekly with a hand mower. Clippings are raked and put in the compost pile, along with any weeds. (Oak leaves that fall in the Ballards' garden are raked and carried to the woods.) Each week throughout the summer the compost pile is squared and dished in the center to catch water. At the end of a year, the "cooked" (well-rotted) compost is put through an electric grinder and used four parts to one of clean, sharp sand for container plantings. Ernesta says this homemade mix provides everything needed by plants in pots.

Bonsai: Tray Plantings

Bonsai, pronounced *bone-sigh* with even stress on both syllables, literally translated from the Japanese, means "tray planting." Simply, it is the art of keeping a tree or shrub dwarfed by confining it to a small pot. In the gardening world it is one of the highest art forms, blending artistic ability and horticultural expertise. Controlling the size of any bonsai is done by pruning the roots and branches at the time of planting. All its life it will be periodically unpotted, root-pruned, and repotted with additional soil to retain its size and shape. It will also demand constant pruning and pinching of new growth.

Traditional bonsai are mostly outdoor plants, although they can also be tropical or subtropical and kept indoors. Even the hardy ones must have protection when temperatures drop below 28° F, owing to the small amount of soil. They cannot withstand exposure to winter winds or continuous freezing and thawing. They must never be allowed to dry out as it will kill them instantly. In most places, this means watering them every day in summer. If your soil is correct, they cannot be overwatered.

There are five basic styles of bonsai: formal upright, informal upright, slanting, cascade, and semicascade. There are variations to these basic styles including forest and clump style. Books on the subject offer inspiration, but experience is better gained through participation in courses sponsored by local bonsai groups, likely connected with the American Bonsai Society or Bonsai Clubs International.

Bonsai pots come in all sizes and shapes. Each tree is styled and shaped and a bonsai pot is selected for that individual. The pots are unglazed inside and have large drainage holes which are covered with ⅛-inch hardware cloth (rugged galvanized screening) cut slightly larger than the holes and wired down. This keeps slugs from coming into the pot and the soil from coming out. Unglazed pots in brown, gray, or terra cotta are generally used for evergreens while glazed pots are used for deciduous trees. The length of the pot should be approximately two-thirds the height of the tree, for proportion. Straight trunks are better in a rectangular pot while curved trunks look better in round or oval pots. Cascade pots may be three to four times as tall as wide or, for semicascade, about as tall as wide.

Always use clean soil for bonsai. A good average mix is equal parts commercial potting soil (sterilized), peat moss, and a large to medium type aggregate. As you begin work with a bonsai, always keep in mind that approximately the same amount of roots and foliage should be removed at any given time. Leave the small hairlike surface roots on the ball. Loosen the root ball, rake away most of the soil, and cut away one-fourth, one-third, or one-half the root system, depending on how much has been cut off the top of the tree. If it has a tap root, cut it out and remove old clumps of dirt under the root. Place soil in the bottom of the container and fit the tree into it, cutting the root to the size and shape of the pot. Straighten all the roots and finish potting, making certain soil is under and around all roots, with no air pockets. Use a chopstick or pencil to achieve this. The plant should be tied down with a long length of wire going through the holes in the bottom of the container and around the base of the plant to secure it. Place the bonsai in a tub of water or sink, filled to the brim. When the soil is entirely wet, remove and place in a semishaded area for a week to ten days. Do not fertilize for a month or two. If new growth appears, pinch back continually. The plant should eventually be placed in full sun and watered daily. If the sun gets too hot, move to filtered sun. Fertilize with bonsai fertilizer or any organic fertilizer in spring and summer, according to directions on the product label.

Some classic plants used as bonsai are:

• *Evergreen:* Camellia, five-needle pine, cedar, Japanese holly, San Jose juniper, Norway

spruce, Shimpaku juniper, boxwood, chamaecyparis, Japanese juniper, Japanese black pine,
dwarf Alberta spruce, podocarpus, Satsuki
azalea, and pyracantha.

• *Deciduous:* Japanese maple, Trident maple,
red maple, hornbeam, barberry, flowering
quince, hackberry, beech, ginkgo, cotoneaster, hawthorn, privet, crab apple, sweet-gum,
flowering apricot, bald cypress, elm, wisteria,
zelkova, and oak.

• *Indoor bonsai* (kinds that can be maintained
year-round indoors, or kept outdoors in warm
weather): *Bucida spinosa, Calliandra emarginata*
(powderpuff), *Carissa grandiflora* (Natal plum),
Cuphea hyssopifolia (false heather, elfin herb), *Eu-
genia uniflora* (Surinam cherry), *Ficus benjamina*
(weeping fig), *F. retusa nitida* (glossy-leaf ficus),
Fortunella species (kumquat), *Ilex vomitoria* (yau-
pon), *Lagerstroemia indica* (crape myrtle), *Ligus-*

trum japonicum and *L. lucidum* (privet), *Lonicera
nitida* (honeysuckle), *Malpighia coccigera* (miniature holly), *Myrtus communis* (myrtle), *Olea euro-
paea* (olive), *Psidium cattleianum* (guava), *Punica
granatum nana* (dwarf pomegranate), and *Serissa
foetida.*

A green lattice structure, ABOVE LEFT, *designed by Bill
Mulligan for gardening columnist C. Z. Guest, stands
next to the tennis court on her property in Old Westbury, Long Island. The begonia is 'Christmas Candy', a
hybrid semperflorens that grows big and beautiful in
dappled sunlight, unexpectedly showy by comparison to
the more usual dwarf bedding begonias. An important
part of the Ballards' pleasure in gardening comes from
collecting the containers,* ABOVE RIGHT. *Here a trailing
rubus, recently introduced by the University of British
Columbia Botanical Garden, spills from an old concrete
vase. Like the wall by which it stands, the container
wears a patina of moss and lichen, and serves to signal
a change of grade in the walkway.*

Movable Topiary and Espaliers

Sally Reath's garden near Philadelphia spreads out and down a gentle slope from the house, itself attached by means of an airy arbor to a greenhouse, garden work center, a slathouse, and adjoining raised beds for propagation and the testing and observance of new plants. In addition there are a series of compost bins, a raised scree for alpine plants, and numerous trough gardens that hold miniature conifers and rock plants. Although renowned for her success in training topiary and espaliers as container plants, Sally forthrightly admits that this passion is currently on the wane, in favor of what she calls the "woodies"—trees and shrubs in every size, shape, and color imaginable. Nevertheless, here are the basics as I learned them from her some years ago.

Topiary (three-dimensional) and espalier (two-dimensional) are closely related plant training techniques. Both require a frame or support, which is one meaning of the word "espalier." Topiary frames come ready-made or you can shape your own—from wire coathangers or a coil of galvanized wire from the hardware store. Stuff the forms with sphagnum moss if working with tiny-leaved plants (i.e., baby's-tears *Soleirolia soleirolii*); larger ones can be trained up from a pot of soil and tied in place to cover the wire form. Frames for potted espaliers can be fashioned from thin bamboo stakes and a classic espalier pattern can be

Chenille plant (Acalypha hispida), ABOVE LEFT, *blooms heavily in spring and summer, and can be trained as a bush or tree-form standard. It is also available in a pinky white form, and a newly introduced trailing species (A. repens) will spill delightfully from a basket or window box. The yellow flower is lollipop plant (Pachystachys lutea), with showy terminal bracts. New Guinea impatiens, like this large basket at Logee's Greenhouses, Danielson, Connecticut,* ABOVE RIGHT, *have colorful leaves and spectacular flowers. Unlike the more usual bedding impatiens of the wallerana type, these require full sun and are ideal for all kinds of container gardens outdoors, as well as summer bedding. The Ballards grow container plants on every shelf, ledge, and table in the garden,* BELOW. *Fred designed and built the mini wheelbarrow to move along narrow paths; a cushioned rubber tire facilitates going up and down steps. A rock outcropping appears in the foreground, with varied plants of alpines and sedums.*

selected based on the growth habit and appearance of the plant to be espaliered. Alternatively, a piece of wire hardware cloth can be secured upright in the pot, and then cut into the desired shape using wirecutters or tin snips.

Some plants suited to growing on a moss-stuffed topiary form include small-leaved cultivars of ivy, *Hedera helix*, such as 'Shamrock', 'Pittsburg', 'Glacier', 'Gold Dust', 'Pin Oak', 'Itsy Bitsy', 'Ivalace', and 'Jubilee'. Also creeping fig, *Ficus pumila*, in numerous varieties; *Selaginella kraussiana* 'Brownii'; hen and chicks, *Sempervivum tectorum*; and Kenilworth ivy, *Cymbalaria muralis*, work well.

Some plants that can be trained on wire forms without stuffing include most ivies, mandevilla, hoya, jasmine, and passion vine. Sally's advice is to "try anything that needs support, even cherry tomatoes."

Potted espaliers can be trained from myrtle (*Myrtus communis* 'Microphylla'), rosemary, calamondin orange, African boxwood (*Myrsine africana*), crown of thorns (*Euphorbia milii*), Natal plum (*Carissa grandiflora*), and false holly (*Osmanthus heterophyllus* 'Variegatus').

Finally there is the tree-form standard, a way of training plants that is easy, great fun, and can be tried on almost any plant. Start with a single stem tied to a stake of the height you want your tree's trunk to be. Keep all branches pinched off until the leader reaches the top of the stake. Then pinch off the tip and succeeding branch tips to develop the tree head. As the head develops, gradually remove all leaves from along the trunk. This works well for the more upright forms of coleus, fuchsia, and miniature rose, most pelargoniums or garden geraniums, myrtle, rosemary, Australian rosemary (*Westringia rosmariniformis*), and *Euonymus fortunei*.

Fourth in my quartet of Philadelphia master container gardeners is Liddon Pennock, a man who is living proof of the adage, if you want something done, ask a busy person. Long since retired as one of America's preeminent florists, Liddon now devotes his life to the private and commercial gardens he is constantly embellish-ing and refining, at Meadowbrook Farms, Meadowbrook, Pennsylvania.

Container plants play an important role in nearly every outdoor garden room at Meadowbrook. Since the nursery is only a few steps down the drive, Liddon has an ever-ready supply of fresh materials, seasonal flowering plants, ivy wreaths and topiaries, and bouquets of cut garden flowers. What he does on a grand scale is not that different from what anyone can do who loves growing plants in containers and bringing them up close as an integral part of outdoor living. All of this spills quite naturally indoors and has a way of turning indoor rooms into winter gardens.

Logee's Greenhouses: The Source

It will be a hundred years in 1992 that the Logee family of Connecticut has been supplying gardeners in the Northeast with some of the rarest and best plants from all over the world for growing in containers.

Here are some of my choices from a recent splurge at Logee's; all require wintering in a frost-free area and all do best outdoors in warm weather:

• Dwarf bougainvillea for hanging baskets in full sun.

• Brunfelsia, a shrub that is generous with large lavender-blue flowers that are fragrant and slowly fade to nearly white, thus inspiring the name of yesterday-today-and-tomorrow.

• Euryops, a yellow-flowered daisy that comes in a green- or gray-leaved form, and will grow into a bushel-size bush in a season.

• Helichrysum in several varieties, varying from a filigree of tiny gray leaves to one with coin-size rounded leaves that are a pale, glowing yellow green. When stroked or disturbed these plants smell of curry.

• New Guinea impatiens with outrageously colored leaves and vividly colored flowers to twice the size of ordinary impatiens. Moreover, these are not for bringing color to the shady garden but for lighting up the sunny ones.

• Jasminum, a botanist's way of saying jasmine: The Logees have an impressive collection. I particularly favor 'Maid of Orleans' for flowers outdoors in summer or in a warm window in winter, and J. tortuosum, a vigorous grower that can be readily trained into an 18-inch wreath, or on some other trellising, has glossy, attractive foliage, and is everblooming.

• *Leptospermum scoparium*, the Australian tea tree, is a twiggy shrublet that trains beautifully into a tree-form standard. It needs to bake outdoors in full sun in summer, then spend fall in a cool, frost-free space. Flowers come in winter and spring.

• Passifloras: Several species are available that can be grown as hanging baskets or trained on a trellis. 'Incense', a hybrid, has proven winter-hardy in the ground against a south-facing wall of a Logee growing house; it is slow to appear in the spring but is tolerant of temperatures to zero or colder.

• *Salvia gregii* is a tender species that can't stay outdoors in winter, but the small, tidy plants are readily kept over in a cool window or greenhouse. Varieties are available in white, crimson, pink, and salmon.

Container Gardening at Templeton

Most of my experiences as a container gardener outdoors have been on Long Island with C. Z. Guest at Templeton, her property in Old Westbury. C. Z. has two greenhouses with several compartments that can be kept at different temperatures, and a sun-heated pit that is used for wintering camellias, potted tree-form azaleas, tubbed figs, and a host of woody subtropicals that spend the summer outdoors on a sunny terrace and around a lattice pavilion at the tennis court. These include abutilon, or flowering maple; citrus; clerodendrum; brugmansia, or angel trumpet; oleander; and tibouchina, or glory bush. The warmer greenhouse compartments are reserved for orchids, cestrum, mandevilla, *Mitriostigma axillare* (African gardenia), geraniums, and rutcya, a little-known and easily grown plant that bears quantities of orange and brown or yellow and brown flowers. C. Z.'s sizable collections of clivias and agapanthus spend winters in a cold but frost-free cottage where they are kept dry.

Some of the lessons I have learned in helping manage C. Z.'s extensive container gardens are: Group plants of a kind together, as well as those requiring similar conditions as to light, temperature, watering, and fertilizing. Avoid little plants in big pots, and vice versa. This helps prevent over- or underwatering and in the case of big plants in little pots, avoids the top heaviness that invites havoc from gusts of wind. When you water, be thorough. If in doubt, turn the plant out of its pot and check to see if the entire mass of soil and roots has been soaked from top to bottom. Because container plantings often have to be watered daily in the hottest weather, nutrients are quickly leached away. This necessitates fertilizing a little with every watering, a result most easily achieved by using timed-release fertilizer pellets such as 14-14-14, or by applying fertilizer at watering time once each week. When container plants have ample water and are not allowed to dry out severely between waterings, they are better able to assimilate nutrients and become inherently stronger and more resistant to insects or disease. The usual aphids, white flies, mealy bugs, brown scale, and spider-mites can be controlled by spraying with insecticidal soap. Small green worms that often attack geraniums can be hand-picked or sprayed with a product such as Sevin. Disease is rarely a problem with container plants in the Northeast if you keep dead leaves and spent flowers picked and if plants are spaced for air circulation.

CHAPTER NINE

OUTDOOR LIVING

To me, no part of the garden is as important as that area set aside as the outdoor living room, a place that is relatively quiet, private, and protected, with furnishings to facilitate relaxing, dining, and entertaining. Since all too many of us in the Northeast pass the Friday finish line flying, literally or figuratively, with or without discernible "colors," the outdoor living room represents escape from the fast lane, to a sanctum where slowness can be celebrated and not necessarily on weekends alone. I marvel that so few apartment terraces reveal any signs of living outdoors. Since my city dwelling has no terrace, my outdoor living room where friends and family come together is more often than not a large rock in Central Park, with a cloth spread on it, a picnic hamper, and, in spite of the crowded setting, a surprising sense of "getting away from it all."

Rooms for Living Outdoors

Despite obvious differences and distinctions, porches, patios, terraces, and decks are remarkably similar in terms of design considerations, furnishings, and ultimate uses. To the purist, a patio is an enclosed court, walled-in by the house, and open to the sky. Since the Second World War the word has come to mean almost any paved area that adjoins a dwelling, and is adapted to outdoor living, barbecue cooking, and dining.

The word "terrace" is even less specific than patio. Classically it can be applied to a colonnaded porch or promenade, to a flat roof or open platform. It can also mean a relatively level paved or planted area adjoining a building, in this application often indistinguishable from the modern patio. Apartments in multi-story buildings often have terraces, which may also be referred to as balconies or, if of wood construction, decks.

The wood deck has a lot in common with porches, patios, and terraces. Usually but not necessarily attached to the house, a deck can solve the problem of where to put an area for

A late summer flowering white hosta spills into the stepping-stone path of the entrance to the Hartwood cottage garden in New Jersey, bordered by bergenia, white sweet-alyssum, echinacea, and self-sown flowering tobacco that is pale greenish white. Beyond the old apple tree, the path leads to a secluded sitting area with bentwood twig settee, sidechairs, and table. Extending into this garden from the house is a conservatory, with many orchids and jasmine.

outdoor living when the terrain is too rough, or falls away in a slope too steep for any other treatment. Even if your house is cottage-size, a deck extending from one or more sides can unify varied spaces, with cut-outs for major existing trees, at once creating an outdoor room more spacious than any you have indoors.

If you have any choice in the size of a patio, terrace, or deck, bigger is usually better. The outdoors tends to minimize the effect of any roommaking attempted there. Small children often play in these spaces and other family members require a place to spread out as well. While porches can get quite dressy, patios, terraces, and decks seem by nature more casual, analogous perhaps to the family or recreation room inside.

Patios and earth-bound terraces can be designed with planting pockets for trees, shrubs, flowers, or your favorite herbs. Bricks or flagstones laid in sand or gravel allow embellishment of the surface by establishing between them, in carefully placed pockets of soil, such pleasing carpeters as creeping thyme and Corsican mint. If you have an extensive flower garden nearby, kinds that readily self-sow from tracked or windblown seeds will often grow up between bricks or stones, especially in less trafficked spots. Left to their own devices these add delightful surprises in unexpected places—here a rollick of Johnny-jump-ups, there a clump of tall white flowering tobacco that scents the evening air.

Container plantings are favored on most patios, terraces, and decks. Exactly what you grow will depend on the amount of sun or shade and the season, but in general it pays to use a few large planters rather than a scattering of small pots, which have the habit of drying out too much and blowing over in the first gust of wind. Be especially wary of any container that could topple from a high place and fall on an unsuspecting passerby, possibly yourself.

Although variety may be the spice of life, the greatest impact from plantings you will be enjoying up close often comes from a finely tuned color scheme and not too many different forms and textures. Ornamental grasses, ranging from 6 inches to 6 feet, and in color from blue-gray to all shades of green, from nearly yellow to glowing scarlet and burgundy, are a recent innovation in gardening. They adapt readily to containerization and offer refreshing motion and sound when rustled by breezes. For more information on container gardening, see Chapter Eight.

Paving Choices

Many different kinds of paving are used for patios and terraces. In general you want a surface that is easy on the eyes—does not create glare—and has a nonskid texture. Absorptive materials are best avoided since they make the cleaning of mud and food stains difficult. Rapid drainage of excess water away from the house is a primary consideration to accommodate natural precipitation as well as the regular hosing off that is a part of outdoor housekeeping. A smooth surface gives solid footing for furniture, eases its rearrangement, permits dancing, and lets the wheels of children's toys roll smoothly. Add to all this the need for a surface in harmony with surrounding architecture and building materials, and you will see that this choice merits careful thought. Here are some more specific guidelines:

Bricks are nonglare and nonskid, unless infested with algae. (Algae thrive in acidic, wet, poorly lighted situations; environmentally safe algaecides are available from at least one manufacturer of insecticidal soaps.) In color and texture, bricks get on well in almost any setting and no extraordinary skills are needed to lay them yourself in a variety of classic patterns.

Concrete, poured in 2- to 4-foot squares, is a frequent choice for patios. It can be finished in a variety of textures, from slick to pebbly, and may even be colored, although this is hard to do evenly or permanently. Wood headers are often used but tend to rot out and require replacement in a few years.

Flagstones are expensive but will last indefinitely if laid well. Colors vary and subtlety is not always possible with their random patterns. As with bricks, they yield an irregular surface that can be a liability in situating furniture, yet in the right setting a flagstone terrace or patio can be a great success, especially when small plants are established in pockets here and there —the previously mentioned creeping thymes, Corsican mint, along with the herb lady's-mantle, and tufted perennials such as dianthus and seapink, *Armeria maritima*.

Tiles, compared to other patio and terrace surfaces, are smooth and dressy. They are expensive but often the best choice, especially where the terrace or patio relates directly to an indoor room floored in the same tile.

Soft materials such as gravel, mill-run aggregates, and crushed brick can be used to supplement a permanently paved terrace or patio, especially the area surrounding a fire pit or barbecue. Food spills and stains can be readily obscured by raking, or the affected material removed and replaced by fresh. Tanbark—the crushed bark of such trees as oak and hemlock, used in tanning hides—creates an excellent surface where children play; it is quick to dry after rain, hard enough for small wheels to roll over, yet soft enough to cushion falls.

Enclosing the Outdoor Room

A need for privacy or to break the prevailing wind may require the addition of one or more walls around the outdoor living room. These can be constructed or be created from plantings of evergreen or deciduous shrubs or trees arranged as hedging or windbreaks. Constructed outdoor walls, whether part of a building, or built specifically to confine the space as an outdoor room, may be made of brick, stone, wood, bamboo, or iron. They may be solid or open, as in classic trellising and the woven fencing found in Japanese landscapes.

While outdoor walls may shield wind and rain, give privacy, and block out unsightliness,

they also afford the garden decorator a place to drape leafy, flowering, fragrant vines, or to espalier woody plants into formal or casual traceries that constitute living art.

The distinction between what is a wall and a fence blurs, although in practice garden walls tend to be part of a larger structure while a fence, which is short for *defense*, is more likely installed as a barrier. Fences have traditionally been erected on newly settled land from materials found on· or near the site—stone, earth, wood. The traditional New England stone wall laid loose, without mortar, is called a dry wall or dry-stone wall, and when pockets of composty earth are added, and plants, it becomes a splendid place for rock gardening.

All outdoor rooms have ceilings, whether or not we perceive them as such. Most expansive and the least controllable is the open sky, with its varied moods and colors, blue, gray, dark, even stormy. Nothing we bring to the outdoor room rivals its opening to the moonlight and all the twinkling stars of the universe. The extent to which we close this off is dictated by the need for shelter and a sense of enclosure, which can be created with plants, with structures, or a combination.

Plants that lose their leaves in cold weather can be a distinct advantage in sheltering the outdoor room. They provide welcome shade in hot weather, yet let in as much warmth from the winter sun as possible. This growth pattern can serve the needs of early spring flowers and bulbs that need sun in cool weather but shade in summer, to help keep the area cool and moist, as inviting for them as for the human occupants.

The extent to which an outdoor room is protected from the elements is dictated by its intended use and the climate. A large, well-anchored umbrella or canvas awning can be the answer for a dining area adjoining the house. The more gardenesque solution could be a pergola with wisteria, climbing roses, or clematis —or all three and more—topped by an all but invisible corrugated fiberglass roof. Tie-back,

plastic-lined canvas panels or draperies may be added at the sides as necessary to secure the interior, thus making it cosy, intimate, and dry even in the midst of a storm.

Doors, arbors, and gates for outdoor rooms offer more than access. They serve as frames for the picture implied by the opening. They are a welcoming device as well. An opening cut in a tall hedge, wall, or fence gives the eye a treat when even the most minimal of scenes is framed, a chair or bench in the distance, perhaps a small table.

The walls of an outdoor room can also have windows, or cuts, that open to a view. Sometimes these are literally cut through, to frame something distant. They can also be of a *faux* quality, more two-dimensional, a place to display an urn with plantings or to hang a bas relief terra cotta or bronze construction. Window cuts in an otherwise solid wall, whether of plants or constructed, serve to give a sense of escape and also permit air circulation that helps control the microclimate within the room. The same as indoors, windows in outdoor walls can be closed, using shutters, for added privacy, or as a shield against inclement weather.

Furnishing the Outdoor Room

Outdoor furniture, like that for indoors, may be new, old, or so indifferent it challenges the makeover artist. Outdoor furniture often transplants successfully indoors, especially where the intent is a gardenlike interior, but furniture intended for indoors seldom serves well for more than a day in the sun, perhaps for a family celebration.

Many outdoor rooms start off being furnished with odds and ends or with here-and-now, relatively inexpensive folding pieces in plastic, metal, aluminum, or a combination. Bright, primary colors are available and make virtually instant furnishings for the outdoor version of a breakfast nook or family room. Be careful of cheap, painted, metal-and-wire chairs; they are inclined to rusting at the joints

The Ballards' outdoor living room opens into the towering trees of Philadelphia's Fairmount Park and serves as a staging place to grow and show off container plantings in warm weather. Seen across the Ballards' only lawn, the outdoor living room, OPPOSITE ABOVE, is bowered by soaring old trees, which they prune and maintain with the same loving care and attention to detail as for their prized collection of bonsai. Grapevines clothe the walls and cascade gracefully from the top. A small balcony (upper right) off the master bedroom overlooks this peaceful scene, with the soothing sounds of splashing water from the fountain and birds singing in the trees. A small pool, OPPOSITE BELOW, at the base of the fountain holds goldfish and supplies the constant standing water needed by cyperus and grassy-leaved sweet flag (Acorus gramineus 'Variegatus'). A fancy-leaved caladium stands on the cocktail table. Other plants nearby include an elaeagnus having highly variegated foliage, numerous tropical ferns, acanthus, and gray-leaved helichrysum. Fruit-bearing plants such as this dwarf apple next to the tennis court in the Cabots' garden in Quebec, ABOVE, are especially enjoyable when included as part of an outdoor space that functions as a gathering place for family and guests. Dwarf fruit trees can be grown in containers the size of a bushel basket or larger, not to mention everbearing strawberrries such as 'Tristar', raspberries, and gooseberries, the latter readily trainable as an espalier or tree-form standard.

where the seat joins the legs, a condition that can readily escalate to booby-trap proportions.

Upholstered garden furniture, including wicker and cushions, is most readily accommodated in a part of the outdoor room that is afforded a measure of shelter, a porch or summerhouse for example. Flowered fabrics, however evocative of the garden they may be indoors, are tricky in the midst of a living garden, which is not to say a finely tuned color scheme and delightful effect cannot be worked out between the various elements of garden and decor.

With the exception of brief forays on the lawn, outdoor furniture is best situated on a solid, level surface. Those who mow lawns are never fond of stopping to move furniture or other objects left in their path. In addition, furniture parts that rest directly on the grass or cast dark shadows can quickly disfigure an otherwise well-kept lawn.

The whole genre of outdoor furniture bears careful thought as to how it will be seen and experienced, often as a focal point or even a distant vista. Furniture choices depend on the style, size, and function of the outdoor room. For sitting or some degree of recline there are chairs, sofas, chaises, benches, banquettes, and stools. There may be dining and side tables as well as a sizable low surface analogous to the coffee table indoors.

Outdoor furniture constructed of milled wood may be allowed to weather naturally, or be stained for an immediate effect of patina. In the event of troublesome splintering, coating with paint is often the answer, at once a measure of preservation and the means for unifying dissimilar pieces or effecting a change in color scheme.

Accessories can be more than our personalized finishing touches for an outdoor room, for in fact one or more may serve as its focal point if not inspiration. A garden dependent for effect on bloom may go off like fireworks one week and lie plaintively spent the next, which will of course be when you are expecting guests. A well-placed antique watering can, a birdbath, or even a heroic piece of terra cotta can make a remarkable difference in how we perceive an outdoor space. However transitory, there is undeniable visual charm in the honest trappings of the gardener at work, the silhouette of a wheelbarrow with long-handled tools and stakes protruding, a trug cradling clippers, seeds, and twist-ties, or the inevitable hamper for collecting deadheads and weeds.

Statuary, sundials, and other ornaments may be classic or contemporary, antique or newly made. Hardly anything brought into an outdoor room has such an immediate effect, often letting us focus on that perfected part as we exercise patience in waiting for the other elements to materialize, in plant growth or construction.

Lighting

Quite apart from the sun, moon, and stars, lighting plays a major and potentially magical role in our experience of the outdoor room. Provisions for it, like water, are ideally accounted for in the planning stages and installed in the due course of construction. The same as indoors, light is needed for general illumination as well as specific spots and floods. Drama, safety, and security may be achieved by the use of an energy-efficient, low-voltage system. It helps if lighting fixtures can be readily adjusted, turned, even moved, so as to play up the outdoor room's best features at any given moment. While vines are supposed to hang leafy curtains over architectural shortcomings, selective night lighting can make a so-so gardener look astonishingly competent.

Mood lighting in the outdoor room may be afforded by candles, hurricanes, old-fashioned kerosene lamps, or a variety of lanterns, including those evocative of a remote campsite, whimsical Japanese paper globes strung at party time and the classic Japanese stone lantern. Tiki torches and citronella candles offer light and some protection from annoying insects.

Swimming Pools and Hot Tubs

Bodies of water designed specifically to invite the physical interaction of people—swimming, lap, and wading pools, whirlpools, and hot tubs—have a way of being integral to if not the main events of the outdoor living rooms in which they are placed. Recent innovations in technology permit designs not previously feasible and the on-going detail of maintenance has been eased through automation and computerization. Besides the usual aqua color, there is also the option of gray, dark blue, or black, which can be less intrusive, especially in a more natural garden setting. Dark-painted pools mirror the sky and absorb more of the sun's warming rays. (Water gardening *per se* is discussed in Chapter Six.)

Besides the pool (for people), other considerations are the surrounding surface treatment, enclosure of the general area through plantings and construction so as to comply with local laws, and how all of this will tie in and relate to the dwelling, other buildings, and any connecting outdoor rooms.

It is well to formulate an overall design concept yourself, but then you will want to involve professionals to ensure sound engineering and installation. The containerization of 30,000 gallons of water, the amount held by the average pool, is no job for an amateur. The swimming pool often represents a homeowner's single largest investment in property improvement, one destined for a continuum of upkeep and repairs which, we hope, will be generously offset by a long life of pleasure-giving. Some considerations relating specifically to the gardener's viewpoint are these:

Sunshine and Shade. Sunbathers obviously want sun, as do most active swimmers. Site for maximum sun in the main swimming season, with no shadows from buildings, trees, and fences during the hours of greatest use. Orientate the deep end of the pool so that divers will leave the diving board with their backs to the sun, rather than facing into direct glare. Shade

can also be welcome, especially in the poolside area used for lounging, cooking, and entertaining. All manner of constructions and devices come into play here, including umbrellas, canvas awnings, cabanas, and a variety of lattice structures.

Wind. Breezes may be welcome in hot weather but winds usually need blocking in order not to chill the swimmers and unduly cool the water. Fences, plantings, structures, and the placement of the pool in relation to the dwelling can keep this from being a problem.

Maintenance. Debris will accumulate, but it can be minimized by siting the pool as far away from trees as possible and at some distance from any source of tracked or wind disbursed debris such as the children's sandbox, a gravel area, or cultivated garden soil.

Filter and pump. The closer to the pool, the better, for this basic equipment, which can be hidden behind a fence or screen, an adjacent garage or wing of the house, or by enclosure in a simple lattice structure that can be enhanced with an arrangement of plants, planted in the ground or in containers.

Pool deck. The paved area immediately surrounding a swimming pool is called a deck whether or not it is constructed of wood. Instead of being a uniform width all around, two or three sides will usually be fairly narrow, a minimum of 3 to 5 feet, with an extended paved section on the remaining one or two sides that will serve the space needs for furniture, accessories, and all the myriad activities of outdoor living.

If wood is the material chosen as swimming-pool decking, it must be splinter-free, either inherently or by treatment. Tile and smooth cement are slippery when wet. Rough surfaces are hard on bare feet and resist efficient cleaning by sweeping or hosing-off. Since it is relatively inexpensive and neither slippery nor coarse, brushed concrete is the frequent choice.

Drainage. Underground and surface drainage are crucial to the short- and long-term suc-

cess of a swimming pool. If ground water collects under the pool, pressure may build to the point of cracking or pushing the pool out of the ground. Avoid this dilemma on a site that has poor natural drainage by installing a system of drain tiles around the base of the pool. Drainage outlets will also be needed to carry away surface water from the pool decking, which should be sloped away from the pool at the rate of one-fourth inch to the foot.

The hillside site. Consult with a geologist and pool engineer. If a pool is feasible, its structural engineering must balance great weight on one side with lack of support on the side that is backfilled. Retaining walls may be used separately or incorporated in the structure of the pool itself. Drainage systems will be needed to carry water around and away from the pool.

Whirlpools, hot tubs, and spas. These miniature swimming pools with water heated to 100° F and aerated bubbles fit into very little

space and can be tucked away for privacy. Not intended for serious swimming, but rather for lounging and soaking away the serious cares of the day, the container itself is usually constructed of redwood or fiberglass, and often comes in kit-form, complete with heater, pump, filter, and hardware.

Compared to a full-scale swimming pool, hot tubs are far less costly, use less than a thousand gallons of water, and require a minimum monthly outlay for gas and electricity. Unless you are able to do the work yourself, figure the

This inviting corner in the Hartwood cottage garden in New Jersey is framed by a stone retaining wall, capped by trellising that shields and protects, also providing a place for vines such as the sweet autumn and other clematis, and, toward full sun, climbing roses and honeysuckle. The bentwood furniture has an organic quality that suits the setting. The potted tree-form standard is gray santolina. Creeping thyme grows between the paving stones, with white flowering tobacco; tree peony leaves are in the foreground.

(130)

cost of installation by a professional contractor at approximately equal to that of the kit itself, with an additional expenditure for the decking and surrounding plantings.

Greater privacy can be afforded by situating the hot tub or spa in a gazebo or trellis structure that can give welcome shade on hot days and shield from wind at night or in cool weather. A solar greenhouse makes a wonderful surround for a hot tub that can be used all year in all kinds of weather. The humidity and warmth given off by the small body of water encourages the cultivation of exotic plants which make a delightful finishing touch for a place that is always cozy, intimate, and inviting.

Plantings for the Pool and Other Outdoor Spaces

Plantings play an important role in poolside areas outdoors. Ground-level beds immediately adjacent to a pool are not recommended be-

cause any run-off of chlorine-treated water can actually kill vegetation. Sizable wood tubs or large terra-cotta pots can be employed in fairly close proximity, a few feet back so that ample decking is clear for foot traffic. Avoid scattering containers on the deck as they are sure to be tripped over; remember, there is safety in numbers and massing creates the maximum effect.

There are endless possibilities for what to grow in and around an outdoor living area that features a swimming pool. Some can be permanent fixtures in the ground and others can

This chair on the Connecticut terrace of Lynden and Leigh Miller invites pausing to rest a bit and contemplate activity at the birdfeeder, if not in the gardens beyond. Matching clay pots hold marguerites or Boston daisies (Chrysanthemum frutescens) in a selection with finely cut gray-green leaves. To the right is a cutleaf Japanese maple and a dwarf pine. The herb lady's-mantle (Alchemilla vulgaris) grows along with creeping thymes between the terrace paving stones. An open pergola ceiling casts sun and shade patterns.

(131)

be in movable containers. Dyed-in-the-wool gardeners who have a way of doing odd bits of pruning, digging, planting, and grooming even when they are supposed to be relaxing with friends and family will be happiest if this area is used for showing a collection of favorite container plants. What better way to unwind and maybe say a little prayer of thanks that a radish cannot be rushed through a facsimile machine!

Seasonal flowering vines make quick cover for safety fences and wind screens. Wisteria, with white or lavender-purple flowers in spring and early summer, is a rampant grower, as well as trumpet creeper, *Campsis radicans*, which produces showy orange flowers mid- to late summer, and silver-lace vine, *Polygonum aubertii*, which is adorned in early fall with a bride's veil of tiny white flowers. There are many different clematis that can be mixed or matched as to color and flowering season, from spring to fall, with silken seed clusters that remain into winter. Hurry-up-and-bloom annuals from seed, such as morning-glory, moonvine (*Ipomoea alba*, sometimes known as Calonyction aculeatum), and 'Scarlet Runner' or 'Hyacinth' beans can be employed while you organize permament plantings.

If you work days and will enjoy your poolside plantings primarily at night, try this idea: Concentrate on white, pale pink, and yellow flowers. That way they will show up better in moon or other night light. Try some petunias, daylilies that stay open at night, white flowering tobacco, impatiens, and four o'clocks. White-variegated hosta and caladium foliage add light, as do moonflower vines.

Plants in living arrangements are especially enjoyable as part of the outdoor living surround. To grow a living picture of succulents, take a 12- x 18-inch wooden flat about 2-inches deep. Fill with planting mix, then add a layer of sheet moss or unmilled sphagnum moss over the surface. Cover with chicken wire or half-inch-mesh wire hardware cloth and tack in place all around. Plant thickly with hen-and-chicks, sempervivum, echeveria, crassula, and

sedum. Keep in a horizontal position until the roots take hold, then hang on a sunny wall. (In absence of rain, remove once a week and soak 15 minutes in a basin of water.)

Large pieces of driftwood with natural pockets are ideal for showing off succulents, such as those just mentioned, along with aeonium. Just tuck a bit of planting soil into the driftwood pockets and they are ready to display in any sunny outdoor living area. If you have more shade than sun, plant the driftwood with ferns, small-leaved ivies, peperomias, dwarf impatiens, or almost any common houseplant.

If you are in a time and space crunch, here is a way to expedite a terrace garden: Sink several small pots in one large container filled with damp peatmoss or bark chips. The community system helps keep roots uniformly cool and moist. When one crop finishes, lift and replace only the pots affected; leave the others undisturbed. This is a proven system for gaining hours of pleasure from minutes of gardening.

Trouble in Paradise

The ticks that carry Lyme disease not withstanding, the Northeast is comparatively free of poisonous insects and snakes. If you are going to walk into weeds, through undergrowth or woodland, common sense dictates wearing long sleeves with snug-fitting cuffs and long pants tucked into boots or taped snugly about the ankles. According to Andrew Spielman, Sc.D., professor of tropical public health at the Harvard School of Public Health, the way to remove a deer tick, the tiny parasite that carries Lyme disease, is to grasp it firmly with tweezers and pull with a steady motion. "By removing the majority of the tick, you kill it and may avoid being infected with the disease. Clean the bite with soap and water, then dab with rubbing alcohol to disinfect it. If any of the following symptoms occur within two to four weeks after the bite, see a doctor: fever, rash, generalized aches and pains, or other signs of illness."

Individuals who are never bitten by mosquitoes have a way of knowing exactly why they are biting you: too much sugar in the diet, too much perfume or cologne, a genetic predisposition, or not eating enough raw garlic. Herbalists say that mosquitoes and other insects are repelled from an area by aromatic herbs, either growing or hanging in bunches to dry, kinds such as basil, anise, coriander, rosemary, and sage. It definitely helps to make sure that there is no standing water—where mosquitoes breed—in the vicinity, and that pools and ponds are stocked with fish since they feed on the larvae. I am categorically opposed to applying directly to my skin or as a spray any petrochemically derived insect repellent, a practice most of my friends have now sworn off as well. The current alternative of choice is an Avon product called "Skin So Soft," which has the incidental side effect of keeping insects at bay (but it does contain petrochemicals).

In case you have not guessed, I have always been the one in a crowd with some magnetic attraction to mosquitoes. On the other hand, I have never gotten poison ivy, so my advice will no doubt be taken with a grain of salt if you get it simply by petting your dogs after they have been out for a romp in the woods. If you know you have been exposed to poison oak, ivy, or sumac, rinse immediately with rubbing alcohol, then bathe under cold running water. Soap is not helpful and do not use a washcloth since it can have the effect of spreading the toxin. Jewelweed, *Impatiens pallida*, which grows wild in wet places throughout the Northeast, in both sun and shade, is a natural neutralizer for the effects of poison ivy and is often readily available to the working gardener. Squeeze out the gelatinous clear liquid from its succulent stems and apply to the area of exposed skin.

If you get stung by a bee, remove the stinger by a flick of your fingernail, or ease it free using the tip of a knife blade. Outright plucking or squeezing is best avoided since it could release more toxin. Ease the pain by soaking in cold water, then applying a thin paste of meat tenderizer containing papain, an enzyme that neutralizes the toxin. In the event of an allergic reaction, such as difficulty in breathing or hives, seek the help of a doctor immediately.

One recurrent problem for gardeners in the Northeast is the yellow jacket, which my dictionary describes as a "social wasp." In my experience they are extremely antisocial if their underground nest is disturbed in late summer. During my season working with the gardeners at the Brooklyn Botanic Garden I inadvertently cut into a yellow jacket nest that was in leaf-moldy soil under English ivy ground cover. Before I realized what was happening the yellow jackets had stung me all over. After getting away from them, my initial thought was to rest a spell and then go back to work. Fortunately a fellow gardener happened by and urged my going immediately to the potting shed. By the time I got there my eyes were nearly swollen shut and I was having trouble breathing. Someone marshalled a car and rushed me to the nearest hospital emergency room where it took an hour or so of treatment with antihistamines to stabilize my vital signs. I lay around at home for several days and did not feel up to par for a couple of weeks. My advice is to give yellow jackets a wide berth and, if bitten, to seek help at once.

The pain or discomfort of minor stings and bites can be alleviated by applying a paste of baking soda and water. The alkalizing effect from the moisture brings almost instant relief. The gelatinous liquid squeezed from a leaf of *Aloe barbadensis*, better known as Aloe vera, will also bring relief to insect stings and bites.

CHAPTER TEN

INDOOR GARDENING

Every Northeastern gardener can benefit from an indoor garden if for no other reason than to serve as a nursery for the outdoor. The tradition of growing houseplants and wintering-over the frost-tender indoors has roots in the Northeast. Today millions of us live in apartments or condominiums where little or no gardening is possible except indoors. Even where gardens surround a home, there is nothing quite like the experience of waking up to find a fragrant rose in a bud vase next to your bed, or walking into a sunny room in the morning and smelling rosemary, rose geranium, and sweet-olive.

A high-rise apartment near what is purported to be one of the busiest, noisiest, most dangerous, and polluted intersections in the world has served as my primary garden and laboratory for plant experimentation for nearly twenty years. I have no terrace, but the windows all face south; a tall building on the opposite side of the street blocks some direct sun at midday, which I accept as a blessing. Fluorescent-light gardens in floor-to-ceiling shelf units stand at either end of an otherwise dark hallway, with cooler growing ferns and seasonal flowers such as cyclamen and primula on the lower shelves, upward to African violets, begonias, and or-

chids, and finally some cacti and other succulents on the top shelves where the air is consistently warmer and drier.

Where window light is not strong enough to grow a plant, I often take advantage of table and floor lamps used for general illumination. Within the circle of brightest light cast by a lamp, whether on a table or the floor, it is possible to show off and even grow an amazing number of beautiful plants. Right now on the lamptables at either end of the living-room sofa there are two 'Dallas' ferns in matching pots that stand on 15-inch white, reproduction Greek columns (made from plaster of Paris). Three-inch-square white tubs in the manner of Versailles stand at the base of each column, filled at the moment with cut roses. There are

This sunny window provides welcome and sometimes intensive gardening activities in all seasons, in all kinds of weather, and at any time, day or night. English ivies are trained as a globe, a wreath, and a bird. Lime-scented geranium is trained on a small bamboo trellis as an espalier. There is also a 'Gold Cloth' fancy-leaved geranium standard, with Deacon Hybrid geraniums in a clay window box. Giant bird-of-paradise stands in a pedestal; spathiphyllum grows in the foreground, shielded from direct sun.

also the 'Compacta' forms of dracaenas 'Janet Craig' and 'Warneckii'. At the back of the tables I have a collection of small sansevierias. These tablescapes rarely stay the same for long; their refurbishment always gives me pleasure and I've noticed that my family and other guests are delighted by close encounters with horticulture in miniature.

Ongoing pleasure from an indoor garden depends largely on the gardener. Outdoor gardens in the Northeast are moved onward inexorably by the changing seasons. Indoors we must take matters in hand. As an apartment gardener, my favorite seasons are spring and fall when neither heating nor cooling units are needed. Central heating and cooling may spell creature comfort, but few plants bask in hot or cold blasts of air. The longer days and warmer average temperatures of spring and summer are conducive to active growth and the attendant needs for potting, repotting, root and top pruning, and fertilizing. Activity slows in fall and winter, although this can be obviated by a warm fluorescent-light garden operated sixteen out of every twenty-four hours, in which case blizzard conditions may prevail outdoors while you garden inside as if it were high summer.

Palms and Other Indoor Trees

Hardly anything has a more dramatic or immediate effect on a room than a large specimen plant. Palms and ficus in variety grow best with direct sun, while dracaenas, pleomeles, and polyscias adapt to bright reflected light with little or no direct sun. Pony-tail palm, also known as elephant-foot plant (*Beaucarnea recurvata*), can become treelike within five to ten years from a seedling, and it will adapt to full sun or light that is merely bright.

A chief problem with palms indoors is that they are not watered properly. The larger the mass of soil, the more difficult it is to judge how much and how often to water. Apply enough water so that the entire mass of soil and roots is moistened through and through. Water again when the surface soil feels dry to the touch. Don't wait until it looks dry; some soils, especially those having high peat content, look about the same, wet or dry. When a palm in warmth is repeatedly allowed to dry out severely, spider-mites almost invariably move in for the kill. These tiny insects seem drawn to stressed plants. If one of your plants is plagued by an infestation, the treatment is to shower the palm in lukewarm water, directing a strong spray to the frond undersides, which is where the mites are most prevalent. When the palm has drained and dried, spray with insecticidal soap, again being careful to thoroughly wet the frond undersides. Repeat weekly until the mites are gone. Meantime, brush up on your watering technique.

Ficus trees suffer the same watering mistreatments as palms, but the consequences are different. A ficus allowed to be severely dry for even one brief period may drop bushels of leaves, or so it seems to the distraught novice. Moving a ficus from a high light level to a low one without any preconditioning can have a similar effect. And sometimes one or two branches will die in the midst of healthy ones, a sign that pockets of soil and roots within the pot are not receiving water. In any event, pick up the leaves, and cut out the dead branches and twigs. Don't do anything drastic, like a double dose of fertilizer, or complete repotting. Hold steady. With a little TLC the ficus will likely recover and become an indoor tree that is uniquely adapted to your conditions.

Indoor Plants If You Have No Sun

Indoor gardeners rarely complain of having too much sun, but most of us could do with more. It's pointless to try growing plants in dark corners. They can't be seen and will languish and eventually die. In brighter spots, with little or no direct sun, lots of plants are capable of adapting and giving pleasure.

Lesson #1 is to start with a vigorous, youthful specimen—one that is on the way up instead of at its peak or already headed down.

Lesson #2 is to go with a proven performer in relatively low light, which is to say bright enough for you to read small print by.

One of the best such species is aglaonema, or Chinese evergreen. There is a rather tall plain green form but today's market is filled with a variety of silver- or creamy-white variegated cultivars that are more compact and showier.

Another choice plant that doesn't need direct sun—it is in fact inhibited by too much light—is the spathiphyllum, or peace lily. This plant is available in several sizes, from 12-inch miniatures to relative giants 4 feet tall or more. In season, each bears white spathe flowers, sized according to the plant, and often the source of a light lemony scent.

Any number of ferns do well in light that is merely bright: Maidenhair ferns (*Adiantum* genus) and tabletop pterises are outstanding, but any from the Boston complex (*Nephrolepis exaltata* 'Bostoniensis', 'Roosevelt', 'Whitmanii', and the recently introduced dwarf 'Dallasi'), rabbit's-foot (*Davallia fejeensis*), and miniature *Polystichum tsus-simense* are delightful possibilities. Bird's-nest fern, *Asplenium nidus*, has potentially dramatic form but quickly shows stress from erratic watering by producing new fronds that are deformed and browned at the margins. A bark-mounted staghorn fern (*Platycerium* genus) makes a wonderful trophy to hang on the wall of a sunporch or greenhouse. Holly fern, *Cyrtomium falcatum*, was favored by Victorian gardeners for its toughness in the face of darkened interiors and widely fluctuating temperatures. It may be too coarse to suit a person who thinks of ferns as delicate and lacy, but to be honest, holly fern is the right choice for beginners.

No beautiful-leaved plant gives me more satisfaction than the calathea, readily collectible in at least 30 different species and cultivars. They vary from 1- to 3-feet tall, all having veined and patterned leaves that fold upward at night—or when under duress from being at once too hot and dry or too cold and wet—in the manner of the familiar (and related) obedience and prayer plants (of the genus *Maranta*). Calatheas don't grow much except in constant warmth—65° to 80° F—and fairly bright light is needed for proper development.

If you are a gardener who loves cacti and other succulents but have little direct sun, don't despair. There are many different and fascinating sansevierias, not to mention peperomias and rhipsalis, the latter a leafy cactus that hails from warm rain forests and makes an excellent choice for hanging in a window that is merely bright. Numerous aloes, including the Aloe vera of cosmetics and wholistic medicine, more correctly known as *Aloe barbadensis*, as well as haworthias and gasterias, make excellent growth in bright light with little direct sun.

Jade plant is often placed in low light, but don't expect the impossible. If this member of the *Crassula* genus is grown in bright light, it will be from pale to dark green, with wide spacing between the leaves. The branches may be too weak to stand without help from stakes. Frequent pinching out of the growing tips will help encourage more compact habit. In full sun the same plant will have a glowing golden green quality with reddish margins and the leaves will be tightly packed along short, stocky stems.

There are numerous plants that will flower quite satisfactorily in a north window, or in the merely bright light I have previously described. These include miniature gloxinias such as *Sinningia pusilla* and 'Tinkerbells', tiny *Begonia prismatocarpa*, white *Oxalis regnellii*, and an unusual relative of the wandering Jew known as *Siderasis fuscata*. Any of these can be brought along nicely when placed within the circle of brightest light cast by a table lamp with a 60-watt or brighter bulb burned eight hours or more out of every twenty-four.

If you want an indoor tree in low light, the

possibilities are fairly limited. I have my best success in this department with two dracaenas, the corn plant 'Massangeana' and the plain green 'Janet Craig'. Make sure you select vigorous young specimens; avoid purchasing any dracaena whose leaves show evidence that numerous dead tips and margins have been scissored off.

Potting Mixes and Nutrients

In a perfect world the indoor gardener uses a potting mix designed to suit the needs of each plant and through this familiarity is able to judge how much to water and what fertilizer to use and when. In the real world most of us constantly bring in new purchases that may not even be growing in soil, but rather in a soil-less mix based on sphagnum peat moss, perlite, and vermiculite. Soil-based potting mixtures are biologically active and tend to produce foliage

plants that more efficiently purify the indoor air than the same plants in a soil-less medium that must be constantly fortified by applications of properly balanced chemical fertilizer. In practice most of us use some chemical fertilizers even on plants in a soil-based mix, but the amount can be reduced or the need eliminated by including in the original recipe such naturally slow-release ingredients as one or more parts well-rotted compost or leaf mold and a sprinkling of bone meal and blood meal. Acid-

Kathryn Taylor's sun-heated pit greenhouse in Dover, Massachusetts, is entirely dependent on solar energy for maintenance above freezing even in the coldest weather. Plastic foam mats are secured over the windows at night and left during cold and darkly overcast days. This scene in late March shows daffodils, camellias, azaleas, and acacias in full bloom. A propagating bench toward the back holds a host of wildflower seedlings, along with pots and tin cans of flowering sweet violets and unusual species primroses.

loving plants such as potted camellias, azaleas, gardenias, and Chinese hibiscus can be top-dressed in spring and again in summer with a sprinkling of cottonseed meal scratched into the soil surface and watered in.

The usual complaint about packaged potting soils is that they are too dense, prone to soggy wetness or turning concretelike when dry. I almost always amend these mixes according to individual plant needs. Recipes, all based on purchased ingredients, with the exception of well-rotted compost and leaf mold which I bring in from a country garden, for a variety of planting needs follow.

General potting mix: flowering and foliage plants. Equal parts by volume of packaged, all-purpose potting soil, premoistened sphagnum peat moss, and clean, sharp sand. Optional: a handful of horticultural charcoal chips to a quart of mix, to facilitate drainage and give a "sweet" smell.

ABOVE LEFT, species, varieties, and cultivars of Abutilon—known popularly as flowering maple, owing to the leaf shapes—bloom on new growth all year, but especially in a situation that is sunny and warm, with a nighttime drop in temperature of at least ten degrees. 'Golden Chimes', a superior cultivar, is shown trained as a tree-form standard, about three years old, in a growing house at Longwood Gardens, Kennett Square, Pennsylvania. Like fuchsias, some abutilons grow strongly upright, while others have pliant branches that tend to cascade—thus becoming perfect choices for hanging baskets—and to spill over the sides of pots and boxes. Breeders have taken an interest in this genus lately, and improved cultivars are appearing nearly every year. There is no nicer way to open up a room and add growing space than to install a lean-to greenhouse, ABOVE RIGHT. Prefabricated models like this one belonging to New York designer Luther Travis, an inveterate collector of orchids who has also added a growing greenhouse on the rooftop of his building, are well engineered and reasonably priced. An automatic vent system facilitates efficient cooling. A small pool in the foreground center is home for colorful tropical fish and water evaporating from it serves to humidify the greenhouse.

Potting mix: African violets and other gesneriads, begonias, and tropical foliage plants such as aglaonema, spathiphyllum, and philodendron. Follow the recipe above for general potting mix, but add a portion of well-rotted compost or leaf mold. You may use instead of the packaged, all-purpose potting soil a packaged mix labeled for African violets.

Potting mix: cacti and other succulents. Amend the general potting mix by using two parts clean, sharp sand instead of one. Or start with a packaged mix labeled for cacti and other succulents and mix two parts of it with one of premoistened sphagnum peat moss or well-rotted leaf mold.

If you have access to what might be termed good garden loam, it can be used instead of packaged all-purpose potting soil. I have not found it necessary, but some gardeners recommend pasteurizing by heating it to 180° F for an hour, presumably to kill any insects, worms, disease organisms, or weeds that might be in it.

If you can't get clean, sharp sand, also known as builder's sand, don't substitute sand from the seashore; it is too salty. Use perlite instead, a packaged product that is widely available.

Plants newly set in pots of fresh soil-based growing medium do not need fertilizer, at least in theory, until their roots begin to fill the pot. In practice most of us are in a hurry and always eager to help our plants grow better. Organic gardeners opt for fish emulsion, liquid seaweed, manure tea, and such top-dressings as cottonseed meal for acid-loving plants and oyster shells (which can be purchased where poultry feed is sold) for those needing more alkalinity or "sweetness." These work well for me with soil-based but not soil-less mixes.

The miracles of chemical fertilizers have been acclaimed through much of this century. Despite my childhood readings of a new magazine then called *Organic Gardening & Farming*, the natural way espoused there took a few decades to sink in—on me and millions of others. Now I am torn. My old habits have produced

beautiful results, but at what cost to the environment? When I buy plants in soil-less mix, is it environmentally correct to give them the chemical fertilizers on which they are dependent, or should I transplant immediately to a soil-based mix with organic fertilizers? I am presently collecting and testing old potting mix recipes that served well before gardeners—and plants—became chemically dependent. Here is one of them, for prize-winning African violets from a book published in 1948: It came from an Iowa farm woman and calls for 3 parts good black soil (gumbo), 1 part peat moss, 1 part compost (about half manure), 1 part rotted leaf mold, and 2 parts sand. To a bushel of this combination, add one 6-inch potful of superphosphate and 1 gallon wood ashes.

In ideal conditions, indoor plants need fertilizing regularly in spring and summer, less in fall and winter. Light feedings every two weeks are probably better than full doses monthly. Less fertilizer usually turns out to be more; double doses almost invariably lead to leaf and root damage if not death of the plant.

Generalist or Specialist?

It is not possible for most of us to grow all kinds of plants. Usually we try a little of this and a little of that and one day we discover, possibly at the observation of a friend, that one plant group is apparently favored. National and local societies devoted to individual plants (see Resources and Index) are an indication of the possibilities. Some leading contenders for specialization are: Amaryllids, including the popular *Hippeastrum*; aroids, including philodendrons; begonias; bromeliads; cacti and other succulents; ferns; geraniums, in particular the genus *Pelargonium*; gesneriads, including African violets; and orchids, last on my list alphabetically and often the choice of advanced gardeners seeking new challenges and new thrills.

Orchids and bromeliads that are epiphytes, or air plants, need special attentions indoors. They respond to the rain-forest cycle of frequent rains followed by sunny, drying breezes. At home this means implementing a drench-and-dry cycle with not much lingering at either extreme of wet or dry. These plants typically need fairly strong sun, warm temperatures, high humidity, and fresh air in order to form new growth and bloom. Thereafter, they keep remarkably well as room decorations until the flowers fade. Some likely beginner orchids are cattleya, laelia, *Brassavola nodosa*, phalaenopsis, paphiopedilum, and miniature cymbidium. Paphiopedilums are ladyslipper orchids and will grow well, particularly those having silvery mottled leaves, in the same conditions as thriving African violets. Pot them in a mixture of equal parts medium firbark chips and a packaged soil-less product such as Pro-Mix®. The other orchids mentioned can be grown in straight medium firbark chips, with the addition of a handful of horticultural charcoal chips to each quart of firbark. Bromeliads are grown in a variety of mixes, from terrestrial to epiphytic. Most will thrive as indoor plants in a mixture of 1 part each medium firbark chips, packaged all-purpose potting soil, clean, sharp sand, and peat moss. Favorite genera include *Aechmea, Billbergia, Cryptanthus, Guzmania, Neoregelia, Tillandsia*, and *Vriesea*. If the leaves of your bromeliad form cups at their bases, or together become a vaselike shape, keep this filled with water; pour out and refresh on a weekly basis.

Small orchids and bromeliads are often sold mounted on pieces of bark or driftwood. As indoor plants these need a dip in tepid water every sunny day and daily or twice-daily misting at other times.

Since orchids and bromeliads need lots of water but can't stand in it, arrange a system that includes a tray for water and pebbles, with a wire rack on top on which to arrange the pots.

Greenhouses

Hardly anything we add to a garden is as useful and delightful as a greenhouse. Adding a bay or window greenhouse to a sunny or bright window is a popular option, or almost any indoor space can be delightfully opened up to an attached greenhouse. Prefabricated units are available in mix-and-match modules, thus permitting considerable customization without added expense. Free-standing greenhouses can look beautiful in a garden setting, but heating may require a separate system and a greater expenditure of energy thereafter.

There is a type of free-standing greenhouse that requires more ingenuity than money to heat. It is the sun-heated pit, an idea from European gardeners that became popular in the Northeast early in this century. A classic book published in 1941 by Charles Scribner's Sons, *Winter Flowers in the Sun-Heated Pit and Greenhouse*, told the experiences of Kathryn S. Taylor and Edith W. Gregg. In an inland area of Massachusetts, not far from Boston, they had adapted the large sun-heated pit idea of the estate gardener and commercial grower to their own needs as passionate home gardeners. I visited Mrs. Taylor in 1974, which is when the photograph in this book was taken, a sunny but cold day in March. It was cozy as a bug down in the pit and flowers greeted us at every step: camellia, freesia, narcissus, sweet-olive, rosemary, and, finally, at the very back, my hostess revealed a cache of neatly labeled tin cans that sported a king's ransom in rare primulas, sweet English violets, and endangered wildflower seedlings which, as it turned out, were Mrs. Taylor's greatest passion.

Garden Indoors to Suit Yourself

I once participated on a panel of experts for a radio talk show devoted to educating consumers. We were asked how to buy plants. One expert thought in terms of proper decor and furnishings—matching plants and containers to early American, contemporary, English country, and so on. Another classified plants as "boy" and "girl," and said that "macho" persons must never grow "feminine" plants, or vice versa. This is nonsense. Buy the plants you like,

the best and most beautiful. What really counts is matching the needs of the plants—light, temperature, moisture, air quality—to the space you can provide.

In my book what really counts with indoor plants is that they be clean and healthy. I would much rather see the most common variety in the world grown well and displayed with respect than the rarest specimen languishing from neglect.

When it comes to arranging an indoor garden, there are essentially two schools: formal and casual. Which you choose probably has more to do with personal feelings about what constitutes a garden than whether you are black tie or punk, new flash or old cash. Personally I have window gardens that are formal, with matching pots and tailored plants, and others that are wildly casual. The renowned English landscape gardener Russell Page once told me that it was not possible to have a garden indoors. He never visited my apartment, but the

Two 20-watt fluorescent tubes, one Warm White, one Cool White, light this bookshelf garden that measures 12 inches by 24 inches, LEFT ABOVE. The focal point is a carved wood statue, with English ivies trained on 6-inch circles as a formalized, leafy backdrop for miniature clipped trees of green and variegated dwarf myrtle and miniature carissa 'Humphreyi'. Two nearly everblooming miniatures, Gesneria cuneifolia and Begonia prismatocarpa, grow under glass globes on either side, with a flowering miniature African violet stage center. Notice the two Lilliputian watering cans. LEFT BELOW, bowls and baskets of potpourri can be ever changing and evolving as colorful or fragrant petals from bouquets are sprinkled over the top, or a hauntingly beautiful withering flower such as this ladyslipper orchid is displayed on the surface. Seasonal flowering plants such as chrysanthemums, placed in baskets or large pots at floor level, with foliage plants clothing the walls, help turn a city apartment into an inviting garden, RIGHT.

similarly distinguished American, Carlton Lees, did. He seemed amazed and delighted at what had been accomplished and observed that my placement of foliage and seasonal flowering plants at floor level had a lot to do with his experience of the space as a real garden

What I find endlessly gratifying about my indoor garden is that it is always changing. Yesterday was a cold, freezing-rain day outdoors. I hardly looked up from my writing. This morning the sun was out and as I began to make my rounds with the watering can there greeted me a pot of blue crocus bursting into bloom, new buds on two evergreen species amaryllis—and a bad infestation of mealybugs on a seedling banana plant. Yin and yang. It all works together. My plants need me and I need them. And since they are indoors, I can practice plants as therapy day or night, rain or shine, dressed or not. Gardening in the nude is considered by some the ultimate experience with plants. Do I? I'll never tell!

Hybrids and species of Hippeastrum, *the amaryllis of florists, grow in the sunny window of an apartment, along with the yellow-flowered orchid,* Dendrobium chrysotoxum, *and 'Maid of Orleans' jasmine trained on a wire wreath. Amaryllis and many orchids soak up the summer sun, storing energy that is returned in the form of flowers, either in winter or early spring, following a period of relative coolness and drying in autumn. Microclimates abound in indoor gardens, the same as outdoors, and can be matched to specific plant needs.*

RESOURCES

PLANTS   SUPPLIES   TOOLS   EQUIPMENT   FURNITURE

Adams County Nursery, Box 108, Aspers, PA 17304; fruit trees.

Allen, Sterling & Lothrop, 191 U.S. 1, Falmouth, ME 04105; flower and vegetable seeds.

W. F. Allen Co., Box 1577, Salisbury, MD 21801; strawberries.

Ambleside Gardens, Route 206, at Oxford Place, Belle Mead, NJ 08502; 201 359-8388; retail only; sophisticated selection of tools, pots, supplies, equipment, plants, and design services; no catalog.

Appalachian Gardens, Box 82, Waynesboro, PA 17268; trees and shrubs.

Appalachian Wildflower Nursery, Route 1 Box 275, Reedsville, PA 17084; wildflowers and ferns; catalog $1.

Bailey's Waist High Gardens, Inc., Box 272, Blue Ridge, Summit, PA 17214; raised planting beds (especially for the physically impaired).

Warren Baldsiefen, Box 88, Bellvale, NY 10912; azaleas and rhododendrons; catalog $3.

Bigelow Nurseries, Box 718, Northboro, MA 10532; fruit trees.

Kurt Bluemel, 2740 Greene Lane, Baldwin, MD 21013; ornamental grasses; catalog $2.

Briarwood Gardens, 14 Gully Lane, RFD 1, East Sandwich, MA 02537; azaleas and rhododendrons; catalog $1.

Lee Bristol Nursery, Box 5, Gaylordsville, CT 06755; hemerocallis.

Buell's Greenhouses, Weeks Road, Eastford, CT 06242; African violets, Buell Hybrid florist gloxinias, and other gesneriads; list 50 cents.

Bull Valley Rhododendrons, 214 Bull Valley Road, Aspers, PA 17304; catalog 50 cents.

W. Atlee Burpee Co., Warminster, PA 18974; seeds, bulbs, nursery stock, perennials, tools, supplies; free catalog.

Caprilands Herb Farm, 534 Silver Street, Coventry, CT 06238; 203 742-7244; a foremost American garden of herbs and herbal products.

Carlson's Gardens, Box 305, South Salem, NY 10590; azaleas and rhododendrons; catalog $2.

Carroll Gardens, 444 East Main Street, Box 310, Westminster, MD 21157; perennials, summer bulbs, roses, scented geraniums, herbs, vines, shrubs, conifers, and trees; catalog $2.

Catnip Acres Farm, 67 Christian Street, Oxford, CT 06483; herbs; catalog $2.

Clapper Company, 1124 Washington St., Newton, MA 02165; garden tools.

Robert Compton Ltd., Star Route, Box 6, Bristol, VT 05443; stoneware fountains.

Comstock, Ferre & Co., 263 Main Street, Wethersfield, CT 06109; flower and vegetable seeds; free catalog.

Conley's Garden Center, Boothbay Harbor, ME 04538; wildflowers and ferns; catalog $1.50.

The Cook's Garden, Box 65, Londonderry, VT 05148; only the best in salad and other vegetable seeds; catalog $1.

Country Casual, 17317 Germantown Road, Germantown, MD 20874-2999; garden furniture; catalog $2.

Creative Gardens, 409 East Saddle River Road, Upper Saddle River, NJ 07458; 201 327-5224; retail; acres of plants and gardening supplies; no catalog.

Cricket Hill Herb Farm, Glen Street, Rowley, MA 01969; herbs; catalog $1.

Crownsville Nursery, Box 797, Crownsville, MD 21032; perennials; catalog $2.

The Cummins Garden, 22 Robertsville Road, Marlborough, NJ 07746; mail-order only; hard-to-find dwarf conifers, Texbury and Knaphill azaleas, small-leaf rhododendrons, and native groundcovers; catalog $1.

Dauber's Nurseries, Box 1746, York, PA 17405; trees and shrubs; catalog 50 cents.

Daystar, RFD 2 Box 40, Litchfield, ME 04350; perennials; catalog $1.

Dehkan Farms, 132 Newton Sparta Road, Newton, NJ 07860; 201 383-9621; retail; vegetable seedlings started organically; supplies and guidance for organic gardeners; no catalog.

P. de Jager & Sons, Box 2010, South Hamilton, MA 01982; bulbs, corms, and tubers.

Dilatush Nursery, 780 Route 130, Robbinsville, NJ 08691; six acres of plants and supplies for all kinds of gardens; list of current stock for three first-class postage stamps.

Donaroma's Nursery, Box 2189, Edgartown, MA 02539; wildflowers and ferns; catalog $3.

Eastern Plant Specialties, Box 226, Georgetown, ME 04548; evergreens; catalog $2.

Eastern Plant Specialties, Box 40, Colonia, NJ 07067; rhododendrons, dwarf conifers, native plants; catalog $2.

The English Garden, Inc., 652 Glenbrook Road, Stamford, CT 06906; trellises, gazebos, pavilions, seats, birdhouses, planters.

Fern Hill Farm, Box 185, Clarksboro, NJ 08020; vegetable seeds.

Field Stone Gardens, 620 Quaker Lane, Vassalboro, ME 04989; perennials; catalog $1.50.

Florentine Craftsmen, 46–24 28th Street, Long Island City, NY 11101; fountains, statues, sundials, urns.

Floyd Cove Nursery, 11 Shipyard Lane, Setauket, NY 11733; hemerocallis; catalog $1.

Foxborough Nursery, 3711 Miller Road, Street, MD 21154; evergreens; catalog $1.

Fox Hill Farm, Box 7, Parma, MI 49269; herbs; catalog $1.

Howard B. French, Route 100, Pittsfield, VT 05762; bulbs, corms, and tubers.

Gardener's Supply, 128 Intervale Road, Burlington, VT 05401; organic fertilizers and pesticides, soil amendments, seeds for green manures, supplies, tools, prefabricated greenhouses.

D. S. George Nurseries, 2491 Penfield, Fairport, NY 14450; clematis; first-class stamp for brochure.

Gladside Gardens, 61 Main Street, Northfield, MA 01360; bulbs, corms, and tubers; catalog $1.

Golden Acres Farm, R.R. 2, Box 7430, Fairfield, ME 04937; vegetable seeds; catalog $1.

Golden Glow Gardens, 115 Sligo Road, North Yarmouth, ME 04021; perennials.

John Gordon Nursery, 1385 Campbell Boulevard, North Tonawanda, NY 14120; nuts.

Hickory Hill Gardens, R.D. 1, Box 11, Loretto, PA 15940; perennials; catalog $1.

Indigo Knoll Perennials, 16236 Compromise Court, Mount Airy, MD 21771; perennials; catalog $1.

Irving & Jones, Village Center, Colebrook, CT 06021; fine garden furnishings; brochure $2.

Janco Greenhouses, 9390 Davis Avenue, Laurel, MD 20707; catalog $5.

Johnny's Selected Seeds, Albion, ME 04910; vegetable seeds.

Kelly Nurseries, Dansville, NY 14437; fruit and nut trees, berries; free catalog.

Kemp Co., 160 Koser Road, Lititz, PA 17543; compost shredder/chippers.

Kinsman Co., River Road, Point Pleasant, PA 18950; cold frames, cloches, arches, baskets, and bird houses; also compost bins and electric chipper/shredders.

Grimo Nut Nursery, R.R. 3, Niagara-on-the-Lake, Ontario L0S 1J0; nuts; catalog $1.

Halcyon Gardens, Box 124, Gibsonia, PA 15044; herbs; catalog $1.

Harris Seeds, 961 Lyell Avenue, Rochester, NY 14606; flower and vegetable seeds; free catalog.

Heart's Ease, Route 517, Fairmont, NJ 07830; 201 832-2708; retail; perennials, annuals, herbs, vegetables, houseplants, orchids, miniature sinningias; no catalog.

Hen-Feathers and Co., 10 Balligomingo Road, Gulph Mills, PA 19428; containers, birdbaths, sundials, benches, tools.

Heritage Rosarium, 211 Haviland Mill Road, Brookville, MD 20833; roses; catalog $1.

Hermitage Garden Pools, Box 361, Canastota, NY 13032; fiberglass garden pools and water features; catalog $1.

M. & J. Kristick, 155 Mockingbird Lane, Wellsville, PA 17365; evergreens.

Landreth Seed Co., Box 6426, Baltimore, MD 21230; vegetable seeds; catalog $2.

Orol Ledden & Sons, Box 7, Sewell, NJ 08080; flower and vegetable seeds.

Legg Dahlias, 1069 Hastings Road, Geneva, NY 14456.

Lilypons Water Gardens, 6800 Lilypons Road, Box 10, Lilypons, MD 21717-0010; aquatics and pool supplies; catalog $4.

Limerock Ornamental Grasses, R.D. 1, Box 111, Port Matilda, PA 16870; catalog $1.

Lowe's Own Root Roses, 6 Sheffield Road, Nashua, NH 03062; roses; catalog $2.

Logee's Greenhouses, 55 North Street, Danielson, CT 06239; a primary source for container plants and herbs; catalog $3.

Kenneth Lynch & Sons, Box 488, Wilton, CT 06897; gates, statuary, fountains, pools, benches, sundials.

John D. Lyon, 143 Alewife Brook Parkway, Cambridge, MA 02140; bulbs, corms, and tubers.

Machin Designs, Inc., 557 Danbury Road, Route 7, Wilton, CT 06897; conservatories.

Mantis Mfg. Co., 1458 County Line Road, Huntingdon Valley, PA 19006; compost chipper/shredder.

Le Jardin du Gourmet, Box 85, West Danville, VT 05873; herbs and gourmet vegetables; catalog 50 cents.

Lennilea Farm Nursery, R.D. 1, Box 314, Alburtis, PA 18011; nuts.

Henry Leuthardt Nurseries, East Moriches, NY 11940; espaliers and other fruit trees.

McNaughton's Nursery, 351 Kresson Road, Cherry Hill, NJ 08034; 609 429-6745; retail; superior selection of shade trees and other plants; no catalog.

Meadowbrook Farms, 1633 Washington Lane, Meadowbrook, PA 19046; by calling in advance, 215 887-5900, organized garden groups may arrange to visit the adjoining private gardens of Mr. and Mrs. J. Liddon Pennock, Jr.; one of the finest small, retail garden centers in the Northeast.

Meadowbrook Herb Gardens, Route 138, Wyoming, RI 02898; herbs; catalog $1.

Merry Gardens, Camden, ME 04843; herbs, geraniums, ivies; catalog $1.

Messelaar Bulb Co., Box 269, Ipswich, MA 01938; bulbs, corms, and tubers.

J. E. Miller Nurseries, Canandaigua, NY 14424; fruit trees.

E. B. Nauman, 688 Davids Lane, Schenectady, NY 12309; evergreens.

Nor'East Miniature Roses, 58 Hammond, Rowley, MA 01969; miniature roses.

Nourse Farms, Box 485 RFD, South Deerfield, MA 01373; small truits.

Oak Ridge Nurseries, Box 182, East Kingston, NH 03827; wildflowers and ferns; catalog $1.

Obal Garden Market, 516 Alexander Road, Princeton, NJ 08540; 609 452-2401; retail; unusually large selection of bulbs; also evergreens and other plants; no catalog.

Oliver Nurseries, Inc., 1159 Bronson Road, Fairfield, CT 06430; rock garden plants and dwarf conifers.

Paradise Water Gardens, 14 May Street, Whitman, MA 02382; aquatic plants and pool supplies; catalog $2.

George W. Park Seed Co., Greenwood, SC 29647; all manner of garden and houseplant seeds, bulbs, supplies, tools, and equipment; free catalog.

Pinetree Garden Seeds, New Gloucester, ME 04260; home gardener-size packets of vegetable, herb, and flower seeds; supplies; books.

Putney Nursery, Putney, VT 05346; wildflowers and ferns; catalog $1.

Raynor Bros., Box 1617, Salisbury, MD 21801; strawberries.

Otto Richter & Sons, Box 26, Goodwood, Ontario, Canada L0C 1A0; herbs; catalog $2.50.

Ringer, 9959 Valley View Road, Eden Prairie, MN 55344; bio-organic products for completely natural lawns and gardens.

D. L. Rohrer & Bro., Box 25, Smoketown, PA 17576; vegetable seeds.

The Rosemary House, 120 South Market Street, Mechanicsburg, PA 17055; herbs; catalog $2.

Roslyn Nursery, Box 69, Roslyn, NY 11576; azaleas and rhododendrons; catalog $1.

Saxton Gardens, 1 First Street, Saratoga Springs, NY 12866; hemerocallis; catalog 50 cents.

John Scheepers, Inc., 63 Wall Street, New York, NY 10005; bulbs, corms, and tubers.

F. W. Schumacher Co., 36 Spring Hill Road, Sandwich, MA 02563; trees and shrubs; catalog $1.

Seawright Gardens, 134 Indian Hill, Carlisle, MA 01741; hemerocallis; catalog $1.

Seedway, Hall, NY 14463; flower and vegetable seeds.

Joel W. Spingarn, Box 782, Georgetown, CT 06829; rare evergreens and alpines; list $1.

Square Root Nursery, 4674 Deuel Rd., Canandaigua, NY 14424; grapes.

St. Lawrence Nurseries, R.D. 2, Potsdam, NY 13676; fruit trees; catalog $1.

Stokes Seeds, Box 548, Buffalo, NY 14240; flower and vegetable seeds.

Stonehurst Rare Plants, 1 Stonehurst Court, Pomona, NY 10907; evergreens; list $1.

Sunburst Seeds, R.D. 1, Box 34, Freedom, NY 14065; vegetable seeds.

Sunrise Oriental Seeds, Box 10058, Elmwood CT 06110; oriental vegetables; catalog $1.

Surry Gardens, Box 145, Surry, ME 04684; perennials; catalog $2.

Thompson & Morgan, Box 1308, Jackson, NJ 08527; flower and vegetable seeds, many rare and unusual; free catalog.

Tomato Seed Co., Box 323, Metuchen, NJ 08840.

Tranquil Lake Nursery, 45 River Street, Rehoboth, MA 02769; hemerocallis; catalog 50 cents.

Tripple Brook Farm, 37 Middle Road, Southampton, MA 01073; seeds, general nursery stock; catalog.

Troy-Bilt Mfg. Co., 102nd Street and 9th Avenue, Troy, NY 12180; rotary tillers and chipper/shredders.

Otis Twilley Seed Co., Box 65, Trevose, PA 19047; flower and vegetable seeds; free catalog.

Twombley Nursery, Inc., 163 Barn Hill Road, Monroe, CT 06468; dwarf conifers, rock garden plants, perennials.

Van Bourgondien Bros., Box A, Babylon, NY 11702; bulbs, corms, and tubers; free catalog.

Vandenberg, Black Meadow Road, Chester, NY 10918; bulbs, corms, and tubers.

Mary Mattison Van Schaik, Cavendish, VT 05142; bulbs, corms, and tubers; catalog 50 cents.

Vegetable Factory, Inc., Box 2235, New York, NY 10163; prefabricated greenhouses and porch enclosures; catalog $2.

Vermont Bean Seed Co., Garden Lane, Fairhaven, CT 05473; vegetable seeds.

Vermont Wildflower Farm, Route 7, Charlotte, VT 05445; wildflowers and ferns.

Vesey Seeds, Box 9000, Houlton, ME 04730; flower and vegetable seeds.

Vick's Wildgarden, Box 115, Gladwyne, PA 19035; catalog 50 cents.

Vixen Hill Gazebos, Elverson, PA 19520; prefabricated gazebos.

Walpole Woodworkers, 767 East Street, Walpole, MA 02081; furniture, swings, picnic sets, weather vanes.

Waterford Gardens, 74 East Allendale Road, Saddle River, NJ 07458; aquatic plants and pool supplies; catalog $4.

Watnong Nursery, Route 10, Morris Plains, NJ 07950; retail; by appointment only; more than four hundred different evergreens; no catalog.

Wayside Gardens, Hodges, SC 29695-0001; perennials, shrubs, vines, "new" old roses, bulbs; catalog $1.

Well-Sweep Herb Farm, 317 Mount Bethel Road, Port Murray, NJ 07865; herbs; catalog $1.

White Flower Farm, Litchfield, CT 06759-0050; perennials, shrubs, bulbs; catalog $5.

Wicklein's Water Gardens, 1820 Cromwell Bridge Road, Baltimore, MD 21234; water lilies, lotus, bog plants, pool liners; catalog $3.

Winterthur Plant Shop, Winterthur, DE 19735; trees and shrubs; catalog $1.

Wolfman-Gold & Good Co., 484 Broome Street, New York, NY 10013; statuary, garden furniture, latticework window boxes, planters.

Wood Classics, High Falls, NY 12440; 914 255-7871; teak and mahogany outdoor furniture, kits or assembled.

Woodruff Seed Co., Box 145, Whitehall, NY 12887; vegetable seeds.

Worley's Nurseries, Route 1, York Springs, PA 17372; fruit trees.

Wyrttun Ward, 18 Beach Street, Middleboro, MA 02346; herbs; catalog $1.

Dr. Yoo Farm, Box 290, College Park, MD 20740; mushrooms and oriental vegetables.

PLANT SOCIETIES   BOTANICAL GARDENS   ARBORETA
HORTICULTURAL SOCIETIES   PERIODICALS

African Violet Society of America, Box 3609, Beaumont, TX 77704.

American Begonia Society, 8922 Conway Drive, Riverside, CA 92503.

American Bonsai Society, 1363 West Sixth Street, Erie, PA 16505.

American Boxwood Society, Box 85, Boyce, VA 22620.

American Camellia Society, Box 1217, Fort Valley, GA 31030.

American Conifer Society, William Schwartz, 1825 North 72 Street, Philadelphia, PA 19151.

American Daffodil Society, Miss Leslie Anderson, 2302 Byhalia Road, Hernando, MS 38632.

American Dahlia Society, Michael Mortinolich, 159 Pine Street, New Hyde Park, NY 11040.

American Fern Society, Dr. Les Hickok, Botany Department, University of Tennessee, Knoxville, TN 37916.

American Fuchsia Society, Hall of Flowers, Golden Gate Park, 9th Avenue and Lincoln Way, San Francisco, CA 94122.

American Ginger Society, Box 100, Archer, FL 32618.

American Gloxinia and Gesneriad Society, Box 493, Beverly Farms, MA 01915.

American Gourd Society, Box 274, Mount Gilead, OH 43338.

American Hemerocallis Society, Sandy Goembel, Route 5, Box 874, Palatka, FL 32077.

American Hibiscus Society, Drawer 1540, Cocoa Beach, FL 32931.

American Horticultural Society, 7931 East Boulevard Drive, Alexandria, VA 22308.

American Hosta Society, 9448 Mayfield Road, Chesterland, OH 44026.

American Iris Society, James Burch, Box 10002, Huntsville, AL 35801.

American Ivy Society, Box 520, West Carrollton, OH 45449.

American Magnolia Society, Richard Figlar, Box 129, Nanuet, NY 10954.

American Orchid Society, 6000 South Olive Avenue, West Palm Beach, FL 33405

American Penstemon Society, Orville M. Steward, Box 33, Plymouth, VT 05056.

American Peony Society, Greta Kessenich, 250 Interlachen Road, Hopkins, MN 55343.

American Plant Life Society, Box 985, National City, CA 92050; amaryllids and other bulbous plants.

American Pomological Society, Dr. L. D. Tukey, 103 Tyson Building, University Park, PA 16802.

American Primrose Society, Brian Skidmore, 6730 West Mercer Way, Mercer Island, WA 98040.

American Rhododendron Society, 14635 S. W. Bull Mountain Road, Tigard, OR 97223.

American Rock Garden Society, Norman Singer, SR 66 Box 114, Norfolk Road, South Sandisfield, MA 01255.

American Rose Society, Box 30,000, Shreveport, LA 71130.

The Arnold Arboretum, Jamaica Plain, MA 02130; 617 524-1718; recorded information, 617 524-1717; 7,000 different trees and shrubs grow on a 265-acre oasis, established in 1872.

The Avant Gardener, Horticultural Data Processors, Box 489, New York, NY 10028; monthly newsletter; $18 per year.

Azalea Society of America, Box 6244, Silver Spring, MD 20906.

Bamboo Society of America, 1101 San Leon Court, Solana Beach, CA 92075.

Barlett Arboretum, The University of Connecticut, 151 Brookdale Road, Stamford, CT 06903; 203 322-6971; 63-acre site features a dwarf conifer garden, an ericaceous collection and small flowering trees.

Berkshire Garden Center, Box 826, Stockbridge, MA 10262; 413 298-3926; 15 acres of gardens and three greenhouses; special emphasis on ideas relating to the home gardener.

Blithewold Gardens and Arboretum, Ferry Road, Bristol, RI 02809; 401 253-2707; spring bulbs, rock garden, water garden, annuals, perennials, roses.

Bonsai Clubs International, Box 2098, Sunnyvale, CA 94087.

The Botanic Garden of Smith College, Lyman Plant House, Northampton, MA 01063; 413 584-2700 ext. 2748; campus greenhouses and gardens contain over three thousand kinds of plants.

Bowman's Hill Wildflower Preserve, Washington Cross Historic Park, Washington Crossing, PA 18977; 215 862-2924; 100 acres of wild flowers, ferns, trees, shrubs, and vines.

The Bromeliad Society, 2488 East 49 Street, Tulsa, OK 74105.

Brooklyn Botanic Garden, 1000 Washington Avenue, Brooklyn, NY 11225; 718 622-4433; 52 acres of visitor-friendly gardens and displays of plants arranged according to their botanical relationships; extensive under-glass plantings in the Steinhardt Conservatory, and a Bonsai Museum.

Brookside Gardens, 1500 Glenallan Avenue, Wheaton, MD 20902; 301 949-8230; 50-acre display garden that always abounds in ideas for the home gardener.

Leonard J. Buck Garden, Somerset County Park Commission, R.D. 2, Layton Road, Far Hills, NJ 07931; 201 234-2677; a series of alpine and woodland gardens situated in a 33-acre stream valley, including wildflowers, azaleas and rhododendrons, and a major fern collection.

Cactus and Succulent Society of America, Box 3010, Santa Barbara, CA 93130.

Mary Flagler Cary Arboretum Institute of Ecosystem Studies, Route 44A, Box AB, Milbrook, NY 12545; 914 677-5358; nature trails, demonstration gardens, collection of lilac cultivars.

Clark Garden, 193 I. U. Willets Road, Albertson, NY 11507; 516 621-7568; this 12-acre botanical garden offers outstanding plantings and educational opportunities in all seasons.

Connecticut Arboretum, Connecticut College, Williams Street, New London, CT 06320; 203 447-1911 ext. 7700; over 200 kinds of native trees and shrubs, the Edgerton Wildflower Area and the naturalistic Landscape Demonstration area.

The Conservatory Garden, Central Park, 830 Fifth Avenue, New York, NY 10021; 212 360-8236; located at 105th Street and Fifth Avenue, at the edge of Central Park; formal gardens and some of the finest herbaceous borders seen in any garden, public or private.

Bayard Cutting Arboretum, Box 466, Montauk Highway, Oakdale, NY 11709; 516 581-1002; 690 acres, of which 130 acres open to the public feature over a thousand different kinds of plants.

The Cycad Society, 1161 Phyllis Court, Mountain View, CA 94040.

Cymbidium Society of America, 6881 Wheeler Avenue, Westminster, CA 92683.

Delphinium Society, 1630 Midwest Plaza Building, Minneapolis, MN 55402.

Duke Gardens Foundation, Inc., Box 2030, Highway 206 South, Somerville, NJ 08876; 201 722-3700; among America's most fabled gardens; advance reservation required.

Dwarf Fruit Tree Association, 303 Horticulture, Michigan State University, East Lansing, MI 48823.

Epiphyllum Society of America, Box 1395, Monrovia, CA 91016.

Fine Gardening, bimonthly magazine, The Taunton Press, 63 South Main Street, Box 355, Newton, CT 06470; $22 yearly.

Flower & Garden, bimonthly magazine, 4251 Pennsylvania Avenue, Kansas City, MO 64111; $8 year.

The Frelinghuysen Arboretum, 53 East Hanover Avenue, Box 1295R, Morristown, NJ 07960; 201 326-7600; 127 acres including flowering shrubs, roses, annuals and a Braille nature trail.

Fuller Gardens, 10 Willow Avenue, North Hampton, NH 03862; 603 964-5414; 2 acres of extensively developed gardens.

Garbage, the Practical Journal for the Environment, published bimonthly, by Old House Journal Corp., 435 Ninth Street, Brooklyn, NY 11215; $21 yearly.

Garden, the magazine about the plant world, published bimonthly by The Garden Society, Botanical Garden, Bronx, NY 10458; $12.95 yearly.

Garden Club of America, 598 Madison Avenue, New York, NY 10022.

Garden Design magazine, published quarterly by the American Society of Landscape Architects, 4401 Connecticut Avenue N.W., Suite 500, Washington, DC 20008-2302; $20 yearly.

Garden in the Woods of the New England Wild Flower Society, Hemenway Road, Framingham, MA 01701; 617 877-6574; 45 acres, subtly landscaped since the 1930s, into one of the Northeast's most wondrous gardens.

Gardens for All, 180 Flynn Avenue, Burlington, VT 05401.

Isabella Stewart Gardner Museum, 2 Palace Road, Boston, MA 02115; 617 566-1401; Fenway Court, an indoor courtyard filled with plants, is something of a mecca among gardeners.

Gesneriad International, Box 102, Greenwood, IN 46142.

Green Animals, Cory's Lane, Portsmouth, RI 02840 (mailing address: The Preservation Society of Newport County, 118 Mill Street, Newport, RI 02840); 401 683-1267; 80 animal-shaped topiaries on a 7-acre estate with many garden features.

Green Scene, published bimonthly by the Pennsylvania Horticultural Society, 325 Walnut Street, Philadelphia, PA 19106; $9.75 yearly, exclusive of PHS membership.

The Hagley Museum and Library, Box 3630, Greenville, Wilmington, DE 19807; 302 658-2400; period garden in front of the mansion.

Hardy Plant Society, Evie Douglas, 11907 Nevers Road, Snohomish, WA 98290.

Heliconia Society International, Flamingo Gardens, 3750 Flamingo, Ft. Lauderdale, FL 33330.

Herb Society of America, 2 Independent Court, Concord, MA 10742; local chapters throughout the Northeast.

The Henry Foundation for Botanical Research, Box 7, 801 Stony Lane, Gladwyne, PA 19035; 215 525-2037; 40 acres of naturalized settings, rock outcroppings, important collections of halesia, lilium, magnolia, ilex, and rhododendron, among others.

Highland Park, Monroe County Parks, Arboretum, 375 Westfall Road, Rochester, NY 14620; 716 244-4640; famous for its lilac collection.

Hobby Greenhouse Association, 432 Templeton Hills Road, Templeton, CA 93465.

Holly Society of America, Mrs. E. H. Richardson, 304 Northwind Drive, Baltimore, MD 21204.

Home Orchard Society, Marian T. Dunlap, 2522 S. W. Miles Street, Portland, OR 97219.

Horticulture, The Magazine of American Gardening, 20 Park Plaza, Suite 1220, Boston, MA 02116; monthly; $24 yearly.

Houseplant Forum, Horticom Inc., 1449 Avenue William, Sillery, Quebec GIS 4G5; bimonthly newsletter.

Hoya Society International, Box 54271, Atlanta, GA 30308.

Indoor Citrus and Rare Fruit Society, 176 Coronado Avenue, Los Altos, CA 94022.

Indoor Gardening Society of America, 128 West 58 Street, New York, NY 10019.

Indoor Gardening Society of Canada, 16 Edgar Woods Road, Willowdale, Ontario M2H 2Y7.

Innisfree Garden, Tyrrel Road, Millbrook, NY 12545; 914 677-8000; 180 acres of naturalized gardens.

International Aroid Society, Box 43-1853, South Miami, FL 33143.

International Carnivorous Plant Society, Fullerton Arboretum, Fullerton, CA 92634.

International Geranium Society, William McKilligan, 1442 North Gordon Street, Hollywood, CA 90028.

International Lilac Society, Walter Oakes, Box 315, Rumford, ME 04276.

International Palm Society, Box 27, Forestville, CA 95436.

Ladew Topiary Gardens, 3535 Jarrettsville Pike, Monkton, MD 21111; 301 557-9466; 15 secluded gardens and an extraordinary collection of topiary.

George Landis Arboretum, Esperance, NY 12066; 518 875-6935; 96 acres of wildflowers, conifers, flowering shrubs, and flowering crab apples.

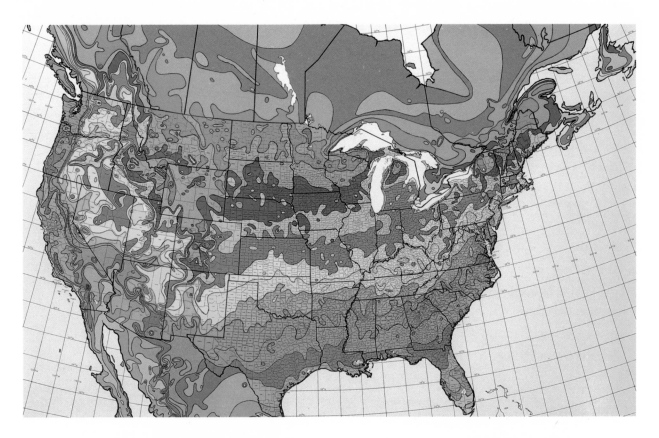

USDA Plant Hardiness Zone Map

The 1990 USDA Plant Hardiness Zone map gives gardeners from every corner of North America guidelines as to which plants can be wintered outdoors in their vicinity. Gardeners in the Northeast and elsewhere are advised to study their own landscape to determine the nuances in temperatures particular to their planting area.

Photo courtesy of the Agricultural Research Service, USDA.

AVERAGE ANNUAL MINIMUM TEMPERATURE

Temperature (°C)	Zone	Temperature (°F)
−45.6 and Below	1	Below −50
−42.8 to −45.5	2a	−45 to −50
−40.0 to −42.7	2b	−40 to −45
−37.3 to −40.0	3a	−35 to −40
−34.5 to −37.2	3b	−30 to −35
−31.7 to −34.4	4a	−25 to −30
−28.9 to −31.6	4b	−20 to −25
−26.2 to −28.8	5a	−15 to −20
−23.4 to −26.1	5b	−10 to −15
−20.6 to −23.3	6a	−5 to −10
−17.8 to −20.5	6b	0 to −5
−15.0 to −17.7	7a	5 to 0
−12.3 to −15.0	7b	10 to 5
−9.5 to −12.2	8a	15 to 10
−6.7 to −9.4	8b	20 to 15
−3.9 to −6.6	9a	25 to 20
−1.2 to −3.8	9b	30 to 25
1.6 to −1.1	10a	35 to 30
4.4 to 1.7	10b	40 to 35
4.5 and above	11	40 and above

Longwood Gardens, Box 501, Kennett Square, PA 19348; 215 388-6741; 350 acres of formal and informal gardens, with more than 3½ acres under glass; seasonal displays; extensive education program and lecture series.

Los Angeles International Fern Society, 14895 Gardenhill Drive, La Mirada, CA 90638.

Marigold Society of America, Box 112, New Britain, PA 18901.

Mens Garden Clubs of America, 5560 Merle Hay Road, Des Moines, IA 50323.

Mohonk Mountain House, New Paltz, NY 12561; 914 255-1000; 15 acres of gardens set in beautiful countryside; annual five-day Garden Holiday program is highly recommended.

Montreal Botanical Garden, 4101 Sherbrooke Street E., Montreal, Quebec H1X 2B2; 514 872-1454; an extraordinary collection of some 26,000 different plants.

Morris Arboretum of the University of Pennsylvania, 9414 Meadowbrook Avenue, Chestnut Hill, Philadelphia, PA 19118; 215 247-5777; 90 acres and 3,500 kinds of plants, laid out in naturalistic style.

Mount Auburn Cemetery, 580 Mount Auburn Street, Cambridge, MA 02138; 617 547-7105; the first garden cemetery in America, has over two thousand identified trees representing more than three hundred varieties.

National Chrysanthemum Society, B.L. Markham, 2612 Beverly Road, Roanoak, VA 24015.

National Fuchsia Society, 2892 Crown View Drive, Rancho Palos Verdes, CA 90274.

National Oleander Society, Mrs. E. Koehler, Box 3431, Galveston, TX 77552.

New Canaan Nature Center, 144 Oenoke Ridge, New Canaan, CT 06840; 203 966-9577. 40-acre property with large perennial border, herb garden, wildflower garden and an education building.

New England Wild Flower Society, Garden in the Woods, Hemenway Road, Framingham, MA 01701.

The New York Botanical Garden, Bronx, NY 10458; 212 220-8700; 250 acres with extraordinary displays in the Enid A. Haupt Conservatory, and extensive plantings on the grounds.

North American Fruit Explorers, Mary Kurle, 10 South 055 Madison, Hinsdale, IL 60521.

North American Gladiolus Council, R. A. Vogt, 9338 Manzanita Drive, Sun City, AZ 85373.

North American Heather Society, Alice E. Knight, 62 Elma-Monte Road, Elma, WA 98541.

North American Lily Society, Dorothy Schaefer, Box 476, Waukee, IA 50263.

Northern Nut Growers Association, Broken Arrow Road, Hamden, CT 06518.

Old Sturbridge Village, Sturbridge, MA 01566; 617 347-3362; 300 herbs, door-yard gardens, and formal gardens.

Old Westbury Gardens, Box 430, Old Westbury, NY 11568; 516 333-0048; 70-acre estate preserved as an example of grandeur in the early 20th century; formal gardens, wild flowers, demonstration gardens.

Organic Gardening magazine, 33 East Minor Street, Emmaus, PA 18098; monthly; $18 yearly.

Palm Society, Box 368, Lawrence, KS 66044.

Peperomia Society International, 5240 West 20 Street, Vero Beach, FL 32960.

Phipps Conservatory, City of Pittsburgh, Schenley Park, Pittsburgh, PA 15213; 412 255-2376; 13 connected greenhouses display more than two acres under glass.

Planting Fields Arboretum, Planting Fields Road, Oyster Bay, NY 11771; 516 922-9201; 400 acres of formal and informal gardens featuring more than six thousand kinds of plants; camellia house contains one of the best collections in America.

Plumeria Society of America, Elizabeth Thornton, 1014 Riverglyn, Houston, TX 77063.

Queens Botanical Garden, 43–50 Main Street, Flushing, NY 11355; 718 886-3800; 39 acres, with thousands of roses and numerous demonstration gardens.

Royal Botanical Gardens Centre, 680 Plains Road West (Route 2), Box 399, Hamilton, Ontario L8N 3H8; 416 527-1158; 40 acres of flowers and gardens; educational programs.

Rutgers University, Research and Display Gardens, Box 231, Cook College, New Brunswick, NJ 08903; 201 932-9325; 30 acres with about 1,200 kinds of plants.

The Scott Arboretum of Swarthmore College, Swarthmore College, Swarthmore, PA 19081; 215 447-7025; 110 acres and more than 5,000 kinds of plants.

Sempervivum Fanciers Association, Dr. C. W. Nixon, 37 Ox Bow Lane, Randolph, MA 02368.

Skylands, Ringwood State Park, Box 302, Ringwood, NJ 07456; 201 327-1782; the only botanic garden in the New Jersey park system.

Soil Conservation Society of America, 6515 Ankeny Road, Ankeny, IA 50021.

Staten Island Botanical Garden, Seaman's Cove, Staten Island, NY 10301; 718 273-8200; a young garden with education programs and opportunities for volunteers.

Swiss Pines, Charlestown Road, R. D. 1, Box 127, Malvern, PA 19355; 215 933-6916; extensive Japanese-style gardens.

The John J. Tyler Arboretum, Box 216, Lima, PA 19037; 215 566-9133; 200 acres of woody plants, native plant trail, fragrant garden, and bird-habitat garden.

Waterlily Society, Box 104, Lilypons, MD 21717.

Wave Hill, 675 West 252 Street, Bronx, NY 10471; 212 549-2055; 27 acres of gardens and a small conservatory filled with treasures; a gardener's mecca.

Winterthur Museum and Gardens, Winterthur, DE 19735; 302 654-1548; 200 landscaped acres in the English naturalistic style.

INDEX

Italic page numbers refer to illustrations and to information in picture captions.